LESSONS
FROM THE EDGE

LESSONS FROM THE EDGE

For-Profit and Nontraditional Higher Education in America

Gary A. Berg

AMERICAN COUNCIL ON EDUCATION
PRAEGER
Series on Higher Education

Library of Congress Cataloging-in-Publication Data

Berg, Gary A., 1955–
   Lessons from the edge : for-profit and nontraditional higher education in America /
Gary A. Berg.
      p. cm. — (ACE/Praeger series on higher education)
   Includes bibliographical references and index.
   ISBN 0–275–98258–0 (alk. paper); ISBN 0–275–98896–1 (pbk : alk. paper)
      1. Education, Higher—Economic aspects—United States.   2. Private universities
and colleges—Economic aspects—United States.   3. Public universities and
colleges—Economic aspects—United States.   I. Title.   II. American Council on
Education/Praeger series on higher education.
   LC66.B46   2005
   338.4′3378—dc22   2004016586

British Library Cataloguing in Publication Data is available.

Library of Congress Catalog Card Number: 2004016586
ISBN: 0–275–98258–0

First published in 2005

Praeger Publishers, 88 Post Road West, Westport, CT 06881
An imprint of Greenwood Publishing Group, Inc.
www.praeger.com

Printed in the United States of America

The paper used in this book complies with the
Permanent Paper Standard issued by the National
Information Standards Organization (Z39.48–1984).

10 9 8 7 6 5 4 3 2 1

For, my mother, Leona

CONTENTS

PREFACE:
EDGING TO THE CENTER

Sam Shepard, the great American playwright, created a memorable image of how communities in the western United States were begun that has stuck with me for years. He describes the citizens of a remote desert town as arriving there after driving aimlessly down Route 66 until they ran out of gas. With no history, no options, no gas, it is there among the cactus, sand, heat, and broken-down cars that they established their new civilization. Actually Shepard was reflecting on his own hometown in southern California (which happens to be mine as well) and his sense of the psychological and spiritual clearing in the desert, where the only evidence of civilization is what is discarded by fast-moving cars passing on the highway and what you bring with you in your trunk and in your head. Everything is possible (maybe), but only if you do it yourself. The other relevant image that persists in my mind is from when I worked as an administrator for Chapman University and visited some of its remote satellite campuses. Although an old and traditional nonprofit, it was a leader in the use of multiple distributed campuses with eighty-some sites beginning back in the 1950s, sprouting up around the country either on remote military bases or areas where no four-year universities existed. While over the years many of these educational outposts have been shut down or evolved into big urban training centers, in the mid-1990s a few still remained. I visited one site in Victorville, California, where I was given a tour of the facility by its director. At the back of a classroom lined with tables and chairs facing forward, I opened a back door and stood staring out at hundreds of miles of desert—whiteboard, markers, and unlimited open desert. With the accessible admissions standards, lack of competition, and edge-of-civilization location, these centers had a missionary feel to them. Chapman University provided an important service to working-class students in those remote locations: On military bases, regular soldiers, often from humble backgrounds, tried to make progress toward a degree, along with many first-generation adult students working at the community's scarce low-paying jobs.

The Sam Shepard image rings true in my mind when thinking about the haphazard way society developed in the West, and the psychological profile of those who are drawn to live on the edge of civilization. The University of Phoenix left California after various accreditation battles and set up shop in the desert, where it was less hampered by the past and the ways of traditional higher education. Both practically and metaphorically, it is a perfect location for the dynamic institution. The other for-profits and nontraditional institutions studied for this book had similar trail-blazing beginnings.

These images were in my mind when I arrived in Phoenix to observe the University of Phoenix Academic Leadership Development Conference. While the observation of this event was informal, and consequently one wouldn't want to make too much of any single impression gathered, it is useful as an entry point for the study of the University of Phoenix and other for-profit higher education in America today. Many of the key issues that arose in the interviews, such as innovation, change, growth, centralized-decentralized balance, academic and business interest equilibrium, and the altered role of the faculty, were all embodied in various forms at this retreat.

The conference was held at a sprawling resort hotel with swimming pools that never closed, light-strung palm trees, and stucco mission revival–style buildings. It was explained to me jokingly that the conference was held in July because of the combination of cheap hotel rooms and 100-plus degree weather that drives attendees into air-conditioned conference rooms. I took it as a test of toughness: like desert lizards, the University of Phoenix's staff and faculty can survive the harshest climate the country has to offer. After all, they've survived twenty-seven accreditation visits. Test of toughness, test of will, an aggressive attitude—"we can do this," they seem to always be saying.

At an opening cocktail party, Craig Swenson, the provost, and Laura Palmer Noone, the president, each greeted me warmly. Many of the casually dressed men and women knew each another, and the mood was friendly and relaxed. As I looked around the group, I was reminded of similar events held at Chapman University—in particular, the annual

"Director's Retreat," an event where the heads of the satellite campuses gathered each year. The groups shared the same unpretentiousness and matter-of-fact, middle-America feel.

Terms and phrases generally used in corporate settings were heard throughout the conference over the next few days. As a gathering of faculty, the common use of this business terminology would undoubtedly surprise or even shock many traditional academics. New academic programs were described like new product roll-outs with corporate phrases like "beta" and "alpha" used to label various versions of the educational product. The customer service emphasis of the organization was evident with the repeated use of phrases like "manage to student perceptions," "manage to them," "ask what the student wants," and "value students." The admonition to "manage" was a key word heard over and over again by conference participants. Phrases such as "relationship management," "manage business in standardized way," "management skills," "managing grievance," and "managing within process" were heard continually. In addition to reflecting the corporate model of the organization, the language tended to communicate an approach that differs distinctly from traditional higher education, where "building consensus" and "shared governance" are ideals. To manage well is a University of Phoenix ideal and goal.

Later in an auditorium, lights dimmed and a video played showing the garage where the organization started twenty-five years earlier. A short film clip of John Sperling was intercut with voice-over narration recalling the origins of the University of Phoenix, when the founder did everything from teaching the classes to collecting tuition. The small-business-started-in-a-garage story in this film is a classic origin story, but very different from the beginning of most universities, which are usually religious, philanthropic, or land-grant narratives. Traditional institutions would never represent themselves in this fashion—the University of Phoenix clearly understands itself to be a business and doesn't attempt to shroud itself in academic mythology. While universities typically talk about either broad community coalitions or religious missions in their origin stories, the University of Phoenix talks about struggling against overwhelming odds, perseverance, and success. A hush went around the auditorium when the president announced a new aggressive target set by John Sperling: 500,000 students by 2006. As I sat in the darkness I wondered: Is the outsider role appropriate for an institution that is fully accredited aiming for half a million students? Is the marginalized University of Phoenix moving from the edge toward the center?

ACKNOWLEDGMENTS

This book was written with the important and necessary collaboration of a number of people, including most especially colleagues on the Study of Good Work in Higher Education, which has been funded by the Hewlett Foundation, Carnegie Corporation of New York, and the Atlantic Philanthropies to study colleges and universities with outstanding undergraduate educational programs. Teams at Claremont Graduate University, Harvard University, and Stanford University, under the direction of Mihaly Csikszentmihalyi, Howard Gardner, and William Damon, carry out the project. I would particularly like to thank Howard Gardner for his comments early on, and the subsequent careful reading of my first draft. I'm greatly appreciative of Jeanne Nakamura and Mihaly Csikszentmihalyi's willingness over the past few years to involve me in the fascinating GoodWork Project.

Additionally, I want to express gratitude to the institutions and the individuals who agreed to participate in this study. I especially would like to thank Terri Hedegaard from the Apollo Group for the extraordinary cooperation she showed in opening the doors of the University of Phoenix to my inquiry. Additionally, Sylvia Williams at the Fielding Graduate Institute and Felicia Horton with DeVry Inc. were of great assistance in coordinating interviews with individuals from their organizations.

I want to thank Susan Slesinger, the executive editor of the ACE/ Praeger Series on Higher Education, for her early interest in my book and support throughout the writing process. I'd also like to express thanks to

Jason Cook of House of Equations, Inc., the copyeditor who carefully helped with the final revisions of this book. Finally, once again I'm indebted to my wife, Linda Venis, for her ongoing encouragement, counsel, and close reading of my work.

CHAPTER 1

Introduction: Building "Educational Hobo Jungles"?

History suggests that cultural, intellectual, and organizational advancements are made at opportune times. The G.I. Bill, which completely altered the composition of the student body in American universities after World War II, was the culmination of years of building pressure on the academy to open its doors wider to minorities, women, and lower economic classes, combined with the public sentiment to reward returning American warriors. Similarly, the Higher Education Act of 1965 providing federal financial aid, without which higher education as we know it today could not exist, came at a moment in time when civil rights and access issues in general were peaking. These defining moments in American higher education could not have occurred earlier. They were successfully implemented because of the particular characteristics of the specific time and place. Are we in a similar moment in time when the next great defining moment in higher education is occurring? Perhaps the approaches that for-profit institutions such as the University of Phoenix and DeVry University take are occurring at the right time and place. We may look back fifty years from now and say that these nontraditional institutions changed higher education at the turn of the century and led the way to important and necessary changes.

Robert M. Hutchins, chancellor of the University of Chicago, in a December 30, 1944, *Collier* magazine article warned that if the G.I. Bill passed, universities would find themselves converted into "educational hobo jungles." In fact, the G.I. Bill led to the enrollment of 1,013,000 veterans in American universities in 1946, instantly doubling the size of the student population. We shall see that according to administrators and faculty members from exemplary higher education institutions in America sixty years later, the focus on access for the underserved has shifted to the adult learners flooding universities, marking a change as significant as the entrance of returning soldiers after World War II. In the interviews conducted for the Good Work Higher Education study, representatives from two-year, four-year, public, and independent institutions spoke about current challenges in general, including the erosion of support for historically underserved groups and the way that access is now being redefined because of the rise of the adult learner. In this context, one begins to see the emerging importance of for-profit and nontraditional institutions designed to serve this new group.

Historically, higher education in America has been a place where social agendas are put into effect—some question this assumption. Derek Bok, former president of Harvard University, in *Universities and the Future of America* (1990), asks whether universities are still meeting this responsibility. Commentators inside and outside the academy have long pointed to a lack of access and an inability to serve the social purpose that is part of the stated mission of many universities. From the corporate perspective, Davis and Botkin, in *The Monster under the Bed* (1995), argue that business is increasingly taking responsibility for higher education in America because it sees a skilled workforce as a key competitive advantage. Simultaneously, higher education in America has come under great financial pressure; demand has grown greatly, while the costs have risen at an even faster rate. In reality, the pressures of economic necessity have been present in American higher education since its beginning. Hutchins, in his seminal book *The Higher Learning in America* (1952), describes what he calls the "service-station conception of a university," which blindly meets the needs of the student "customers" rather than leading with an assertion of academic quality and values. He describes this vocationalism as a natural outgrowth of the sources of funding for the university and the resulting emphasis on empirical research, rather than liberal studies. Criticism of overly applied curricula and vocationalism seen in the literature is particularly relevant in the debate about how best to meet the needs of underserved populations. At the beginning of the twentieth century, African American institutions moved toward a vocational emphasis and W.E.B. DuBois condemned this strategy, arguing that college was needed to educate students in the dominant system of power, not just to master skills to make a living. Revenue pressure, vocationalism, and the applied curriculum for minority groups are all central challenges that emerge from the interviews. More current problems center on an academy increasingly out of touch with the needs of society and faculty and often preoccupied with obscure research that doesn't address the needs of a new type of student.

Over the past two decades, higher education in America has witnessed an enormous shift in the demographics of students, while at the same time technology has enabled increased access to formal higher education. By the late 1990s, national attendance figures showed that 42 percent of the undergraduate and 59 percent of the graduate students attended part-time (UCEA, 1998). Of those part-time students, the largest average segment was women thirty-five years and older. Clearly, there has been an important shift in the past twenty-five years in the profile of the average college student, which is changing the American university. In addition to putting pressure on the university for an increasingly vocational and professionally oriented curriculum, this shift is also leading to pressure for the general accommodation of the working adult student through more convenient scheduling and location of courses. These changing demographics, combined with the severe revenue pressure felt throughout American higher education, now dramatically press the academy to change. The entrance of the adult learner into undergraduate education marks a major shift in direction for higher education, one perfectly in line with the missions of many for-profit and nontraditional institutions.

For-profit universities need to be taken more seriously. American higher education is respected worldwide and students flock in increasing numbers to universities across the country. What could successful universities possibly learn from for-profit institutions? Nevertheless, when a group of experts were asked about institutions that they felt were most innovative, the name of the University of Phoenix continually surfaced. Why?

To begin to appreciate the importance of for-profit higher education, we need to examine the state of higher education in America today. Although there are many challenges facing higher education, I point to four major pressures: (1) diminishing financial support, (2) the call to serve adult learners and first-generation college students, (3) a need to balance applied and liberal arts curricula, and (4) the subsequent necessity of maintaining and evolving institutional mission.

More than ever, concerns about revenue and balancing budgets are central for leaders in higher education today. Most important, institutions are increasingly pressured to alter their mission because diminished public funding has resulted in further dependence on donors and corporations. Particularly for public institutions, reduced funding is leading to fee increases, resulting in a smaller percentage of their overall budgets being supported by the state government. This shift may begin to change the mission of these institutions. Independent universities are also forced to behave in more entrepreneurial ways, often developing new educational programs outside of their traditional missions. Overall, stakeholders are more numerous and are pulling institutions in different, sometimes conflicting directions. While economic pressure on universities has been chronic throughout history, the apparent difference is that such strain is causing universities to behave in new ways.

Perhaps the biggest change in higher education over the past few decades has been the entrance in large numbers of adult learners, who are specifically targeted by the for-profits. The question arises of whether or not with the rise of the adult learner a liberal arts education is necessary or appropriate. Administrators from the for-profit institutions sometimes claim that adults, unlike traditional eighteen- to twenty-two-year-old undergraduates, are already formed and have values based on experience and knowledge gained to that point in their lives. Consequently, they are not seeking a traditional education. Additionally, adult students are less patient with faculties and universities who believe they know what is educationally best for students. A paternalistic attitude of "we know what's best for you" doesn't sit well with adults who increasingly look at universities with the jaded eye of a consumer. Perhaps those training for professions will return to school later in life looking for the liberal arts education they missed as undergraduates. Recognition of both applied and humanistic forms of knowledge may require a lifelong education. This realization of the extended learning life-span would mark an important evolution of the undergraduate degree in American higher education from one centered on a rite of passage of eighteen- to twenty-two-year-olds into society, to a more integrated grounding in the humanities, as well as competency in applied fields spread over a lifetime. In this way, the undergraduate degree may be changing its function in society.

In recent years we have seen the increased dominance of professional programs in higher education. While liberal arts courses have been losing enrollments to business and applied coursework for years, the move away from traditional undergraduate subjects is perhaps more overt than ever. Indicators such as a survey of freshmen students across America undertaken by the Higher Education Research Institute at UCLA suggest that a primary reason for attending college is to increase personal income. Educators from various types of higher education institutions regularly express concern that the traditional liberal arts education is increasingly de-emphasized. Additionally, higher education institutions continue to report severe problems with poor student preparation for college, particularly in writing. This student limitation may be pulling institutions even more toward a vocational curriculum. On the other hand, the liberal arts curriculum could become something available only to the privileged in elite schools. Ethnic minority youth may be ghettoized in applied courses of study, because it is easier for institutions to accomplish applied learning objectives, and it is more in line with the interests of businesses needing a vocationally educated workforce. For-profit higher educational institutions have redefined the affirmative action debate by encompassing class rather than just race, and by trying to serve diverse learners in business terms as customers. There is a long debate in higher education about whether the emphasis should be on a traditional liberal arts education or on applied fields in undergraduate education. Perhaps we can learn from the for-profits what an undergraduate education for the twenty-first century should look like given the new majority of adult learners.

So we see that higher education today is confronted with revenue constraints, while at the same time wrestling with deciding the direction and purpose of a college education. The traditional liberal arts education may be further abandoned for applied programs, because of the entrance of adult learners, minority populations, and the demand of society for a skilled workforce. How do universities protect what is valuable and useful about themselves, while responding to these pressures and the changing environment?

As these challenges weigh down traditional institutions, the for-profit universities rise up. The challenges listed earlier are handled by the for-profit universities by their very structure as for-profit companies organized to achieve efficiency and growth. Additionally, they specialize in applied curricula aiming to meet the need of businesses for a workforce skilled in specific ways. They are managed professionally as businesses and continually question and refine their organizational missions. Last, they are constructed specifically to meet the needs of adult learners.

This book grew out of research linked to the Study of Good Work in Higher Education (see Appendix A). Since 1995 the GoodWork Project (GWP) has been investigating how individuals are able to carry out "good work" in their chosen professions when conditions are changing at unprecedented rates and when market forces are enormously powerful. By "good work" is meant work that is at once of high quality, socially responsible, and beneficial to the worker. It is my argument in this book that good work by this definition is occurring at nontraditional institutions, including some of the for-profits.

There is a large amount of disinformation—sometimes willful—about for-profit universities. Although unique in some ways, the University of Phoenix has come to represent the for-profit university more generally, and can be used here to shed light on some of the specific characteristics of these nontraditional universities (in Chapter 3 I look in more detail at specific for-profit and vocational education history and data). First, the University of Phoenix is a for-profit, publicly traded company, a fact that generates much of the disdain administrators and faculty members from traditional universities display for it. Second, it is remarkably successful, with over 130,000 students and a 30 percent annual growth rate. In fact, the University of Phoenix is expanding internationally and has set a target of 500,000 students. Third, its mission is clearly defined as educating working adults. Both "working" and "adult" are central to this mission. Fourth, it has a specific teaching approach that includes five-, six-, and eight-week single-course terms, learning teams, the incorporation of work experience, standardized course materials, and heavy emphasis on learning objectives and assessment of student learning. Fifth, it is not primarily a distance learning university. In fact, only one-third of its courses are taken over the Internet; mostly students attend courses in regular face-to-face classrooms. Sixth, it has few full-time faculty members and instead relies on a "practitioner" faculty model wherein work experience within a specific profession is seen as more desirable than teaching or research. Finally, the University of Phoenix isn't just about making money. Although it is a for-profit company, it is critical to understand that the university faculty members and staff express a clear social agenda. While few for-profit institutions are as successful as the University of Phoenix, key characteristics such as the emphasis on working adults, intensive formats, and the use of practitioner faculty are similar.

For-profit universities lead the way in many of the critical areas where higher education needs the most work. They have led in targeting the needs of businesses, focusing on working adults seeking to complete degrees, and in creating economical, standardized content. The for-profit universities have also led in assessment methods, creating and maintaining responsive student services, and innovations such as the recent development of customized digital textbooks at the University of Phoenix. They have been leaders in distance learning. In fact, collectively they are altering the domain of higher education as a whole. As a result of years of pitched battles with regional and professional accrediting agencies, they have honed their arguments. Rather than simply complying with accreditation guidelines as most institutions regularly do, the University of Phoenix and others have engaged in a debate about the essence of the standards. For instance, rather than be held to a notion of quality based on resources and the number of full-time faculty, they have insisted on quality as derived from stating what they intend the students to learn, and then proving that they have done what they said they'd do. In addition, they've taken on the long-held value of seat time in higher education, and argued against this measurement of quality, again asking that the essence of what higher education institutions are doing be understood. As a result, accrediting agencies are refocusing their guidelines on self-determined institutional objectives based on a "culture of evidence" rather than the older measurements of resources and number of full-time faculty. This is indeed a major shift in higher education.

Let me give specific examples of innovation shown at for-profit institutions. For more than a decade, for-profit universities have offered online degree credit programs. They initially began by using simple course management software, realizing early on the advantage of keeping their courses low-tech to accommodate students and that the importance of distance learning is as a communication tool (computer-mediated communication, commonly known now as CMC). Other universities with less of a student focus have repeatedly made the mistake of overloading their online courses with multimedia elements, causing problems for student users. Especially for more selective institutions, the tendency to insist on graphic-intensive online courses has led to a belief that distance learning is not economically viable because they are spending too much money on course development. At the same time, these institutions have run into trouble with distribution and technical support. In the past couple of years, most have learned their lesson on this point, but a look at the for-profit model early on would have saved these institutions a great deal of time and money.

Many of the for-profit universities had an already existing model for teaching and learning that fit nicely with the online environment. Their face-to-face models often emphasize learning teams, practitioner faculty, and standardized curriculum. Research indicates now that group learning is particularly effective in online learning environments in creating a sense of community (Berg, 2002). The learning teams formed for in-person courses work well when adapted to the online environment. The practitioner faculty model, which emphasizes the use of professionals working in their fields, is a natural in the online environment, where working adults can integrate school and work effectively. Furthermore, through the computer, the ability to access course materials and communicate with the faculty and other students while at work further encourages this work-learning integration. Finally, the standardized materials make the scalability of the online courses more possible and provide content without having to rely on individual faculty members. This is a key advantage for the for-profits, because they have "unbundled" the faculty from the course content. Where the slow process of encouraging sometimes-resistant faculty members to develop online courses has weighed down traditional institutions, the for-profits have been able to quickly convert their content and then hire and train faculty to teach online courses.

The for-profit universities concentrated on a culture of evidence in face-to-face courses, and this led them to quickly adapt to using assessment in online courses. With regulatory pressures and a customer/client focus, the for-profits have always set clear learning outcomes, and then measured success in meeting those goals. With the spotlight thrown on distance learning and the suspicion from traditional educators, this concentration on assessment has allowed the for-profits to be leaders in providing proof of the effectiveness of distance learning as an approach. While many traditional institutions have employed various methods of assessment for distance learning courses, they are primarily using the same methods employed in the face-to-face courses. These methods for the most part are faculty centered, and not nearly as aggressive and detailed as the for-profits' methods. As a result of the size of their distance learning operations and the scope of measurement, the for-profits are far ahead of other institutions in understanding and ensuring uniform quality in their distance learning courses.

There is a long history in American higher education of using various blended formats for course delivery, going back over a hundred years to the Chautauqua movement, during which adult students would attend summer educational retreats and then continue to learn the rest of the year at a distance, often in "reading" groups. Now the University of Phoenix and other for-profit universities are leading the way on the blended delivery front by combining face-to-face with online learning. Students in these courses meet in person for part of the course (the first and last meetings at the University of Phoenix). The other meetings are held online. This blended format has the advantage of still including face-to-face learning at the crucial introductory and final meetings, while retaining the convenience and networked capabilities of online courses. Other traditional universities are offering similar programs, such as the MBA program at Duke University and the EdD program at Pepperdine University. However, once again, none has the advantage of the large scale and established methods of the for-profits.

What may prove to be the biggest innovation thus far by a single for-profit higher education institution is the new e-textbook effort at the University of Phoenix, which switches the course content over to digitized custom textbooks. Pushing the textbook companies with its growing clout, the University of Phoenix is revolutionizing how course content is created and distributed. In its initial stages, not only will this new program make the books available to students in digital formats, but also the books will be customized for the University of Phoenix. This innovation will perhaps lead individual universities and faculty members to construct custom books for their courses in the future. The possibilities for customization and integration with online learning resources are obvious. This challenge to textbook companies will lead to a changed higher education economics and more, important, is liable to force changes in how universities think about course content. While some may bristle at the notion of standardized curriculum as used at the University of Phoenix, traditional universities have been dependent for years on textbook publishers for standardized curriculum presented in textbooks, particularly for lower-division undergraduate courses.

Taken altogether one can see that for-profit universities are often remarkably innovative. The for-profit institutions have had poor reputations in academia for years because of their proprietary status, unorthodox methods, and combative posture toward mainstream higher education. Nevertheless, traditional universities have much to gain in looking at the for-profits' approaches to dealing with the challenges faced today in higher education. While certainly there are many differences between the for-profit universities and traditional institutions in mission and method, there is common ground in needing to better understand ways to confront the increasing revenue pressure, sustain institutional mission, harmonize applied and liberal arts curricula, and meet the needs of adult learners.

PERSPECTIVE AND ORGANIZATION OF THE BOOK

It is not my intention in this book to make a qualitative judgment about for-profit universities—the regional accrediting organizations have this responsibility. As with the subject of distance learning, many want to enter into a debate about for-profit higher education—I don't believe this is productive. Instead, I intend to look deeply at the specific characteristics of for-profit higher education with the goal of learning what might be useful in their approaches and particular methods. I am suggesting one way of looking at the for-profit universities and their place in the changing setting of higher education today.

My own professional background has been primarily in continuing education divisions within traditional universities. Consequently, I've been intimately involved in nontraditional forms of education and training, including corporate, contract, grant funded, and distance learning. Furthermore, I am primarily accustomed to serving adult learners and assisting them in meeting their ongoing professional development needs. Additionally, continuing education divisions in America are generally self-supporting. As a result, the extended education division in most universities tends to be the most closely associated with market models by their very nature and design.

Moreover, I'm interested in improving higher education. Usually discussions of reform focus on K–12 education, not higher education. It is my experience that the general public is often puzzled by discussions of reform in higher education, believing that in comparison to primary and secondary school the problems are minimal. I disagree.

This book is organized in the following manner. I begin Chapter 2 by looking at current challenges in higher education as represented by faculty and administrators from exemplary higher education institutions. I then consider how traditional institutions are confronting these issues and the way their solutions intersect with those offered by the for-profits. In Chapter 3, as a way of introducing the current information on for-profit institutions, I give a description of the development of vocational and for-profit higher education in America and patterns of meaning derived from this review. In Chapter 4, I reflect on the unique missions at for-profits to serve working adults and special characteristics of how mission functions within the organizations. In Chapter 5, I examine the culture and rhetoric of the universities as represented in symbolism and forms of communication, as well as common attitudes and approaches to work. Additionally, some of the more dynamic aspects of the organizations such as their propensity for innovation and openness to internal debate are analyzed. In Chapter 6, I turn to organizational structure and examine the role that charismatic leaders play in the for-profit universities, the balance between centralized and decentralized functions, and risk-taking. In addition, topics such as awareness of public policy, participatory management style, and staff development are addressed.

In Chapter 7, I look more closely at the decision-making process at the for-profits. How is the creative tension between academic and business interests maintained? How is change managed? How can traditional universities find a faster decision-making process? In Chapter 8, I consider faculty members at the for-profits, including the practitioner model, the lack of tenure, and the nature of personal investment in the organization. I also look at related pedagogical issues, such as the problem of poor student preparation for college-level work and the use of standardized teaching materials. In Chapter 9, I discuss the apparent challenges that the for-profit universities face, including maintaining order during vast growth and drawing talented administrators and faculty to the organization. I conclude the book with a look at the distinguishing characteristics of the for-profit university in the context of higher education as a whole, and what might be of use to traditional institutions during a time of great flux. I reflect critically on the larger debate about for-profit higher education and the future of higher education in America.

In writing this book I intend to neither be a cheerleader for the for-profit universities, nor a blind critic. As with any large human organizations, they are a collection of motives and efforts, good and bad. My sincere intention is to be fair, honest, and truthful about the for-profit universities and their role in higher education today. Nevertheless, I start from the position that there is something new, interesting, and worthwhile going on at for-profit institutions that others might learn from. This is not without basis—it is in fact what many experts in the field are saying.

Let me suggest another way to read this book. It is quite clear to me that in many ways for-profit higher educational institutions (especially the University of Phoenix) are uniquely American inventions and hold great interest as cultural artifacts. With colorful and fiery founders, origin stories of beginnings as garage businesses, their populist beliefs in providing educational opportunities to first-generation college students, their Yankee innovation, hardworking, participatory management, and pure bravado, they are American as can be. For me, the University of Phoenix particularly represents the America seen arising like the proverbial phoenix in various manifestations from the turbulent 1960s and 1970s. In many ways it signifies a twist on the capitalist system that only could have happened by design from those emerging from that influential time period in America.

The University of Phoenix and other for-profit educational institutions are both an expression of American culture at the start of the twenty-first century and an indicator of things to come in higher education. The increasing focus and scrutiny by the general public on the mysterious ways of the academy is largely the result of its successes. Americans have come to understand the value of a productive university to the economy, the culture, and the personal well-being of citizens. As the importance of the university is widely recognized, scrutiny grows. Some of those looking from the outside wonder why the university cannot be more efficient, inexpensive, accountable, and responsive to society. We shall see that some tentative answers to these questions may come from the for-profit universities.

DEFINING THE TOPIC: FOR-PROFITS
AND NONTRADITIONAL INSTITUTIONS

Initially, I set out to write a book on the University of Phoenix alone. After consultation with various colleagues and editors at different presses, I decided that this was too narrow and enlarged the scope of the book to include other for-profit and proprietary institutions. In so doing, I soon realized that for-profit or nonprofit status wasn't really the determining factor in characterizing these institutions. After all, the number of regionally accredited for-profit institutions is very small, and the larger discussion in the academy is really about market models applied to traditional higher education. To highlight the misunderstanding of for-profit institutions in America: When I asked experts in the field for recommendations on for-profit institutions I should look at, they mentioned the Fielding Institute, Heritage College, Monroe College, and the New College of California—all nonprofit institutions! While one could ascribe this misclassification by the experts to various things, I suggest here that their uniqueness is more about these institutions being nontraditional and on the periphery than their official profit/nonprofit status.

Additionally, when one looks at the great diversity of type in American higher education, center and edge notions are a bit murky. So let me here give some basic definitional guidelines. I define a "nontraditional" institution as an institution of higher learning that in mission, teaching method, or administrative and governance structures operates outside of the norm. The University of Phoenix is nontraditional because its mission is to serve working adults exclusively, it uses materials-based intensive-format courses, and it is managed as a business without a faculty governance scheme. Although a nonprofit, the Fielding Institute is nontraditional because it also serves adult learners, and utilizes a unique distance learning pedagogical approach. While some more traditional postsecondary institutions also have like characteristics, they are generally constituted quite differently in overall mission and/or methods. At any rate, the institutions studied here are not ones that you will find highlighted in the *U.S. News and Report* rankings, and are not often mentioned in discussions about selective institutions. Yet we will see that there is much about them that we can all learn from. Therefore, in this book I focus on for-profit regionally accredited institutions, and use selected examples of nontraditional, nonprofit institutions for contrast.

I began this chapter by asking if the for-profits and nontraditional institutions are changing higher education, and that question will undoubtedly be answered over time. However, I propose in the course of this book to provide indications why this might be so, particularly as instruments of providing access to the educationally dispossessed, and in improving the professional management of higher education. In the following chapters we will look in detail at what I suspect Hutchins would think is the perfect representation of the "educational hobo jungle" he foresaw with so much dread.

CHAPTER

Soft in the Middle: Current Challenges in Higher Education

It is difficult to appreciate the uniqueness of the for-profit and non-traditional institutions profiled in this book without looking at these institutions in comparison to traditional higher education. This chapter serves to illuminate some of the main challenges faced by higher education across institutional type and will provide a context for better understanding the importance of organizations like the for-profit University of Phoenix and nontraditional Fielding Graduate Institute. In the interviews conducted for the Study of Good Work in Higher Education, subjects were questioned about their views on challenges now facing their institutions as well as the ones on the horizon. I looked at the emerging patterns and themes that surfaced and how the exemplary institutions in this study are meeting those challenges. In addition, administrators and faculty members were asked about their impressions of "new providers" entering the higher education marketplace and culture. The indirect debate or dialogue that arises from these responses helps focus the key issues and challenges in higher education and suggests how the for-profit and nontraditional institutions may provide some direction. How are the current problems different or similar to the recurring issues encountered over the past two centuries? How are exemplary institutions responding to these challenges? These questions drive the investigation in this chapter.

CHALLENGES

Revenue Pressure

According to a recent Rand report (1997), *Breaking the Social Contract: The Fiscal Crisis in Higher Education*, if the present trend of rising costs and demand of higher education and lessened funding continues, within a few years millions of Americans will be denied a college education. The reasons? Public support per student has remained flat while real costs per student grew by 40 percent between 1976 and 1994. Overall, government spending priorities changed. The average real tuition per student adjusted for inflation doubled between 1976 and 1995. If it doubles again in the following twenty-year period, an estimated 6.7 million students will be priced out of the system. According to the Rand report, streamlining and restructuring are needed to get additional public funding—simply requesting more and more funding from government sources no longer works. Why hasn't higher education as a whole responded more quickly to this crisis? "The main reason why institutions have not taken more effective action is their outmoded governance structure—i.e., the decision-making units, policies, and practices that control resource allocation have remained largely unchanged since the structure's establishment in the 19th century" (Rand, 1997, p. 13). The Rand report ends by recommending structural changes in governance system, performance-based assessment, greater mission differentiation among institutions, and the sharing of resources. Universities need to focus on core competencies in connection with their unique missions.

One of the dominant themes found in the Good Work Higher Education study is the increasing pressure on institutions to raise revenue. While certainly not a new issue in higher education, this particular need for funding may be leading to new behavior. The demand to meet budgetary shortfalls, continually noted in the interviews, generally centered on how these pressures influence objectives and strategies—and even the core mission—of the institution. There has been much discussion in higher education circles for years about the pressure to raise funds and subsequent concerns that the donors influence university direction. Clearly, now more than ever, this is an issue in higher education. Some describe what they see as an inevitable temptation to adjust institutional mission to please donors: "I think that when you get down to the sort of micro level, there are temptations to tweak your goals at times to please donors." However, this same interviewee later indicates that there might be advantages to donor pressure in that it can prompt the university to innovate: "It might be actually a financial source that spurs you to be innovative." This discussion of the academic/business balance is an important one for institutions in the study, and central to the for-profits' solution to current challenges.

The changing demographics of students attending higher education institutions and their need for low-cost education adds further pressure to the economics of education: "I think one of the challenges we will be facing is the cost of higher education; whether we can afford to do the style of education we're accustomed to doing here." Moreover, not only is the issue of institutions' inability to offer low-cost education a primary concern in higher education today, but financial support from the public has lessened as need has increased.

What effect does the lack of revenue have on faculties? One member characterizes current interest in budget information as a possible indication of increased awareness in financial issues affecting their institutions. This awareness leads to inevitable criticism of the influence of revenue on decision making. As one faculty member puts it: "I think many times the bottom line gets in the way. Because of the bottom line, we end up making decisions that are not the most humane. I see that at this institution." With less revenue to spread around, the distribution plan becomes increasingly political and strategic, forcing institutions to prioritize and reflect more on core values. One respondent expresses concern about differing goals for corporate and academic interests in her university: "I just believe that the goals of the corporate sector aren't necessarily consistent with the goals of providing an education to our students; and when that's going to conflict and money is involved, then we're going to be in trouble." Of course, this is a central concern expressed by traditional academics about for-profit institutions—that quality is negatively influenced by profit motive.

What does it mean when an institution puts revenues heavily into recruitment and recreational facilities? Does it indicate a change of mission focus or priority? A faculty member describes the difficult choices that are made because of economic pressures, commenting on how resources are directed to activities outside of the core educational mission such as recreational facilities. Aggressive recruitment tactics usually tied to for-profit institutions also seem to be a trend at traditional institutions. Administrators at various institutions indicate that one result of the revenue emphasis is the attention paid to recruitment. As recruitment leads directly to additional revenue, much like a sales department in a business, it is becoming a core activity for the contemporary university. A university that has a successful admissions department benefits from increased revenue, academic reputation (selectivity), and a bigger donor pool. The pursuit of outside funding in the form of contracts and grants from public

and private sources, and other alliances with business, are other ways institutions respond to the revenue challenge.

Interview subjects talk about how revenue pressure leads to a closer
alliance with businesses in the offering of products and the displaying of
advertising. In the past few years, this "commercialization" of higher education became a core concern for many in the higher education community who are fearful that it changes the essential nature of the university's
role in society. Indeed, one of the most serious complaints found in the
interviews is that revenue pressure leads institutions away from their
missions—particularly social missions that are expensive or unlikely to attract funding sources. Administrators and faculty members from schools
with a strong social mission connect the search for revenue with the ability to support students from lower economic groups: "Probably the biggest struggle we have is to sustain the population that we have brought
on to the college. . . . To serve the population we have [today], and give
the discount we give, we don't need $50 million in the endowment, we
need $150 million." Revenue links to access for lower-class students in a
direct manner.

State government–funded institutions clearly differ from independent
universities in many ways, but especially in their mandated mission to
serve the citizens of their respective states. In recent years, a great deal
of discussion has ensued both within the academy and through the press
about the reduced funding for state-supported institutions, and the ramifications of this change are reflected in fee/tuition increases. For example,
in their annual report, the College Board found a 9.6 percent increase
during the 2002–2003 school year in tuition for four-year public colleges.
One danger of this reduced funding, as many of the interviews made clear,
is resulting pressure on these universities to limit or change their missions
because of economic necessity:

> We get less than 30 percent of our budget from the state, yet the state
> still views us as a public institution and has some say over what we
> see our mission as and how we fulfill that mission. So there's not the
> freedom that there is with privates. I don't think states want to let
> that go, but they also don't want to fund it, so I think that all the
> large publics are going through a kind of redefining of self.

If most of the funding for an institution increasingly comes from sources
other than the state, at what point does it become necessary to redefine
the institutional mission?

State governments are often asking institutions to act more aggressively
in raising funds for support, yet the latter is hampered by a social mission

sometimes at odds with these actions. The following respondent suggests that the mission of the American land-grant institutions likely faces permanent alteration because of reduced funding: "I don't think state funding is ever going to go back to the level that our state seemed to think was appropriate: this was really the access and upward-mobility idea that a university education should be available to all its citizens at a modest cost. Well, that's gone. States are not willing to put in that money." This is a particularly important point because of the strong social service mandate of the land-grant institutions in America. If these institutions are no longer funded by the state, can they still serve as an instrument of democracy in bringing higher education to all who desire it?

Another ramification of slack funding at the state level is that it has led to increased competition between two- and four-year institutions. This is particularly difficult for four-year institutions that operate with higher expenses. One administrator asserts that the competition between the two-year and four-year institutions is so great that it jeopardizes the existence of some institutions. The result of this change in funding for one interviewee means less educational services aimed at undergraduates. So the results of less revenue at state institutions are less access and the further de-emphasis of the undergraduate program.

One outcome of revenue pressure is to focus on making universities more efficient and run like businesses. Tenure is a prime target when looking at traditional university's claimed inefficiencies. A trustee describes how tenure, which lies at the heart of the organizational structure of traditional universities, is not good management practice:

> You could have a faculty that is non-functional and because they have tenure, they're here forever. Whereas in business, at least when I was responsible for hiring or firing, if somebody didn't do their job, they were gone. Period. End of statement. That's in conflict for how things are done in academia, because we have this whole idea of academic freedom and we have this whole idea of "everybody may look at things differently." And so how are those conflicts handled? Most often they're handled covertly.

Notice how the result of this cumbersome management scheme leads to what is described as "covert" methods of getting things done. The same respondent criticizes the inefficient manner in which resources are allocated. The interview subject points out the connection between allocation of resources and mission—an inability to move resources to primary activities hinders the ability to serve the mission: "We're very democratic and we want to make everybody happy. So we take what we have and we cut it up into smaller and smaller pieces and send it out to everybody. As opposed to saying to these areas, 'No. You're not getting anything. What we would've given to you we're going to focus over here.'" What this trustee indicates is that the result of faculty governance is a democratic division of resources that is not in the best interest of the institution, or in the service of the mission. In a day-to-day sense, respondents speak about how a revenue shortfall leads to such things as lack of proper office and classroom facilities. The lack of revenue especially impacts institutions where this has been a chronic problem. More important, one respondent explains what money means for institutions in terms of charting overall institutional direction: "Money is important because it limits, given a lot more money, hiring people with decent vision. You've got money and vision, you solve problems." The effects of lack of financial resources are directly felt in the classroom, and indirectly felt through a limitation on the ambitiousness of institutional objectives.

Thus, in sum, revenue pressure is identified by those interviewed as a primary concern because it might alter the institutional mission by lessening access, devalue the undergraduate program, commercialize the academy, and lead to increased reliance on grants, donors, and businesses for support. Furthermore, lack of revenue is focusing criticism on the academy for inefficient management schemes.

Identity

Not since the nineteenth century, when there was a great proliferation of American colleges, has there been such a need for institutions to differentiate themselves. Academic reputation is the most prized of all things in the academy, and a closely held part of institutional identity. A recurring theme in the Good Work Higher Education interviews, and those conducted separately for this book, is a focus on maintaining the unique identity of the institution given current challenges: "I think preserving the goals and the mission of this institution is going to be a difficult problem to maintain in this environment." The challenges to maintaining identity indicated by administrators and faculty members include changing demographics of the populations served, competition, maintaining academic reputation, and fighting elitism.

Some speak about the challenge of communicating the uniqueness of their institution in combating competition from new providers. The issue of maintaining identity in an increasingly heated competitive environment emerges as a common theme: "We're looking at the issues of marketing ourselves and niche identity as well." The same administrator, from a Catholic women's college, talks about the changes that occurred when programs aimed at working adults and males were added:

> About thirty-five percent of our students are not Catholic, and what does that mean? Niche identity, and that really follows along with the co-ed and religious questions. If we are marketing to a co-ed weekend college and a co-ed allied health evening program and co-educational graduate program, then how do we also market to a traditional liberal arts baccalaureate and associate programs primarily for women?

However, is differentiation enough? What if the students don't need or want your institutional uniqueness? The issue isn't only differentiation, but also relevancy and consistency of organizational presentation to the student audience.

Academic reputation has always been of utmost importance to educational institutions, but now, with increased competition and less public funds for support of land-grant institutions, it is a top priority. One faculty member at a selective institution expresses concern over how academic reputation is maintained and passed along to a new group of caretakers: "One thing I'm worried about is how the new group of people pick up whatever this is that causes [a subject's institution] to have this kind of reputation? I don't know what it is. Nobody's kind of put their finger on that—what maintains that." Subjects complain about the practice of tying academic reputation to selectivity in admission practices. While institutions fight the sometimes arbitrary notion of academic reputation, they understand its increasing import. The tension is that if academic reputation is more critical now because of competition, access needs to be restricted to increase selectivity ratings.

Along with a high academic reputation sometimes come charges of elitism. An administrator from an historically black college describes the challenge of battling misperceptions of elitism in its local community, despite a long history of giving access to an underserved population. Awareness of community perception is required with a mission to serve a particular population—it cannot seem to be turning its back on the main institutional objectives. Here again, the conflict between raising academic reputation and the mission to provide wide access to higher education resources is evident.

Maintaining and differentiating institutional identity, then, is a particular challenge in the current environment of increased competition, revenue pressure, and changing demographics. For those institutions with a social agenda, lack of revenue is clearly putting pressure on their mission. It is interesting to consider here the similarity of the exercise in emphasizing uniqueness for these traditional institutions, to businesses seeking product differentiation.

Social Consciousness and Diversity

Notions of diversity may have changed in both content and intensity. Administrators and faculty members speak very directly about the need in higher education to pursue the goal of providing equal opportunity to earn a college education. However, some lament the slowness of higher education to move forward on diversity issues. Traditional preoccupations with the ethnic composition of the student body and faculty remain common concerns. An administrator from an elite school speaks about the importance and difficulty in attracting a diverse student body: "I think diversity, getting students of color here, has always been a challenge, and I think it will continue to be a challenge." One administrator focuses on the diversity of faculty, especially full-time faculty, as a primary concern. Of course, this has been a problem for many years, and there is some evidence (Finklestein, Seal, & Schuster, 1998) that progress toward a more diverse faculty nationally has been made. Universities appear to be paying great attention to recruiting faculty who better represent the ethnic diversity of the community. In fact, administrators from community colleges speak about the difficulty in competing with four-year institutions for ethnic minority faculty.

More generally, administrators and faculty members talk about diversity in the broader context of changing demographics. One of the historical strengths of higher education in America is to serve the traditional college-age student of eighteen to twenty-two years old in a structured, residential experience. However, this scenario is clearly no longer the primary experience for those pursuing undergraduate degrees. Unlike traditional students, adults worry about a child at home and their partners, and are involved in a career while attending night school. They also demand and need more responsive student services. An administrator from a community college speaks about the inflexibility of some research institutions to accommodate working adult students: "One of the biggest issues we have is that you really need to be a full-time student at the UC's [University of California]. . . . How can they work with our students when the majority of our students are part-time?" While some of the more selective institutions can still afford to ignore the adult learner, most of the institutions I studied have already changed in some way because of this new force.

Diversity remains an issue in higher education and is increasingly important because of the entrance of the adult learner. While there have been improvements, administrators and faculty members acknowledge the slowness of change, and the difficulty in attracting minority students and faculty. One important difference to note here is how for-profits have broadened the affirmative action debate from ethnic-based to class- and age-based definitions of diversity. It will be interesting to see how the for-profit institutions key in on this distinction and awareness.

Teaching/Learning

As always, faculty issues are central to higher education as both a challenge and an opportunity. Slowness to make decisions, recruitment, and the use of part-time faculty are central concerns. On the learning side of the equation, poor student preparation is repeatedly pointed to in the interviews as a primary problem.

The struggle for universities to recruit the most qualified faculty remains an ongoing challenge for universities. One faculty member focuses on the difficulty of universities in areas with high costs of living to recruit faculty. Others connect the ability to recruit top faculty directly with academic institutional prestige: "We have to be able to hire and keep the good faculty members, 'stars,' as the word is frequently used." One faculty member reflects candidly on the attitude of faculty toward their profession and the common concerns for better compensation and reduced teaching loads: "Our faculty members want: A: raises. And they want B: decreased teaching loads. . . . Where in the world is the university going to get these things?" Additionally, a recurring issue in the transcripts is the focus on the increased use of part-time faculty in American higher education. Some connect this use of part-time faculty with distance learning.

The lack of preparation of students by their secondary schools for higher education has been a concern since the beginning of higher education in America, and remains one today. Because education in American developed from the top with higher education institutions rather than K–12 schools leading the way, maintaining standards has always been a challenge. The primary and secondary educational institutions have always had difficulty preparing students for college-level coursework. Furthermore, the large number of colleges in the nineteenth century placed a strain on the number of qualified faculty members. Overall, higher education can be seen as often aiming higher than it has been capable of sustaining on an academic level. The relationship between college and high schools or preparatory schools has been difficult, with college administrators often complaining that they are forced to do the work that high schools do not accomplish in properly preparing students for the demands of college.

In addition, the general failure of high schools to prepare students for college has often become coupled with a lack of attention to undergraduate education. Interview subjects repeatedly note a lack of sufficient preparation for incoming students. A key indicator of the economic challenge of providing remedial education is the increased use of part-time faculty to teach these courses.

Thus I hear from respondents that teaching/learning in the academy is now challenged by the recruitment of qualified faculty, the increased use of part-time faculty, and poor student preparation. Although not new problems, the degree of challenge they now represent may have increased.

Business Models

> I think, to some degree, they [for-profits] are driving us to be uncomfortable, which is a good thing.

While some respondents view the increased use of business models by the university's management as a threat, others see it as an opportunity to innovate. The connection between governance schemes and change is an important one. Many commented on the slowness of traditional academic joint governance: "If the world ran by the kinds of committees that academic institutions run by, we'd still be in the pre-Cambrian ooze." Some speak about the rise of faculty in institutional governance and the challenge this represents. Administrators focus on the resistance of faculty to change toward business models of governance. Overall, many administrators and faculty members see the rise of business models as a response to management problems in the academy.

On the positive side, some interviewees reflect on how the new providers supply an impetus for change at traditional institutions: "They're forcing everybody to be quality focused. They're forcing everybody to be customer focused." Why are the for-profit institutions having such a big effect? Some faculty members and administrators comment on the sensitivity of institutions such as the University of Phoenix and other nontraditional institutions to the particular nonacademic needs of their adult student population. Many of the administrators and faculty members speak about universities now viewing students more as customers than traditional students. Generally, this student-as-customer movement focuses primarily on student services. However, some see a danger in using a customer/student-centered approach when it comes to academic issues. Administrators comment on how the new consumer attitude of the students leads to less institutional loyalty: "That whole consumer view of higher education doesn't lend itself to some of the old-fashioned views of loyalty and bonding to the institution." A similar lack of loyalty is also evidenced in faculty, and according to the administrator leads to a lessening of investment in institutional mission.

The business model is seen by many as a threat because of the efficiency and customer orientation running counter to traditional higher education culture. Others do not see the reason for alarm and refuse to view students as customers. One particular strand of analysis to recognize here is the connection between the use of a business model in higher education and serving the adult student. As noted by one faculty member, the rise of this model in higher education is encouraged by, and is well-suited to, the adult student population, now the majority in undergraduate education nationally.

Applied Curricula

> The aim of the higher training of the college is the development of power, the training of a self whose balanced assertion will mean as much as possible for the great ends of civilization. The aim of technical training on the other hand is to enable the student to master the present methods of earning a living in some particular way . . . we must give to our youth a training designed above all to make them men of power, of thought, of trained and cultivated taste. (DuBois, 1973, pp. 13–14)

There is a long and rich debate within the historically black college and university community about how applied the curriculum should be for the population they serve. Some argue that ethnic minorities need a practical education that leads to a higher standard of living, while others see no reason students should be denied that same whole person, liberal education received at elite institutions. In this context, many of the for-profit and nontraditional institutional approaches come under fire for serving a minority population with an applied curriculum that does not give the students the broader education a liberal arts institution has to offer: "If we all become technical training schools we've changed the nature of the beast again. We're redefining what it means to be human."

The attitude and position of faculty and administrators from Xavier College on this issue are particularly important and revealing. First, the objective of promoting spiritual values is part of the institutional mission: "[T]he idea of the African American community that it largely serves has a spiritual core." One faculty member points to the value of a broad education in the real world and asks, "Which students would be better prepared to exist in the real world? Being prepared in an institution like Xavier gives you an awful lot of flexibility in terms of your options." He argues that liberal arts education is more practical because it gives students an education that is not dependent on the sometimes unsure future of specific trades.

A faculty member from a religious-based institution speaks about the need to address deeper values and human development beyond learning an occupation: "There is within the school a sense that it's about more than just learning a trade. That there are deep recesses in a human being that need to be fulfilled and nurtured." One interviewee criticizes the practical and applied nature of the education received by students at for-profit institutions like the University of Phoenix and laments the long-term negative influence on a lack of humanistic education on the human race, and asks, "What's it going to do to the nation?" The following respondent describes the debate over applied versus liberal arts curricula, now informed by what is meaningful to the student: "I know what that student needs, and that is an academic core of classes they have to have to be a general-educated student. There's that view; then there's also the view that asks the question, is that meaningful to a student?" Here is exhibited the tension between what the institution thinks is best for the student, and what the student wants. This tension is particularly strong for adult learners, those from lower economic backgrounds, and students of color.

Administrators and faculty members generally question the sole focus on applied knowledge. This debate has a long history in higher education, but is particularly central to current concerns and the for-profits when discussing the impact on minority students.

SOLUTIONS FROM TRADITIONAL INSTITUTIONS

It is not surprising that institutions identified as "exemplary" by experts in the field of higher education have solutions for resolving the current problems. Generally, these can be termed routes or specific initiatives rather than fully developed plans detailed in particular interviews. These solutions from traditional universities concentrate on meeting revenue demands, increasing student readiness, emphasizing institutional uniqueness, balancing academic and business interests, prioritizing objectives, and retaining an awareness of social issues.

Find Additional Sources of Revenue

As indicated earlier, state institutions in particular are struggling with how to find additional sources of revenue. What strategies are they using to raise much needed revenues? Two distinct general approaches emerge: (1) use various means to supplement traditional forms of financial support; (2) increase stakeholder awareness of budget issues.

Administrators describe how their public institution emphasizes recruiting full-tuition-paying, out-of-state students in order to increase revenue because the out-of-state tuition is a lot more than in-state tuition. Even tuition discounting—usually an independent institution practice—is used by public institutions for out-of-state students: "It's giving this out-of-state student who's going to pay $10,000 a $1,000 scholarship so they're happy to come here and you're still getting $9,000 out of them." Searching for private and public funds to support specific program areas is another avenue of subsidizing revenue streams for the institution. Administrators speak about the need for both increased marketing and diversification of their educational "product": "We have to market ourselves and we have to diversify ourselves, just like any good organization. We have to look at the kind of programs that we're offering, making sure that we are not investing ourselves entirely in one area. Any good liberal arts college that has survived and is prospering has diversified." Many institutions indicate a need to communicate a better understanding of budgetary restrictions. Administrators talk about the practice of sharing budgetary information with faculty, such as the income/cost ratio for every program so that they understand constraints.

Scholars in recent years have commented on the means taken by institutions to find new sources of revenue, including alliances with business and industry, aggressive student recruitment, grants, and the creation of entrepreneurial units within the university. Additionally, institutions in the study try increasingly to discuss budgets internally and raise generally awareness of funding limitations.

Prepare Students

The solutions to the student readiness problem offered by institutions studied concentrate on using existing university services such as placement exams and writing centers. Additionally, they advocate trying to understand the impact on the students of lengthening the time needed to attain a degree. Some focus on the need to investigate the best methods for remedial education. Faculty members comment on the need to direct students to campus resources designed to address remedial education needs. Other institutions use placement exams to put students in special courses that incorporate review sections.

Administrators and faculty members comment on the issue of time with remedial students. One mentions the importance of not letting remedial courses delay the attainment of a degree. One of the advantages of a private institution is the one-on-one assistance. One administrator focuses on the challenge of needing longer amounts of time to develop knowledge than the students are willing to spend: "They're still in too much of a hurry, given the skills that they've come into school with." A faculty member describes a technique of encouraging retention through enrolling for fall courses in the spring.

In summary, the traditional institutions are facing remedial education problems with various assessment aids, utilizing campus resources, and concentrating on retention strategies.

Emphasize Uniqueness

> There are not too many people pursuing the under-prepared, under-privileged students like we are. (Administrator at religious-based institution)

Exemplary institutions emphasize their uniqueness in mission and culture. As the quotation indicates, identifying a mission that separates the institution from others is crucial. Respondents from a small religious-based school speak about how the strength of traditional universities is in providing in-person access to students, and believe this is something that distinguishes them from nontraditional providers. Respondents expressed little concern for competition from new providers because of a belief in the base value of their educational product: "There is always going to be a market for what we do." One faculty member talks about the need to increasingly emphasize whole person and service learning approaches to distinguish their institution from new providers: "It makes it a little more imperative to us to be sure that we build in that sense of service to others as the purpose of their education, not just money and comfort." Administrators talk about a strategy of viewing identity in terms of maintaining an institutional culture: "I think we're very much dependent on our culture for it to work." However, it is not just high-minded intellectual pursuits and a culture of service to the community that draw students to these high-performing schools, as this comment from an administrator at a large public institution reveals: "The people who come here come for the social life, for the beer and football, and stuff like that."

Exemplary institutions tend to feel confident about who they are and clear on their unique mission and cultural characteristics. Consequently, the increased competitive environment doesn't appear to unsettle them. The strategy in the face of increased competition is to concentrate on presenting what is special and unique about the institution.

Balance Academic and Business Interests

One key issue for institutions facing revenue pressure is to find ways to properly balance practical financial demands with academic objectives. One immediately applicable technique is simple awareness of the specific ways that an imbalance may occur: "I think it's good for us to be conscious of the tension, because once we cease being conscious of the tension, we'll probably neglect one or the other." Conversely, some faculty members describe a willingness to accommodate administrative budget constraints when necessary because of the belief in the overall mission. Balance then in traditional institutions is achieved by engaging in an increased dialogue with faculty over priorities. Later on in this book, it will be clear that faculty involvement is very different in the for-profit models.

Prioritize

One necessary strategy for organizations is to prioritize objectives and distribute resources appropriately: "I guess the bottom line isn't just financial. It's philosophical. . . . [We] would never surface a program just because it's a money maker. If we don't feel it meets a particular need or answers some call, then it never comes to the table." Notice the connection of the decision making in this quotation with mission and their "call." One administrator characterizes the earlier referenced conflict between academic and revenue concerns as prioritizing. Administrators and faculty members see an emphasis on recruitment as a result of this prioritizing. Faculty members comment on the distribution and prioritization of academic programs, often with applied science programs taking priority over less lucrative liberal arts subjects. Other administrators comment on the low priority remediation programs are given.

The tough financial times cause leading universities to reflect upon their main values. One administrator at an Ivy League school speaks about the need to focus on core programs and recognize that even the most prominent institutions cannot do everything they wish to do: "We really have to recognize that we can't do everything." One strategy mentioned by a respondent in regard to this focusing on core values is to look at issues increasingly in an institutionwide context. This big picture admonition links to the trustee mentioned earlier who expressed frustration with the shared governance structure and the seeming inability to effectively prioritize.

Exemplary institutions consciously try to prioritize academic activities in line with their core mission. However, these decisions are made within the traditional joint governance scheme and therefore must battle the democratic structure that tends to spread rather than concentrate resources.

Social Consciousness

In the face of economic pressure that is pushing many institutions away from their social mission, how are exemplary institutions responding? One respondent speaks about the broader role universities are coming to play in the community and throughout the lives of their students: "Colleges and universities are not just simply home away from home for four years for the young. But hopefully they're becoming centers of learning for all of society and centers that affect society, the social fabric of society, and their communities. I feel like we're all evolving into that. We always have a responsibility, because where else does that happen." Social consciousness and public service goals are encouraged in exemplary institutions through community service and service learning—a trend for the past few years. Furthermore, institutions such as Mount St. Mary's in Los Angeles demonstrate an increased attempt to better understand community needs and to tie the service learning program directly to identified problems. Therefore, social consciousness means a continual awareness of changing needs in the community.

According to one administrator, distance learning is an obvious solution for adult working students who do not have the time to attend traditional face-to-face courses. In this way, distance learning and flexible formatting is part of the way institutions try to meet their social missions: "We need to accommodate for that population of students who really can't make it to campus every week for three hours a session or three times a week." However, a faculty member expresses a common concern that distance learning will be used for lower-class students, and face-to-face education reserved for the wealthy: "We'll send all the elites to be on campus at Brown where they get to mingle with different kinds of people, know the professor, find out how to deal in the real world, how to be leaders, and then we'll let the Hispanic kids take their courses online in a cheap vocational way that does not help integrate them or turn them into leaders." Thus, depending on how pedagogically successful faculty see distance learning, increased access is seen as either real or meaningless.

Exemplary institutions indicate that they discuss social consciousness in broader terms of public service programs, using technology for access, integrating multicultural perspectives within the curriculum, and promoting service learning opportunities. It is interesting to reflect on how this expression of social consciousness at these institutions has a mature quality, both in an organizational evolutionary sense and as a reflection of the older student body they now serve.

CONCLUSION

In this chapter I found consistency in the challenges American higher education faces. In order to better understand the uniqueness of the for-profit institutions, I began by describing the challenges and the approaches to addressing problems taken by exemplary traditional higher education institutions of various types. The dialogue that emerged from these responses helped focus the key issues and challenges in higher education, and demonstrated areas where the for-profits and nontraditional universities may provide some direction. In the next chapter I turn to specific data on for-profit universities presented within a larger context of the history of proprietary and vocational postsecondary education in America.

CHAPTER 3

The Surprising Story of For-Profit and Nontraditional Higher Education in America

If I were to judge for-profit higher education by some of the panicked articles written in the past few years, clearly the downfall of civilization is near. According to these accounts the for-profits are stealing students from traditional institutions by using aggressive and perhaps misleading marketing tactics, exploiting part-time faculty in tenureless systems, using mindless and prefabricated curricula, and taking advantage of minority populations in urban areas. What has led to this hysteria and what is the truth about for-profit institutions?

Proprietary, vocational, for-profit, and corporate education and training has a long, complex, and varied history not lending itself to simple generalizations. Even with the emergence of the University of Phoenix, the overall percentage share of the higher education "market" taken by these for-profit upstarts is much smaller than often assumed. Additionally, the growth rate of for-profit education is also much lower and less significant than usually reported. Surprisingly, for-profit organizations do not necessarily concentrate more on revenue-generating activities than do traditional institutions. For-profits mainly serve first-generation college student populations rather than ethnic minorities. Finally, those operating for-profit institutions often have socially conscious motivations for their work, much like one finds in nonprofit higher education.

In this chapter I survey the landscape of what has been variously called for-profit, proprietary, and vocational education. It is hoped that this exploration of the history of vocational and proprietary education in America provides for us the background to better understand the current heated environment. Additionally, I look at the broader social debate and reaction to what has been described as the commercialization or commodification of higher education.

FOR-PROFIT HIGHER EDUCATION: NINE QUESTIONS

Let me begin by narrowing the subject of for-profit higher education. There is enormous variety in the education available for those over age eighteen that might be described as for-profit education in a general sense. However, since most of the organizations offering this type of training are not regionally accredited, they are not directly parallel to traditional higher education (regional accreditation is the important minimal standard all traditional four-year universities in America must have). While I at times in this book glance at these other forms of education, the central focus is on regionally accredited institutions. There is a great deal of misunderstanding about for-profit higher education in America, and it is useful from the start to address some of the confusion so that the reader begins to get to the authentic issues quickly.

Question One: Is For-Profit Higher Education Growing so Fast That It Threatens Traditional Higher Education?

The simple answer is no. The primary reason for the misunderstanding is that most of the for-profit information is about non–regionally accredited institutions. According to Kelly (2001) in a report for the Education Commission of the States (ECS), there was a 59 percent growth in enrollment at for-profits between 1989 and 1998 (the Education Commission, a nonprofit research group based in Denver, tracks and helps develop education policy). Furthermore, there was a 266 percent growth in the number of four-year for-profits between 1989 and 1998. This seems very impressive, but only 10 percent of the for-profits have the all-important regional accreditation and only 2.5 percent of all higher education students are enrolled in for-profits. This is an important point, because only regionally accredited institutions really compete with traditional nonprofit universities.

Subsequent to that study, the *Chronicle of Higher Education* (Borrego, 2001) published an article on the growth of for-profits citing the preceding report by Education Commission of the States with the finding that among four-year institutions, for-profit degree-granting colleges showed from 1989 to 1999 that their number grew to a total of 194. In comparison, those in the public sector grew 3 percent, to 613, while the number of nonprofit private colleges increased 4 percent, to 1,536. However, once again, most of the data cited referred to non–regionally accredited institutions. Furthermore, the growth referenced of the for-profits is calculated on a very small base. As a result, these data presented in the ECS report and the subsequent article in the influential *Chronicle* are misleading to those who do not look closely to evaluate their meaning.

The National Center for Education Statistics (NCES) lists over 700 for-profit postsecondary institutions nationally. However, only 98 of this group have some form of regional, state, or professional accreditation, and just 61 grant degrees. Furthermore, only 6 are listed as having regional accreditation (some institutions such as the University of Phoenix, DeVry, and the Keller Graduate School of Management have multiple regional accreditations because of their widespread presence). While the NCES list is probably incomplete, it gives one a sense of the actual rather than perceived scope of the for-profit higher education phenomenon. The large number of unaccredited for-profit institutions comprise a wide range of professional and trade schools, most of which are not in any way attempting to compete with traditional higher education. However, because of changes in federal financial aid requirements, and the shifting marketplace, some of the largest for-profits have sought and gained accreditation.

Generally, regional accreditors treat for-profits the same as others. Only two accreditors have specific standards for for-profit institutions. The ECS report noted that the regional accreditor's substantive change requirement (which can take two years) slows for-profits' ability to respond quickly to the market. Additionally, the independence (or lack there of) of their boards poses the greatest problem for for-profits seeking regional accreditation.

In reality then, the majority of for-profit postsecondary institutions do not offer degrees and are not regionally accredited. Additionally, one institution, the University of Phoenix, dominates the list of accredited for-profits. Most for-profit institutions have some sort of accreditation, often from a national association. However, according to another report published by the Education Commission of the States (ECS, 2000), despite the growing number of for-profits, very few have regional accreditation—at this time, just sixty-four total nationally, with many of these simply multiple campus locations of the same institution. Even counted separately, the ECS estimates that just 2 percent of all regionally accredited institutions are for-profit.

Question Two: Do For-Profits Exploit Ethnic Minority Populations?

One of the common criticisms of for-profit and vocational institutions is that they intentionally concentrate on recruiting minority students who are unable to gain admittance to traditional institutions. Detractors argue that the reason for success has to do with an emphasis on marketing and recruitment, low admission standards, and perhaps even misleading, exploitative practices. In 1998, *Black Issues in Higher Education* (Collison, 1998) published an article finding that for-profits serve minority populations to a surprisingly large degree. Of the top 100 institutions conferring degrees on people of color, there was a large rise in the number of proprietary colleges particularly in the fields of engineering-related technologies, computer science, and business. In fact, the top producer of minority baccalaureates in engineering-related technologies was ITT Technical Institutes in California, and the number two and three institutions conferring bachelor's degrees in computer and information science on African Americans were Strayer College and DeVry Institute of Technology. By one account, for-profit institutions enroll only 8 percent of postsecondary students, but they enroll 16 percent of all black students, 14 percent of Hispanic students, and 4 percent of Native American students (Evelyn, 2000). Tuition cost on average is cheaper at private for-profit than at nonprofit institutions. Clearly, for-profits are serving minority populations to a large extent. Depending on your point of view, this is either exploitation or better service of these underserved populations.

The practical question that should be asked is why are these schools so popular with minority students? In business terms, the institutions have identified a market of minority adult learners needing and wanting to pursue degrees. The proprietary institutions have focused on recruiting this group and adding services such as convenient formats, which are attractive to their student body. The applied curricula, concentration on facilitating financial aid access, and lack of expenditures on noninstructional resources such as residential life make them well-suited to minority populations. The *Black Issues in Higher Education* article quotes Harold Lundy, executive director of the Association of Collegiate Business Schools and Programs, as saying:

> Proprietary schools like DeVry and ITT are making significant inroads among minority students who are turned off by traditional educational institutions who put up barriers to entrance. . . . A whole segment of students has been written off as uneducable because they don't have the requisite score on the ACT or SAT. But these institutions are more open and amenable to inner-city students.

As minority students make up a larger proportion of students seeking higher education, many are choosing for-profit colleges. The success for-profit colleges have in attracting minority students challenges the conventional wisdom on how to achieve diversity in higher education. For-profits rarely have any special programs or services for students of color. In fact, the ethnicity of students attending these universities is in a real way ignored. While many for-profits obviously do consciously market their programs to these underserved populations, they do not seem to have academic or student services specifically designed to accommodate ethnic groups. Furthermore, the for-profits, which are priced higher than public institutions, dispel the typical argument that minority students often do not pursue higher education because of expense.

The often narrow focus on professional training at many for-profit colleges is one important reason why they attract minority students. As first-generation college students, the practical applicability of the degree they earn is especially important to them. What's more, in an era when publicly supported outreach programs are being curtailed, many for-profits specifically market their educational programs to minority populations, typically advertising in Spanish-speaking publications and on Black Entertainment Television.

In addition, many first-generation college families are unaware of federal financial aid programs, and incorrectly assume that they will not qualify. For-profits realize this and emphasize financial aid counseling and make sure these services are available at night and on weekends. Campus locations also contribute to high minority enrollments at for-profit institutions, with many placed in metropolitan areas near large concentrations of minorities. Another important difference is the cultural perceptions connected to the residential college experience. For many families with a history of going to college as eighteen-year-olds, the experience of leaving home and living in a residence hall is strongly connected to the quality of the educational experience. However, often for first-generation college students, the residential experience is less important. Close family ties and cultural attitudes about staying close to the family are often more important.

In sum, it appears true that for-profits do appeal to a great extent to minority populations because of their attention to educational attributes that adult learners value such as practical degrees, financial aid, and convenient locations, and formats. Charges of exploitation for regionally accredited for-profits are difficult to substantiate because of the strict standards applied to them and their rigorous assessment practices.

Question Three: Are Students at For-Profit
Institutions Uniformly Poor Academically?

Anecdotally, in the first graduate course I taught for the University of Phoenix in preparation for this book, out of eight students I had one student who was a graduate of Harvard and another of Yale (yes, class sizes are usually small, approximately eight to twelve students each course at the University of Phoenix). It is not uncommon to find extremely well-educated professionals in the classroom at for-profits. Certainly, there are students who are distressingly underprepared, probably more so than at most four-year institutions. While some for-profits have strict admission standards, a defining characteristic of for-profit institutions is a willingness to educate students where they are, rather than only teaching those with similarly stellar backgrounds. This open admissions policy is a limitation and a challenge for the for-profits. Nevertheless, one is mistaken to assume that all students at for-profits are uniformly underprepared.

Question Four: Do For-Profit Institutions Concentrate
More on Revenue Than Do Nonprofits?

As publicly held for-profit institutions, the officers of the company are required to focus on financial returns for the stockholders. However, many nonprofit institutions are also struggling to survive and are necessarily extremely conscious of revenue as well. Nonprofit institutions must concern themselves with financial stability. Particularly for smaller, less selective universities, decisions need to be made with the economics of the institution in mind. Moody, the financial service group, defines at-risk universities as having less than 3,000 students and accepting more than 70 percent of applicants, with financial resources per student less than $50,000. Using this definition, there are 1,593 colleges in the United States that might be considered at risk (Moody's Investor Service, 2003). For-profits and nonprofits alike must be very aware of the budget or face their own demise. We will see later (Chapter 7) that this question of revenue focus leads to a constant balancing of academic and business concerns.

Question Five: Are Those Who Run For-Profit Institutions
Businessmen and Businesswomen Primarily
Concerned with Profits?

This is the second part of the previous revenue question, about the values of those who run for-profit universities. While there are certainly many MBAs and corporate-experienced managers at the for-profits, one also finds top administrators who come from research institutions, accrediting agencies, and religious and charitable organizations. Furthermore, many of those interviewed for this book identified a clear social agenda related to their work in education, and expressed values consistent with those of professionals associated with traditional institutions.

Question Six: Do For-Profit Institutions Especially Threaten Community Colleges?

Some believe that because of the practical, skill orientation of the curriculum and the similarity in study bodies, community colleges and for-profits directly compete. Clowes (1995) uses the medieval castle as metaphor for describing the role of community colleges and proprietary schools in higher education hierarchy. Traditionally, community colleges function to protect the castle keep, and proprietary schools in the hills beyond the fields just try to stay alive. Community colleges then are the first line of defense against the roaming for-profit savages. However, community colleges have changed their mission over the years for various reasons. One primary shift has been away from their historical role in transferring students to four-year institutions—in fact, the percentage of students who transfer from community colleges to four-year institutions is extremely low. As a result, in the early 1970s community colleges decided to focus more on training than on transferring students into four-year institutions (Honick, 1995). In this way, they have shifted more toward the trade or technical school institutional mission. Consequently, regionally accredited for-profit and community colleges generally do not directly compete.

Question Seven: Is For-Profit Higher Education New?

Yes and no. Regionally accredited for-profits are relatively new, but proprietary vocational education has been in existence since early colonial America and is consistent with our national character. From its origin, higher education in general has had an interest in the practical application of knowledge. In fact, the earliest universities were dedicated to training for law, civil, and religious careers. Wilms (1974) claims that vocational education began in America as early as in Plymouth Colony in 1635. Practical training through apprenticeship was of fundamental social and economic importance in the English colonies in America. According to Seybolt (1969), vocational apprenticeship training was the most fundamental educational institution of the colonial period. In fact, the Massachusetts Bay Act of 1642 emphasized that children should be brought up to be educated in both book learning and labor. Apprenticeship in the early colonies took place usually in what are now the high school and undergraduate years, the usual term of apprenticeship was seven years and must not be completed until the apprentice was twenty-one years of age. The rise of vocational schools is said to have occurred through the rapid industrialization of the United States combined with the inefficiency of the limited apprentice system. Many large proprietary schools grew in the nineteenth century; the largest was the Bryant-Stratton chain, founded in 1852 (Lee & Merisotis, 1990). Initially most of the students in vocational programs had not graduated from high school, but by the 1930s, 64 percent were graduates.

Over the years, the belief in technology and in practical arts has pushed higher education in America in the direction of vocational education. A prime example of this emphasis is the landmark Morrill Act of 1862, which set forth the system for public higher education in America. The Morrill Act offered each state 30,000 acres of public land for every member of Congress from that state, with the land to be sold and proceeds invested as a permanent endowment for at least one college designated by the state legislature. The colleges founded or designated under this act were required to stress agriculture, the mechanic arts, and military arts. The overall objective was stated as to educate "industrial classes" in professions (Rudolph, 1990).

The military and war efforts contributed greatly to the further development of American vocational education. During World War I, the Federal Board for Vocational Education worked with the U.S. Army to determine the need for an estimated 200,000 mechanics, then found them suitable training. In World War II, existing vocational education systems greatly helped in providing trained inductees for the war effort. Additionally, men were the majority of the students at first, until women entered the schools seeking cosmetology training. Although the influx of veterans into the university after World War II had a significant impact, less than one-third of the G.I. Bill students went to a college or university. Instead, they attended on-the-job training, farm training, or proprietary schools (Lee & Merisotis, 1990).

On the public policy level, the Smith-Hughes Act of 1917 defined and provided support for vocational education (Henry, 1943). Compulsory public education began with the Supreme Court ruling in *Meyer v. Nebraska* (1923), which said that the state could compel children to attend school and establish standards. This decision effectively brought vocational education into the mandatory public school system. The Vocational Education Act of 1963 was significant because it expanded and redirected the federal investment in vocational education (Thompson, 1973).

According to the research literature, the differences between the management of proprietary schools and traditional higher education institutions are great. In proprietary schools, the owners or corporate directors are more likely to make critical decisions regarding the direction of the school, program mix, admissions, or other academic standards. Generally, they tend to keep faculty out of nonacademic decision making. Conversely, nonprofit and government institutions respond to stakeholders and consequently have more layers of decision making. Faculty influence in proprietary schools is minimal, facilities are often leased, extracurricular activities are not emphasized, and there is no residential element. Scheduling at proprietary schools varies from 8 to 152 weeks, whereas universities typically have quarters and semesters. Nevertheless, this distinction is changing as universities with programs focused on adult learners move to shorter, 8–12 week terms. In general, studies show that students of proprietary schools are more likely to be low-income, female, and members of a minority group compared to traditional university students. Finally, up until the 1980s proprietary schools were generally regulated by state licensing, rather than regional accreditation agencies (Lee & Merisotis, 1990).

In the mid-twentieth century, the proprietary sector exercised lobbying power and got itself included in federal grant and loan programs. Starting with the Veterans Education Benefits program after World War II, and continuing with student aid, proprietary schools have used government grants and loans to encourage enrollment in their programs. Proprietary schools served more students on the G.I. Bill than any other institutional type. The watershed 1972 amendments to the Higher Education Act provided full and equal participation with traditional higher education students. This single change in public policy was very controversial and led to charges against for-profit vocation education institutions of abuse and lack of quality control by higher education institutions. According to Merisotis (1991), 78 percent of all proprietary school students receive federal assistance. A U.S. Department of Education study showed that proprietary schools student accounted for 36.7 percent of all those who borrow for school in 1989. Nationally, 79 percent of all proprietary students receive some federal aid, compared to 29 percent of all students (Honick, 1995).

In the early twentieth century, reformers attacked the legitimacy of the proprietary schools. By the mid-1980s, proprietary school students were identified as having higher default rates on student loans than borrowers from other sectors. As one-fourth of all federal student aid went to these students, government officials became concerned with this problem. In their defense, proprietary schools explained the data by pointing out that their students were to begin with higher risks for loan default (Lee & Merisotis, 1990). During the 1990s, 1,300 proprietary schools were removed from eligibility for loan default, which added to the ongoing poor reputation of the for-profit universities (Kelly, 2001).

As a result of this increased scrutiny, the Higher Education Act of 1992 altered the method by which recruitment personnel are compensated. In the past, proprietary schools had used incentive compensation, but this now was halted. The overall impact of the reliance on federal financial aid has been to push for-profits to be more in alignment with traditional institutions by becoming regionally accredited. Thus, while for-profit education is not new, the development of regionally accredited for-profits only came about to a large extent at the end of the twentieth century. This important accreditation puts it more directly in competition with traditional higher education.

Question Eight: Are Corporate Universities the Same as For-Profit Universities?

Corporate universities are related to the for-profit higher education movement because they emphasize an applied curriculum and in some ways they were developed in response to inadequacies or service gaps in traditional higher education. Additionally, to some extent they both are aimed at educating the American corporate workforce. However, corporate universities concentrate specifically on indoctrinating employees in their company ethos and mission, train them for job specific skills, as well as make them generally more productive in their work.

Large corporate America has been a leader in creating corporate universities. IBM created its first education center in 1933 and by 1969 had a faculty of 3,417 with 40,000 equivalent full-time students. In 1955 General Electric launched Crotonville as the first recognized corporate university. In the 1970s corporate education grew tremendously and there was a surge in corporate training into the late 1980s. By 1982, AT&T had 12,000 courses at 1,300 locations per year, and had a training staff of 10,000. Corporate America as a whole had twenty-six major educational facilities by 1987 (Meister, 1998).

Some estimates show that 10 percent, or $60 billion, of the total education budget is spent on workplace training and that over an eight-year time span in the 1990s corporate universities grew from 400 to 1,000 institutions while at the same time 200 colleges closed their doors. Although much of the education at these corporate universities is oriented toward applied skills, there is also crossover into traditional academic subjects. In 1998, 18 percent of American companies offered remedial math and reading skills courses (Schiller, 1999).

In-house corporate training in part is a result of the need for proprietary control of knowledge. Particularly for the large multinational organizations, corporate universities build ways of sharing practices internationally. One can see the development of the corporate universities as part of what happens when learning becomes a function of work. More generally, corporate education often focuses on creating and emphasizing corporate citizenship, developing a contextual framework for the individual, as well as ensuring that employees possess core competencies. Some corporate universities have a notion of embedded learning whereby workers are educated as part of their daily work without even realizing they are learning. Corporate universities have led in the use of distance learning, collaborations with universities, and models of market-driven educational systems and in these ways are similar to for-profit institutions. The primary difference is that while corporate universities concentrate on educating their own employees, for-profit institutions focus on a broader population.

Question Nine: Do For-Profit Institutions Represent the Further Commercialization of Higher Education?

To the degree that traditional institutions adopt for-profit approaches, there is a commercialization result. However, the changed methods do not necessarily mean altered values in the academy. One might argue that the commercialization fear in American higher education has its roots in early efforts to make the curriculum more practical, and in the so-called Yale Report of 1828, which was a reaction to the trend toward a more applied curriculum and promoted a return to a course of study based on the classics. Later, Veblen argued in *The Higher Learning in America* (1954) that the university president is the main channel whereby business values enter the university. His book was a critique of pragmatism and vocationalism, and a criticism of the president's role in leading America down this path. Veblen saw the principles of business organization—the focus on control and achievement—applied increasingly to learning. In more recent times, the debate can be traced to Robert Nisbet's 1971 book *The Degradation of the Academic Dogma,* a criticism of how government-sponsored research was affecting the university.

Although one can see that the debate over the applied nature of the curriculum, the use of technology, and the connection to business is not new, it became increasingly heated in the latter half of the twentieth century. Changes in university patent policies in the 1970s helped pave the way for cooperative relationships, and universities had a clear economic incentive to establish partnerships with businesses. During inflationary environment in the late 1970s universities began applying double-digit tuition increases, beginning the trend of spiraling costs that continues today. Staff positions created without considering workload, private secretarial support hired without need, low-paying appointments leading to an environment of low productivity, excessive management layers and decentralization, long vacations (closure during holidays and the entire summer), and generous benefit packages were all pointed to as reasons for spiraling expenses (Lenington, 1996). Bowie (1994) claims that in the 1990s there was both financial trouble for universities and increased public scrutiny.

In *The Monster Under the Bed,* Davis and Botkin (1995) argue that we are seeing a transition of higher education from government control to business control as a result of the changing needs of students and the role of education moving increasingly toward job preparation. Public policy makers are looking increasingly toward business for answers. Government expects universities to do much more for society and at the same time is becoming what Burton Clark (1998) described as an "unreliable patron." Overall, there is a decrease in unrestricted funding and subsequent increased dependence on external funding sources for universities. Critics such as Slaughter (1990) warn that privatization of higher education transfers what was once part of the public domain to the private. She sees corporate-university partnerships as inherently antidemocratic.

Derek Bok (2003) points out that a focus on revenue is a chronic condition in higher education where institutions continually struggle to have the best students and faculty. On the other hand, university administrators do not have strong incentives to lower costs and achieve efficiencies. Furthermore, university presidents and deans lack the experience of corporate managers: "In sum, the ways of the marketplace are neither consistently useful nor wholly irrelevant in trying to improve the performance of research universities. That is what makes the problem of commercialization difficult" (Bok, 2003, p. 33). Bok further points out that big time athletics programs show the willingness of the university to sacrifice academic standards to make money. In order for the for-profit model to work in higher education, Bok claims that students must know what they need, students must be able to evaluate alternative choices, and their choices need to correspond to the larger needs of society. In particular, the last connection is usually not the case. Earlier in his career, Bok (1990) expressed concern that if the university is perceived as a commercial enterprise, then its stakeholders may change the nature of their relationship to the university for the worse. He was troubled that in the public's eyes, the traditional university desires to seek the truth and disseminate knowledge might be supplanted by the profit motive. Bok argued that as a university grows more aggressive in seeking funding, its image changes, thus making it harder to appear to be a nonprofit institution.

On the other hand, Bowie (1994) claims that the biggest problem with corporate ties may be that such partnerships do not work. In fact, they may end up costing universities money. Bowie cites the statistic that only one in ten patented discoveries recover the money spent on filing the patent, one in a hundred make between $20,000 and $50,000, and only one in a thousand is a major moneymaker. For-profits do connect with the need in traditional higher education for greater productivity and an applied curricula. However, the commercialization of higher education seems to be occurring without for-profit institutions.

We see here then from these nine questions that many of the assumptions commonly made about for-profit and nontraditional institutions are incorrect, or at least more complex than they appear. In the following section, we look at some of the specific institutions studied for this book.

PROFILES OF FOR-PROFIT INSTITUTIONS

Three of the largest for-profit, regionally accredited higher education institutions in America are the University of Phoenix, DeVry Inc., and Education Management Corporation (EDMC), which owns a number of for-profit institutions including Argosy University, and are all highlighted in this book. The following are brief profiles of each institution using official descriptions and then the more personal origin stories gained through interviews with the leadership at the individual institutions.

University of Phoenix

John Sperling, a former faculty member at California State University–San Jose, founded the University of Phoenix in 1976. In 1978 the University of Phoenix received accreditation from the Higher Learning Commission of the North Central Association. In 1989 its pioneering online campus was established. The university has three colleges: College of Undergraduate Business and Management, College of Information Systems and Technology, and College of Graduate Business and Management, and also now offers doctoral degrees through the School of Advanced Studies. It offers in-person courses at 120 campuses and learning centers across the United States and in Puerto Rico and British Columbia. Through the online campus, the university reaches students the world over. Enrollment is estimated at 129,035 (for 2001, as reported to the U.S. Department of Education in 2002), with plans for expansion to half a million students within five years. The student population is 44 percent male and 56 percent female; 61 percent white, 18 percent black, 11 percent Hispanic; average age is 34 years. The university currently has a faculty of more than 17,000. Approximately 285 faculty members are full-time. Faculty is 36 percent female and 64 percent male; 71 percent white (University of Phoenix, 2003).

As we saw previously, the stories told about how the University of Phoenix began are quite different from traditional institutions. The University of Phoenix's story is much more like a successful business created by a solitary owner with strong vision and willpower, than a university beginning with a religious or state government affiliation. When one discusses the culture and rhetoric of the University of Phoenix, the starting point is the charismatic leader, John Sperling. The themes presented in the origin story for the University of Phoenix begin with the formative life of John Sperling. As related in many American business success stories, he speaks about his working-class jobs at a young age: "At the end of the Depression, I worked as a stevedore, a clerk, went to sea, had all sorts of shit jobs." In particular, his experience as a merchant marine seems to have led to a turning point in his life where he found personal direction: "Going to sea is a very quiet occupation, and you have lots of times to think, and it's very quiet on a ship. . . . I was able to look over things and decide that what I'd been doing wasn't such a good idea, so that I better make something of myself." This life-changing experience led him to seek education:

> Went off to what is now City College. Then it was San Francisco Junior College. And then the war came, and I went into the service. Then I came out and finished my college under the GI Bill. . . . I went to Reed College, and Reed College is an intensely intellectual college. And as I say in my autobiography, you almost have a moral obligation to get a PhD.

Notice that his transforming experience was in a community college, in some ways the institution closest to how the University of Phoenix is formulated. Reed College, a nontraditional liberal arts school, was also a strong influence on Sperling's thinking about higher education. As also revealed in Dr. Sperling's published autobiography, his story is one of conflict and symbolic expulsion from traditional higher education, where for many years he earned degrees, successfully taught, and was involved in faculty leadership roles:

> I started the Institute for Professional Development . . . at San Jose State, and they were having none of it. As a matter of fact, I had an acquaintance that was then Vice President for Development at Stanford, Frank Newman, who's now head of the Education Commission of the States. . . . He said John, "No public institution"—bureaucracy he called them—"No public educational bureaucracy will ever accept innovation. No private institution that is financially healthy will accept innovation. You've got to find a private institution that is in deep financial difficulty, and then you might have a chance." And so I said, "Can you find me one?" He said, "Well I'll try." A couple of months later he called me up and said, "I found one for you and would you like to meet the President?" And I said, "Boy, would I." And it was the University of San Francisco. USF had a new President, Bill McGinnis, who'd been President at Fairfield University, and he'd been brought in to save the university. And I presented this to him, and he said, "What the hell. Let's give it a try." And within a year we had 1,500 students, almost as many as they had on campus. So it was an immediate success. But the success drew the hatred of the educational establishment. To make a long story short, the establishment drove me out of California.

The story related by Sperling was repeated numerous times in various forms in the interviews at the University of Phoenix. What is central to this story is the statement "no public education bureaucracy will ever accept innovation," a belief at the root of the history of the University of Phoenix—something that informs its culture deeply. At other points in the interview, Sperling elaborates on this description of his expulsion from the higher education establishment:

> You don't run Stanford for the students. You run Stanford for the professoriate. And you don't like to have any of the cultural artifacts or the economic interests of the professoriate disturbed. You protect tenure as though it were God given, etcetera, etcetera, and I broke

those "shibboleths" I call them. And it infuriated you and your colleagues and they vowed to do everything to destroy me.

When Sperling broke away from San Jose State University with his
adult education program, he could not find investors: "No one ever invested in it." This small business story has a happy ending for Sperling
when his small investment turned into millions when the company offered stock: "I started with $26,000 of savings, and I owned almost 100
percent of the company when I went public, so I was very wealthy from
that event." The self-made man mythology is used in this origin story:
"I just felt that it was a very steep hill to climb, and I knew I felt alone—
I was alone." Alone, and against the world: "I didn't give a God damn
what the professoriate or the establishment thought about me." Against
the odds, Sperling made it work: "No one thought it would be a business
success."

Sperling's life story is one of working-class origins wandering from job
to job until in a moment of calmness out at sea he found direction in his
life: higher education. The routes he took through first the open access
community colleges and then the nontraditional private college, Reed,
are clear influences on his approach in forming the University of Phoenix.
Reed is particularly interesting because of its emphasis on real-life work
experience linked to higher education (and its liberal/progressive political influence). Sperling clearly had this institution in mind when he decided to emphasize practitioner faculty and incorporating student work
experience into the curriculum. His subsequent fight with the education
establishment at San Jose State University and break with traditional
education is a declaration of both the need to innovate and the necessity of going outside the academy to do so.

Personal financial investment in the organization is an important part
of the history of the University of Phoenix. A longtime leader of the
institution describes the importance of the implementation of a profit-
sharing plan:

> Bringing in an incentive system. I know that sounds very business-
> focused and all of that. But the truth is we have always been a for-
> profit institution, but we were never really profitable [laughter]. We
> were for-profit on paper, but we were never profitable until we in-
> troduced incentive systems for the staff. It enabled them to create
> more wealth for themselves, depending upon how well they func-
> tioned. So it was sort of a management by objectives approach. I have
> to say that when that happened the University of Phoenix began to

take off. We got our business structure in focus and lined up the way it should be, so that we could then have greater resources to put back into our academic side. And getting that lined up was key to the University's long-term success.

This correlation of financial self-interest with the objectives and success of the organization is an important point getting at the root of the possible advantages of the for-profit model: self-interest and a capitalist model energize the employees and the organization as a whole. This is a central point of the University of Phoenix origin story: The for-profit model leads to a better educational organization. Another interview subject relates a story describing how employees came together in a time of crisis. This institutional story is useful to see because it informs the team structure and personal and financial investment in the organization found in such prevalence: "One defining moment—at least for me—was in 1985. And it was a very bad time. We almost went under. And a number of us were told that we needed to contribute in the form of deductions in our paychecks to keep the university afloat. So we did that." Clearly, another important event in the history of the organization, and a subject of institutional storytelling, is the public offering of stock in the University of Phoenix.

A faculty member speaks about the opportunity given to invest in the University of Phoenix when the initial public offering was made:

> I will tell you one of the defining moments that comes to mind is when they went public, and faculty were offered the opportunity for the initial public offering to actually purchase stock in Apollo Group. Well, isn't that bizarre? Talk about different. Now that I think about it, though, it is pretty typical of the culture—that we are going to try something different. We are going to go public and sell stock in Apollo Group, the University of Phoenix's parent company. I thought, well that's strange, but, oh, what the heck.

In the following quotation, the subject describes the cultural changes that occurred as a result of Wall Street influence:

> If you look around at what we do, we're a very different organization from most academic organizations. What makes it work is the discipline that we bring to what we do. And that added more discipline to it. Yes, we are highly regulated. We've always had accreditation reviews and lots of state boards and state regulatory bodies look at us. But this added another layer. Now we have Wall Street analysts

looking at us. And we had all of these analysts parading through when we first went public who had never been associated with any kind of nontraditional education. In fact, most of them who had been educated at traditional upper-tier organizations were very skeptical. Then we had to have the discipline of explaining ourselves to them and to the outside world in a way that we never had before.

One commonly repeated story heard in the interviews was the haphazard manner in which the leadership came to the University of Phoenix. The following is a representative story:

> I wandered in here just to say, "If you have any employment opportunities . . ." I needed to make some money while I was taking classes. And they showed me how it was organized and things. And I said, "Well, do you have an enrollment advisor's position?" So they gave me that position and I did that for a couple of years. Then they made me the director of enrollment, and I took over campuses.

Staff seem to enjoy perpetuating a story of involvement with the university that denies in some sense the seriousness of the organization and its mission to serve working adults. They seem to be saying to traditional institutions, we don't take ourselves as seriously as you do—we are not pretentious.

The origin stories at the University of Phoenix depict a visionary founder coming from a working-class background struggling to build a nontraditional institution relevant to a first-generation college audience using real work experience in the curriculum, and energized organizationally by personal and financial investment of the leadership. While undoubtedly the origin of the University of Phoenix is not in reality so simple, we shall see the story connects directly to its operations.

DeVry Inc.

The history of DeVry is one involving changing ownership, acquisitions, and mergers. DeVry can be traced back to 1931, when Dr. Herman DeVry established DeForest Training School in Chicago to prepare students for technical work in electronics, motion pictures, radio, and television. The name was changed to DeVry Technical Institute in 1953, and then became DeVry Institute of Technology in 1968. Over time, the DeVry system expanded its curricula and degree offerings. In 1957, DeVry Institutes achieved associate degree-granting status in electronics engineering technology, and twelve years later was authorized to grant bachelor's degrees in the same discipline.

In 1966, Bell and Howell Education Group purchased DeVry, and the company continued to expand growing from two campuses in Chicago and Toronto to eleven locations in eight states and two Canadian provinces. In 1987, DeVry merged with Keller Graduate School of Management after the graduate school, founded by two former DeVry executives, completed a leveraged buyout of DeVry Institutes from Bell and Howell. Keller Graduate School of Management, begun in 1973 as the CBA Institute, had been established to provide a practitioner-oriented approach to management education. Founders Dennis J. Keller and Ronald L. Taylor launched the school's master of business administration degree program in 1976 and expanded the school to five sites in Chicago and Milwaukee, Wisconsin. This is the point of origin for the contemporary organization called DeVry Inc., created in 1987 through the merger of DeVry Institutes and Keller Graduate School of Management. The company completed its initial public offering in June 1991. Further acquisitions followed including the Becker Professional Review in 1996 and Ross University in 2003, one of the largest medical and veterinary schools in the world. Currently, the collective organization has over 50,000 undergraduate students, 10,000 graduate students, and 50,000 students in training programs.

The personal history of DeVry Inc. concentrates on some of the important events mentioned earlier. Ronald L. Taylor, the president and co–chief executive officer, describes how the contemporary origin of the company occurred through meeting his future partner, Dennis J. Keller, at Bell and Howell in the early 1970s. Bell and Howell at the time owned DeVry and a couple other schools, including a paralegal school. Both of the founders had recent MBAs, from Stanford and the University of Chicago, and were beginning corporate careers. In 1973 they started what is now the graduate division of DeVry University, then called the CBA Institute for Post-Graduate Education Business Inc.—a name that gave them what Taylor describes as the longest business cards in higher education. The two young businessmen had the concept of taking the core of a good two-year MBA curriculum and format it in such a way that liberal arts graduates would have the important skills of an MBA to allow them to enter the job market even though they had a liberal arts degree. It was a full-time daytime program that didn't work well for a number of reasons according to Taylor: "We started in the fall of 1973 with seven students, one was our secretary who didn't pay tuition." Two years later, after having lost their initial investment money and raising additional money, they finally figured out a model that worked. What they did was to unbundle the curriculum so that courses were in groups of skills leading one into another and offered them in the evening. They used practitioner faculty, specifically business people who taught in the area that they managed—the idea was to think about the skills that their boss would have and recruit similarly skilled faculty members. They also concentrated on marketing at a time when other institutions did little more than put together an institutional catalog. They grew this company until, in 1987, they acquired DeVry from Bell and Howell in a "highly leveraged transaction."

With the addition of DeVry they added general education and gained regional accreditation. DeVry went public in 1991 and recently acquired Ross University of Medicine and Ross University School of Veterinary Medicine. Taylor points to the decision to continue during the early struggling days as a defining entrepreneurial moment. The merger of Keller Graduate School of Management with DeVry and moving the private company DeVry to the public arena in 1991 were pointed to as integral to the present composition of the institution. Taylor noted that it was unusual for the two founders to be still involved in the company they began. Other longtime administrators at DeVry pointed to the decision to have a distributed, multicampus structure as key to their success. They also point to the student body they serve as being special about their organization:

> We serve a population that is generally not well served by traditional education and we serve students who are first-generation college students, and make available to them programs that give them a good start in careers. They are neglected to a certain extent by traditional higher education. DeVry has developed an approach, a way to reach these students, recruit and serve these students that makes a meaningful contribution to society.

DeVry sees itself in its undergraduate operation as serving first-generation college students who have not had a history of college in their family and with their degree can get jobs with a decent wage. In its graduate programs at Keller, they target currently employed middle managers: "What we do in that area we provide them convenience, a lot of service, and sound, solid skills that allow them to move forward in their careers."

Argosy University

Argosy University came into existence through a merger of three different institutions: American Schools of Professional Psychology, Medical Institute of Minnesota, and the University of Sarasota. The American Schools of Professional Psychology was founded in the early 1970s with a concentration on the preparation of psychology practitioners emphasizing practical training. The Medical Institute of Minnesota was established to prepare skilled allied health care personnel for careers in hospitals and clinics. The University of Sarasota provided a practice-oriented program of study that met the needs of working professionals. These three schools merged to form Argosy University in 2001. A leader of the university describes how she came to the institution: "We want to start a school you create the curriculum, hire the faculty, the way you think it should be done, at no financial risk, we'll fund it. How many times in your life do you get that opportunity?"

PROFILES OF NONTRADITIONAL NONPROFITS

In order to gain additional perspective, I've included profiles of two nontraditional higher education institutions that were studied, Heritage College and Fielding Graduate Institute. These two unusual nonprofit institutions have different approaches to serving similar audiences as those found at the for-profit universities.

Heritage College

Heritage College is a nonprofit, independent, nondenominational, accredited institution, with the stated mission of providing quality higher education to a multicultural population "that has been educationally isolated." The programs are specifically intended to meet the special needs of multicultural and rural populations. In its literature, Heritage College emphasizes the low student to faculty ratio and how it was recognized in the 2003 *U.S. World News* ratings as having "the highest percentage of courses under 20 in the West." "Knowledge Brings Us Together" is its institutional motto and the college emphasizes respecting the dignity and potential of each student. Additionally, the institutional rhetoric speaks about considering diverse cultural backgrounds as an asset and about seeking to provide leadership in supporting cultural pluralism.

Heritage College is a successor to Fort Wright College (formerly Holy Names College), founded in 1907. A new institution was born in 1981 through a change in name and ownership. Dr. Kathleen A. Ross, the founding president of Heritage College, led this college from 85 students in 1982 to its present enrollment of more than 1,300 students. According to the published institutional information, Heritage College is not affiliated with any church or religious group, but the college's "educational values" have been influenced by the original sponsoring religious Catholic order, the Sisters of the Holy Names of Jesus and Mary. The institutional vision statement focuses on the recognition of a basic principle described as spiritual that "each human person is endowed with inalienable dignity and gifted with unique potential." The institution emphasizes the need for dedicated staff to sustain this mission. "They Shall Rise on Wings as Eagles" is the name of a twelve-foot sculpture representing the vision of Heritage College.

As with most institutions, the personal history is often more textured than the official description. Dr. Ross describes how as a Catholic sister she was pushed by her order, as many others were from the 1930s through the 1980s, into the leadership of educational institutions. When initially asked to take control of the newly formed Heritage College she describes her reaction as, "You've got to be kidding." She began her career as a high school teacher and then became involved in teacher development. Dr. Ross was asked to be academic vice president at Ft. Wright College without ever having been a full-time faculty member. Later, the board of directors decided that they were going to phase out Ft. Wright College, including an outreach site on the Yakama Indian Reservation. Lacking an institution in the remote area to serve the first-generation college students on the Indian reservation, Dr. Ross describes how her friends Martha Yallup and Violet Lumley Rau, who said, "Let's start our own college," encouraged her. Reluctantly, Dr. Ross assumed the presidency of the new college because there was "no other option for those on the Indian reservation." Her religious order told her it could not support the new institution financially, so it would need to be nondenominational, but they would support her work because it fit their mission. Dr. Ross was told, "See if you can make it work."

Fielding Graduate Institute

Fielding Graduate Institute was founded in 1974, in Santa Barbara, California, by Frederic Hudson, Hallock Hoffman, and Renata Tesch, educators who envisioned a graduate school serving midcareer professionals who wanted to pursue an advanced degree and whose educational needs were not being met by traditional institutions of higher education.

According to the official institutional history, the founders recognized that students seeking advanced degrees would be midcareer adults who wanted to enhance their professional skills and were interested in being part of a lifetime-learning community. Additionally, the founders realized that adults learn in ways that differ significantly from those of adolescents. The traditional pedagogical method of education would not be appropriate to this new experiment in adult professional education. To accommodate the learning styles of its adult students, Fielding developed a learning model that they characterize as "flexible, adult-centered, self-directed, task-oriented, and competence-based." Fielding is a small institution with only 1,400 students and 80 faculty members. The median age of students is 46, and 68.5 percent are Caucasian. Fielding Graduate Institute offers graduate degrees within three schools: Psychology, Human and Organization Development, and Educational Leadership and Change.

An administrator at Fielding describes how Frederic Hudson and Hallock Hoffman were sitting in a decision therapy workshop where a lot of master's level practitioners kept talking about how they wanted to go back and get their doctorate, but had no way of doing that. Hudson reportedly said, "I'm going to start a school." Hudson was in adult education and had been a university dean. Hoffman was the son of Paul Hoffman who helped shape the Marshall Plan after World War II, and came to Santa Barbara with Hutchings from the University of Chicago to set up the Center for Democratic Institutions. The founders were influential people with big ideas.

Administrators speak about coming to Fielding from traditional higher education attracted to its mission and innovative adult learning model. One administrator talks about leaving a research one institution because of frustration with traditional higher education's values and priorities: "I felt out of sync with the institutional values there. In speaking with my colleagues it was clear that they made the decision to be outliers in the institution, and I'm not comfortable when I'm that out of sync with the institution. At Fielding the institutional values, mission, purpose were so much more congruent with my personal ones." Nevertheless, administrators coming from traditional academic institutions and careers admitted some reluctance and suspicion of Fielding before accepting a position there. One faculty member and administrator speaks about being attracted to the values, friendliness, and ability to make an impact with a small, developing institution. Another faculty member and administrator coming from the corporate world describes her interest in Fielding: "I've become more attracted to it [higher education] because it has gone from a slow-paced industry to a pretty fast-changing industry. And I find that challenging."

CONCLUSION

In this chapter I addressed some of the fundamental questions that are typically asked of for-profit higher education. I learned that while there has been some growth in for-profit education, it still represents a very small portion of the degree program market in America. Furthermore, most of the data presented on for-profit institutions fail to make the important distinction between regionally accredited universities and those that are only accredited by state agencies or professional associations. This is important because for-profits lacking this accreditation are not really in the same competitive marketplace as traditional institutions. I also learned that there is a long history of vocational and proprietary education in the United States, which served to provide a skilled workforce. Additionally, changes in financial aid legislation beginning with the G.I. Bill have led to the growth of for-profit higher education. By the end of the twentieth century, for-profits began seeking and gaining the crucial regional accreditation for their degree programs. Minority populations are enrolling in for-profit institutions to a surprisingly large degree, but for-profits tend to focus their programs more generally on serving first-generation students rather than in accommodating particular racial groups. Although for-profits tend to have open admissions, their student bodies are varied and include a mix of highly qualified as well as underprepared students. For-profit institutions do not necessary concern themselves with revenue more than nonprofit universities, but can be seen to parallel the general development of what has been labeled the "academic capitalism" movement. Overall, neither two- nor four-year higher education institutions are directly threatened by the growth of for-profit institutions at this time. Furthermore, in this chapter I've profiled some of the for-profit and nontraditional institutions studied. With the official description and baseline statistics about these institutions, brief impressions of the organizational origin from some of the leadership were included to give more depth to the profile.

In the next chapter, I look closely at the mission of for-profits and nontraditional institutions. I examine how mission functions at these institutions, and the way for-profit values and aims contrast with traditional higher education.

CLIPPINGS

The "clippings" sections of this book are designed to serve two purposes: first, to give the reader some additional specific information about nontraditional institutions; and second, to provide a feel for how the institutions are regarded and presented in the press.

Love it or hate it, says Ted Marchese, vice president of the American Association for Higher Education, "it's [University of Phoenix] the most discussed university in the country in faculty lounges." (Miller & Haederle, 2000, p. 87)

BEVERLY SCHUCH, HOST (voiceover): John Sperling is about living, reborn several times after close brushes with death. In fact, he's a lot like the mythical bird the phoenix, having risen from the ashes of his own adversity. He was born the son of an impoverished sharecropper who beat him regularly. As a youth, he worked the farms in the Ozark Mountains shucking barley. He didn't learn to read until he was 16. He faced bankruptcy twice and cancer once. But John Sperling is a fighter and has overcome these hardships to soar to the highest level of entrepreneurial success. (Schuch, 2001, p. 1)

Adult learning scores high marks on the Street, judging by Strayer Education (STRA), which soared from 48 in March to 66 in June. It's now at 57. (Marcial, 2002, p. 89)

Ronald Taylor recalls the day in September 1973 when he and his partner, Dennis Keller, opened the Keller Graduate School of Management in a Chicago office building. "Dennis and my wife and I had to carry a 12-foot chalkboard up 21 floors because it wouldn't fit in the elevator," Taylor says. (Forbes, 1991, p. 304)

"We are, in a sense, a boutique of graduate-education programs," says Mr. Markovitz. Argosy, with headquarters in the same downtown office building where the Illinois school of psychology is now based, also owns the Ventura Group, a publisher of review materials for psychology-licensure exams, and two small businesses, the Medical Institute of Minnesota and PrimeTech Institute, which offer training in health care and information technology, respectively. It is moving into legal education as well. (Blumenstyk, 2000a, p. A46)

DeVry has been authorized to grant a four-year bachelor of technology in electronics engineering, a four-year bachelor of technology in computer information systems and a four-year bachelor of business operations. However, when the accreditation was granted, then vice-president of academic at the Southern Alberta Institute of Technology (SAIT), Barbara Samuels said, the decision would negatively impact public institutions offering similar degree programs. SAIT is a publicly funded post-secondary technical institute. The University of Calgary faculty association concurred with Samuels. "Alberta's university system has been weakened over the last decade with the dramatic loss of provincial funding and the incursion of college applied degree programs," said John Baker, U of C faculty association president. "The move to degree programs offered by the private sector is yet another serious blow to Alberta's universities." (Bolan, 2001, p. 25)

National University has turned its distance-learning program, started in 1996, into a for-profit venture called the Spectrum Pacific Learning Company, the university announced last month. The decision reflects the 31-year-old nonprofit university's effort to build on its success in operating another for-profit entity, the College of Oceaneering, which the university purchased about a year ago. (Forter, 2002, p. A38)

Consolidated degree enrollments for all of the Apollo Group Inc. institutions at Aug. 31, 2002 increased by 26.4% to 157,800 students compared to 124,800 students at Aug. 31, 2001. Degree enrollments at The University of Phoenix (excluding University of Phoenix Online) were 84,300 students at Aug. 31, 2002 compared to 74,200 students at Aug. 31, 2001 representing a 13.6% increase. Degree enrollments for University of Phoenix Online at Aug. 31, 2002 increased by 70.2% to 49,400 students compared to 29,000 students at Aug. 31, 2001. ("Apollo Group Inc. Reports," 2002, p. 1)

CHAPTER 4

Mission: Who Are You?

I would almost describe what we do as noble because we're really fulfilling a need for what has been an almost forgotten segment of the population: adults.

—University of Phoenix administrator

Missions at institutions such as the University of Phoenix and DeVry University are particularly important to analyze because their for-profit status runs counter to traditional higher education in America, with origins in either religious-based institutions (for independents) or serving social agendas (in land-grant public institutions). This legal position has led to many large misunderstandings about the for-profits. The first surprise is that many for-profits have a social mission. Of course, one must be careful not to assume a formal statement of mission is authentic. Nevertheless, in my interviews with administrators and faculty members, this sociopolitical focus was found repeatedly in origin stories, discussions of mission, and stated objectives of individuals. Contrary to what many detractors believe, the mission of the for-profits is not just about making money. If this were the case they would be less interesting, and probably less successful. One of the fascinating aspects of studying the mission of the for-profits is to understand how the demands of the marketplace are balanced with a social agenda. This is particularly true in the current environment, where traditional universities are behaving increasingly like businesses in the pursuit of funding sources, in management style, and in their collaboration with corporations in research. There is much to be learned from the for-profits and nontraditional institutions in how their missions are made clear and relevant, are tested regularly, inform the educational objectives, incorporate diversity, and transform the domain of higher education as a whole.

While proprietary postsecondary institutions with purely applied curricula—which in some ways the for-profits most closely resemble—have existed for years in the United States, none has been as successful at making inroads into the traditional higher education marketplace as regionally accredited for-profits such as the University of Phoenix, DeVry University, and Argosy University. A primary reason for their success is revealed in the role mission plays in the organizations. Based on interviews with these institutions, the following characteristics of the mission clearly emerge: constant testing and questioning of mission, focus on core mission and competencies, mixing social agenda with attention to marketplace, alignment of mission with clear pedagogical objectives, increased diversity through customer service focus, use of technology to increase access, redefinition of the domain to assert mission, and educational community formation. Many looking at this list will recognize that it reveals a curious mix of terms from both corporate and higher education worlds. For instance, what would traditional institutions in higher education think of diversity and customer service together, or pursuing a social agenda with attention to the marketplace? This fusion of business and the academy is at the center of the uniqueness of the for-profits' approach to educational mission. This chapter analyzes mission at the University of Phoenix and other for-profits and nontraditionals in regard to clarity, providing equal access and educating working adults, responding to shareholders' expectations, and creating efficient learning environments, alignment with pedagogy, and compliance or mission within the domain.

CLARITY

The mission of helping adult and traditionally underserved students is constant and clear at the for-profit and nontraditional institutions. As one would expect from any institution that is performing well, the consistent understanding of the mission repeatedly emerges as administrators and faculty members are interviewed. The root reason for this clarity is interesting to consider because it seems to come from both a sociopolitical belief system, as well as an understanding of the need for market segmentation. Throughout the interviews, representatives frequently comment on the clarity of the institution's objectives as this administrator from the University of Phoenix reports: "People are interested in a lot of things that we're doing and they wonder how it works and why it works. Probably the biggest single reason is that our mission is to service the educational needs of working adult students. Period." Another characteristic of the clarity reported by those interviewed is that the mission permeates everything they do and is sustained in daily practices: "I think it comes about just by virtue of the way that we all talk about it [mission], in the sense of what we do. We're here to serve the needs of working adult students whose access to education might otherwise be restricted." Is the mission as clear for the faculty as for the administrators? A faculty member comments on awareness of mission among faculty members:

> I think the faculty understand it in that it's really a thread in every-thing that's communicated to us and things that are asked of us. . . . There are really core faculty that want to grow and learn and understand and support the mission. And I see that hand-in-hand with the campus administrator, because there really is consistency of dialogue and consistency of meaning.

Conversation, debate, and consistent meaning are the main components of the clarity of mission particularly at the University of Phoenix. Inter-estingly, when asked about mission one faculty member spends a great deal of time talking about the for-profit nature of the University of Phoenix—this is never a focus for administrators, who are perhaps a little more guarded. Furthermore, the uniformity of belief and understanding of the mission is remarked about repeatedly by administrators—less so for fac-ulty. One should note here that most of the faculty at University of Phoe-nix do not have full-time appointments, often teach at other institutions, and are probably less likely to have consistent exposure to institutional mission than administrators. Still, some longtime faculty do connect with the mission and are invested in organizational objectives.

Other respondents at the University of Phoenix feel that as the orga-nization has grown, it has been harder to communicate the institutional mission, particularly at the lower administrative levels: "I think at the upper levels you will find great understanding of it. And at the lower levels maybe less understanding." Some also comment on the challenge of com-municating the mission, especially to new staff and faculty—orienting and articulating that mission to them is a constant challenge. A longtime administrator explains more specifically how the original mission has become diffused over time with growth and points to the transformation of the mission into "features and benefits," moving it away from the peda-gogical and social mission. Even for a relatively new institution such as the University of Phoenix, it is interesting to see how there is a tendency to separate pedagogical practice from the philosophy at the core of the approach. One should also note on the positive side that this slippage has been observed by the administrator and is a cause for concern.

Despite some problems of dissemination as the organization grows, the University of Phoenix is still very much an expression of the personality and attitudes of its founder, John Sperling. While the mission is very well defined, the implementation is not expressed in broad goals, but rather in pursuing particular directions. John Sperling characterizes this approach as having directions rather than goals. He explains how goals have an endpoint, whereas directions lead to continual pursuit. This notion of directions rather than goals is revealing because it indicates how the founder of this institution views mission as something impermanent and evolving. Furthermore, directions are more active; they require monitoring and adjustment on a continual basis. This notion ties in very nicely with the observed tendency of the organization to test constantly the mission.

A crucial strength that the following respondent indicates is that the mission is regularly under examination and revision. Notice how the mission is tested through debate, sometimes through a notion of finding the "core business":

> I think that's been a strength, that it's said we're for working adults and we're going to define that as 23 and older with a job. We're debating if that was a good definition, that age thing, that maybe it should be 60 credits someplace else. But that mission for a specific type of demographic and relooking at ourselves to see where our strengths are—our core is business. . . . But I think it's very clear in our minds who we are, what we are, and what are the philosophies driving us. I've never been at an educational institution so aware of educational philosophies.

This self-awareness and constant organizational self-analysis keep the mission fresh and relevant. At the same time, in a business sense, it focuses the organization on core competencies.

Finally, clarity of mission is a strength of the University of Phoenix. While respondents spoke about challenges with growth and new directions, the mission is still remarkably fresh. A distinguishing characteristic of this clarity is that the organization constantly tests organizationally the mission and in this way remains relevant. Furthermore, it is a mission infused with personal meaning for many of the respondents.

At the other for-profits the interviewees express a similar self-awareness. At Argosy University, administrators speak about professional-oriented career preparation. At DeVry, administrators tell of their students achieving the knowledge and skills to be productive in the workforce at various levels. At the undergraduate level, the curriculum is approximately 25 percent general education. Positioning themselves somewhere in the middle between the University of Phoenix and traditional liberal arts institutions, DeVry attempts to give students a solid grounding in general education to support the students' interest in lifelong learning to complement the practical applications they learn. Administrators at DeVry believe the general education component helps prepare students for lifelong learning that will improve their workplace productivity. The stated learning objectives for their students include both functional knowledge, whether it's computer technology or telecommunications management, and a series of broader skills that range from verbal and written skills to cultural understanding, teamwork skills, and general analytical skills, "generally what one would expect of a person who has a college degree."

The nontraditional nonprofits studied for this book are very clear on their unique missions and lean more toward the traditional liberal arts emphasis, but are also very concerned with the practical application of the disciplines they teach. At Fielding Graduate Institute, respondents speak about providing opportunities for students to learn how to learn. Second, they emphasize the integration of personal, professional, academic knowledge and the self. Generally, administrators at Fielding stress growth and personal reflection for their graduates. Fielding Graduate Institute leaders feel that their institution is unique in both its delivery system and teaching methods. In terms of the delivery system, they are dispersed across the country, do not have traditional academic terms, and utilize a competency curriculum. Neither the faculty nor the students are located at their central office facility in Santa Barbara, California. They use a method that accommodates the characteristics of the adult learner, and focus on "conversations" rather than lectures. Like the for-profits, Fielding's uniqueness comes partly from "the recognition that people over 40 have a lot of other things going on in their lives." When describing learning outcomes at Fielding, administrators focus partly on value acquisition: "We want them to be socially conscious individuals with a commitment to a multicultural ethic."

At Heritage College, the mission is to provide a high-quality educational opportunity at both the bachelor's and master's levels for the multicultural population inhabiting their local valley area in Washington state. As the president describes their emphasis, "The college is primarily geared to meeting the needs not being met by someone else." In their mission, administrators point to providing quality education for underserved populations, skills to live in a multicultural world, in accessible and flexible formats to meet student needs. What they describe as "cross-cultural communication competency," which is a little different than just a view of diversity, is a unique feature of the curriculum they offer. In a course specifically designed to encourage the development of this competency, they break the students into diverse groups of three or four students, give them a community project, and then afterward reflect on what has been learned together. A characteristic of the for-profit and nontraditional institutions studied for this book is a singular mission focus on underserved populations.

THE SOCIAL AGENDA: ACCESS AND DIVERSITY

One should first be clear that mission statements represent commitments and not proof of adherence to goals and ideas. Nevertheless, the mission of the University of Phoenix and the other nontraditional institutions studied for this book have a sociopolitical basis similar to that found at many other higher education institutions. The differences lie in the for-profits' business model, the concentration on creating convenient student-centered learning environments, and their focus on career issues and outcomes rather than inputs or selective admissions practices. Furthermore, the social mission is connected to serving a diverse audience, and incorporates a central role for the use of technology to provide access. In the case of the nontraditional institutions, particularly Heritage, there is an especially deep commitment to providing access to ethnically diverse populations.

Throughout this study, those interviewed point to the importance of diversity as an institutional objective, and this social agenda and awareness is evident. Administrators appear clear in the belief and support of their institutional mission and understand the social ideals behind it: "The university's [mission] is to provide access to working adults to the kind of education they wouldn't have had access to before. I get behind that."

The influence of John Sperling on setting the mission for the institution, as the founder of the University of Phoenix, would be hard to underestimate. Sperling characterizes his personal beliefs that inform his social activism: "I suppose each is designed in one way or another to ameliorate the condition of mankind and to get as far as you can from Hobbes' concept of life as nasty, brutish, and short." According to Sperling, his activism started more broadly in 1995, when he began to fund major drug law reform initiatives, first in Arizona and California. He was one of the primary backers of the medical marijuana initiative in California, and his support partially led to the decriminalization of drugs in Arizona. Since then, he's led similar initiatives in Oregon, Washington, Alaska, Colorado, and Maine. Sperling self-effacingly downplays his social consciousness. However, his support of political causes and socially relevant research (such as water desalinization and aging prevention) is clearly shown. Furthermore, Sperling shows a willingness to support causes that cost him money, particularly providing access to lower-class students, and expresses fiery criticisms of those who do not share his point of view.

How does the social consciousness mix with making money? An administrator speaks about how Sperling and the organization as a whole balance its pursuit of profit with a social agenda. He argues that one can do socially relevant and important work and make money at the same time: "John has this thing that everything he does has a social, political purpose. And he makes money off of it." Not only is there a belief that both objectives can be simultaneously pursued, but there is also an understanding that they are each more likely to succeed if done together. This belief is translated into practice, for example, by the University of Phoenix's applied educational curriculum, designed to help first-generation college students succeed economically. Sperling articulates what he sees as a "moral responsibility" to provide applied educational opportunities:

> What we try to do is to give the students the skills to deal with the world that they live in, and that's our moral responsibility—to make them able to prosper in that world. And you have to take that world as a given. You can't say, "We're going to teach these people an ethic that transcends the present." I don't think that is really very ethical if you give them the set of ideas and attitudes of the kind that make their path through life more difficult, that would not be ethical in my view.

This real-world concern leads to an emphasis on an applied curriculum. Here is the theme repeated often in the interviews—the social role of the University of Phoenix is to make the path through college and the work world less difficult. Later in this interview Sperling contrasts the corporate as opposed to the academic view of training:

> They [corporate trainers] start with where the learner is. If they've got Mexican-Americans or Hispanics who can't speak English, it's English training. If they don't know math, it's math training. So

wherever the worker is, they begin there and try to create a worker who is really efficient and effective. And any lower—I don't want to say lower class—but any of the workers from the lower socio-economic background who can start and stick to a job at Motorola for three or four years, they're infinitely better equipped to deal with the world than they were before they started.

Observe how Sperling points out that the corporate approach to training begins with evaluating the needs of the employees and increasing their productivity—thus benefiting both the employer and employee. Sperling's argument is that the focus on the employee (or customer in the University of Phoenix's case) leads to a more beneficial education for traditionally underserved classes.

Putting this approach in context, an administrator from the University of Phoenix points to the elitist history and nature of higher education in America: "When you think back to its [higher education's] roots, it was a country club deal. It was for the rich. It was for the people that had the money." Tying this elitism to inflexibility, an administrator points to how traditional higher education's intransigence has led to a lack of meaningful access for diverse audiences:

For an adult learner to go back to school for a second career, which is so much the trend in society these days, it's not very convenient at most of the institutions that I'm aware of for someone with a family and a full-time job to go back and pursue a career. Maybe they've been in police science and they want to learn something else and get a license to do counseling. . . . The linkage to provide someone that second career really doesn't exist in a very smooth way. The classes are taught during the day, the clinical experiences are limited to places that are open nine-to-five. Well, I don't know how a working adult is going to do that.

Observe how commitment to student focus is tied to diversity in the University of Phoenix's mission. This customer or student focus sets the University of Phoenix and the other for-profits apart from public and independent institutions with access social missions. Administrators at the University of Phoenix tie the access mission to a concentration on meeting student needs and in so doing, differentiate themselves from traditional higher education. In the past decade, many traditional institutions have attempted to reorganize specific areas, particularly student services, to be more responsive to student needs. However, higher education has generally resisted evaluating its own academic programs based so completely on meeting student-perceived needs. These interviews reveal that for the University of Phoenix, as well as the other for-profits, customer service is linked to providing access for underserved populations.

Furthermore, the objective in the University of Phoenix's mission for access is integrated into its learning model and is related closely to the student or customer focus. In the following interview with an administrator, the institution's particular approach to defining educational quality indicates a shift from the traditional concentration on measuring inputs (the qualifications of students entering college) to outputs (demonstrated attainment of stated learning objectives):

> We've got to change the paradigm. I think we have to drive the change of a paradigm that says higher education is only appropriately offered to a select number of people. And we base our evaluation of the quality that you bring to the higher education table on the inputs. . . . The assumption is you can only have a quality institution of higher education if you're like Harvard, which bases their quality on exclusivity.

Here the University of Phoenix very pointedly counters criticism of its open admissions policy with accusations of elitism. The value that seems to underlie the notion of access is that anyone who wants an education should be able to receive it. Instead of depending on the qualifications of entering students for a baseline level of quality, administrators look instead at measuring success in meeting specific stated learning outcomes for each course.

While the social agenda is more class- than race-based, the university's mission also connects directly with more traditional notions of diversity. Anecdotally, it was obvious to me that the student population is very ethnically diverse. Particularly at some of the University of Phoenix's urban locations, one sees great ethnic diversity in both administrators and students: "There's a genuineness of diversity and the philosophy about diversity. It isn't lip service." An ethnic minority faculty member comments further on diversity at the University of Phoenix, noting in particular the flexibility for working adults and the lower admission barriers: "I think this school is in a better position to capitalize on that situation than anybody else. . . . This is an opportunity for them [students] to come in quick and go out quick. And they get a degree while they are working." So the University of Phoenix maintains it meets a social need by serving, to a great extent, underserved and diverse populations.

As reported in Chapter 3, while it is common to think of the University of Phoenix as an Internet university, in fact the online division is actually only one-third of its operation. Nevertheless, the institution's use of technology in the online and face-to-face courses ties in directly with its mission of access. A faculty member voiced a position commonly heard at the University of Phoenix about the role of technology in providing access: "My dream is that education should be free for everybody." This dream of access through technology was echoed frequently in the interviews. Phrases used by those interviewed such as "you can teach yourself" connect with the bedrock American belief in and respect for the self-educated man. The University of Phoenix is a very American institution, linking to beliefs in a work ethic, pragmatism, and democratic ideals of equal opportunity. An administrator comments on multiple delivery systems as a way of increasing access for populations with different needs in the future: "The part-time student, the working student, the mix of online and on-ground, I think that kind of thing is going to be readily available. There is going to be a whole menu of options for people that want to pursue their higher education." University of Phoenix administrators make a distinction between the working adult and the traditional eighteen-year-old undergraduate in the use and appropriateness of technology and thus indicate clarity not only in understanding what they are as an educational organization, but also in excluding what they are not.

Although the educational mission at the University of Phoenix is sociopolitically based, often those interviewed downplay any larger aim in their work. Furthermore, time and again, both administrators and faculty members fail to connect with a more traditional and religious-based notion of a "calling" to work in higher education. In the following quotation, which is typical of responses to this question, one can see that the focus is on doing "interesting" work more than being occupied by religious or social aims:

> Q: Is the notion of a calling to work in higher education meaningful to you?
>
> A: No. I don't get real spiritual about it, if you will. It is fun for me. It is interesting, and that really has driven my choices in what I do the last, oh, five or six years. Does this sound interesting? Is it something that would be fun for me, that I would enjoy doing?

Nevertheless, a faculty member expressed the importance of her work at the University of Phoenix for the social good: "I think I can contribute to the betterment of society, if you will. Students who learn become better citizens." Thus I have the impression that when administrators talk about a larger purpose, the "calling" to work at the University of Phoenix is generally more sociopolitical than religious.

While the evidence of DeVry's sociopolitical mission isn't as abundant as at the University of Phoenix, administrators at DeVry also speak about meeting the needs of historically underserved populations. Serving fewer working adults than the University of Phoenix, DeVry concentrates more specifically on employment: "If you interview students you will find that the most immediate need is for a job—the symphony can come later." However, the administrators do not want only a skills-based education: "We don't want to just train them for a job and not give them any perspective on the human experience." DeVry sees its role as serving this first-generation college group by providing more affordable education. An administrator describes three kinds of public higher education institutions: the privates or nonprofits that have to fund themselves primarily through tuition and donations, for-profits that are funded by public investment capital that want a return on their money, and the selective institutions that charge very high tuition. He argues that the public institutions are also high cost but they are offset by public taxes, leading now in recessionary times to a rationing situation. Given the limited number of publicly funded openings, how do you decide who gets in? Thus its role: "DeVry and others like us have to be about how you deliver the best education for the lowest cost." Their MBA now costs approximately $25,000, far less than at other institutions.

On a personal level, the leadership team at DeVry speaks about the importance of education in their lives. One talks of immigrant parents from Eastern Europe after World War II. While they didn't have a chance to get a higher education in their own lives, they instilled in their children the need for higher education from a very young age: "Education does transform lives and create opportunity like nothing else." Another administrator at DeVry focuses on the personal satisfaction in teaching, not the administrative work: "I get a lot of personal satisfaction and see value personally from teaching. I think the administrative pieces are much like any other industry." One leader in the organization tells the story of how he came to work at DeVry:

> I was in a training program for liberal arts graduates who wanted to learn something about business. This was after the 1960s—"business" was a bad word in the sixties. We were all history or political science majors who needed skills because we found ourselves in business environments. That was a time when Abby Hoffman went on

and became an insurance salesman. . . . I had a terrific experience working here with Dennis and Ron in the CBT Institute and it seemed so cool. It was business, but it was doing good while having the opportunity, it seems such a cool production—education—to be involved in and make a career in.

Still another administrator at DeVry was a member of the Peace Corps. Was there a connection between his young adulthood in the Peace Corps and his work in a for-profit? "I have always had strong feelings about education. It is great being in school; I believe in the education process." Having begun a career first in the healthcare industry and then moving into education, he feels that he has had a consistent social service interest and believes that his work at DeVry fits his values. The notion of a "calling" to work in higher education is meaningful to the leadership at DeVry, and their work with adult and historically underserved populations has a particular resonance for them: "I think that at DeVry we know that we could probably make more money somewhere else if we wanted to, but for almost everyone here there's a true desire to help people." Although this belief in the mission of the institution is similar to that found at traditional institutions, the leaders at DeVry point out that the difference in working at a for-profit is that there is "more structure to get things done." Facilitating social mobility and contributing to society are values in which the leadership at DeVry expresses belief. One leader in the institution describes watching students walk across the stage at graduation and the meaning that it has for him:

> You sit there and realize that you have impacted people's lives that have been marginalized by the traditional higher education system and I think you get a good feeling. Whether in the aggregate that adds up to a sense of a calling, I don't know. I think there is a sense of satisfaction, sense of contribution, sense of doing something that otherwise would be missing in society.

Similarly, at Argosy, a leader of the organization speaks about turning away from a career as a clinical psychologist in private practice to work in education because "I realized I would have a much bigger impact on people in education."

At the nontraditional, nonprofit Heritage College, its uniqueness and purpose are clearly social, described by the president as "uncovering talent that has been overlooked, and neglected by the mainstream higher educational system." She argues in a way not dissimilar to the for-profit representatives that while selective schools have elitist assumptions about education, "talent is distributed randomly across the population." Heritage serves a student population that comes from an extremely low economic level—60 percent of the students have a family income of less than $20,000. Second, the population is multicultural—although they are located on an Indian reservation, the major group is Mexican immigrant because of the agriculture fields located nearby. While Heritage has a student body that is clearly distinctive, their president nevertheless feels that their model could be duplicated in urban areas where people feel isolated, where there isn't a fair share of the educational resources. Heritage also emphasizes small classes and personalized attention, which is distinct to many liberal arts college but unusual given a student body like Heritage's.

At the other nontraditional nonprofit, the Fielding Graduate Institute, the institutional leaders express a strong belief in the work they do to educate adult students. One administrator speaks about her belief in the broad and important role of education for the individual: "I never think of higher education as vocational training. I think of it as establishing a different relationship to themselves, to the world around them." Very much in keeping with its methods based on adult learning theory, one leader at Fielding speaks about her work in higher education as facilitation and stewardship:

> My calling is one of facilitating people or students. Many of the students have a vision or dream. And many of them see education as a vehicle for achieving that. For some, education leads to a career. For some they started school in their thirties and now are in their sixties have come back to school. So it's personal achievement. To me, I have the greatest job, and they have all these great stories, and we have the honor of helping them. It's really kind of like stewardship.

Evidenced throughout the interviews and the histories of the organizations themselves, the for-profits and nontraditionals were clearly conceived with and retain a strong social mission. In this way they are similar to many other higher education institutions, particularly public institutions. The key difference is in the approach. Starting from a for-profit business model and a belief that this structure can provide better access to underserved populations, the for-profits concentrate on creating learning environments tailored to meet the needs of working adults through convenience, focus on benefits in the workplace, and meeting learning objectives rather than using selectivity in admission policies to maintain quality. Furthermore, the social mission is connected to serving a diverse audience with a central role for the use of technology to provide access.

SHAREHOLDER EXPECTATIONS

As publicly traded companies, the for-profit universities must be conscious and attentive to shareholder expectations. Although many critics express concern that the demands of the shareholders lead to a lack of attention to the students, John Sperling argues that this is a false dichotomy: "I see no conflict at all. If the employees know that they should be devoted to the welfare of the customers and then through that devotion, the company continues to grow and prosper, and the shareholders are happy as can be." In fact, Sperling points out that the for-profit publicly traded status has spurred better performance because of access to capital. However, the founder of the University of Phoenix also talks about the performance pressures that come with this access to capital: "You miss your numbers and the punishment is swift and absolutely relentless."

When asked about defining moments in the history of the University of Phoenix, an administrator points to the change brought about with the selling of stock in the company on Wall Street. Note in particular how the administrator discusses the change as bringing in outsiders to the operation: "All of a sudden now we were open to a host of outsiders who were looking in and who had their own set of expectations. And that changed some of the culture as well. We now had things to think about we hadn't thought about before. Wall Street, analysts, expectations." While this quotation certainly reveals the pressure brought about by the expectations of shareholders, another administrator points out that the budget demands are not much different from those in traditional higher education: "You have to satisfy the analysts in order to keep the stock price up. Yeah, there are always concerns at the end of the quarter. If we're coming up close, we might put on a hiring increase for a month. But that's no different from academic institutions, when you run on a budget, that's the same kind of thing." Another longtime faculty member speaks about the for-profit nature of the University of Phoenix, and how its social-political objectives have changed over the history of the organization. In particular, the faculty member asserts that while the mission is preserved by longtime employees, newer employees hired after the organization went public do not understand it well, so that an impression of a changed mission exists: "I think that handful of people who started the company still have those missions—a sense of mission. People who have been hired after that—after the school went public—I think the stock price profit got a little more important to them." While educators are concerned that academic quality may be compromised by profit expectations, administrators at the University of Phoenix repeatedly point to John Sperling's influence in maintaining high standards in the face of Wall Street pressures. Balancing academic quality with profit expectations is a central concern for all for-profit institutions, an issue considered in depth in Chapter 7.

Another respondent at the University of Phoenix comments on how going public increased external criticism of the organization: "I can clearly remember sitting in a NCA meeting and hearing somebody say: 'It wasn't bad enough that they're for profit. Now they have the audacity to sell stock!' And I thought: Oh my! Yet another reason to love the University of Phoenix." This negative reaction to going public from many in traditional higher education is undoubtedly common; however, both administrators and faculty members indicate limited change in the overall mission. Generally, they contend that shareholder expectations have not substantially changed the organizational mission.

The for-profit status of DeVry, much like the University of Phoenix and Argosy University, has given it venture capital. The leadership at DeVry claim that this gives them much needed funding and flexibility. How does this status affect their mission? "The for-profit structure means that we have the financial objective that is parallel to the educational objectives. But any organization that is going to be economically viable has an economical/financial component to their objectives, whether they overtly discuss that or not." The recent downturn in the technology education market led to diversification at DeVry. Administrators point to the Wall Street pressure as part of the reason for moving so quickly to diversify. One leader at DeVry characterizes the most important aspect of being for-profit and publicly held as the focus and willingness to respond to the marketplace. He asserts that the for-profits are the ones that will be able to meet the current crisis in higher education of increasing costs and demand because of their access to capital.

At Fielding Graduate Institute, leaders admit that they are sometimes confused with the much maligned for-profit universities and administrators feel that some of the confusion comes from the fact that they are nontraditional. One administrator at Fielding voices reservations about for-profit institutions because of a potential conflict of interest in pursuing profits over the welfare of their students. She points out that Fielding has a no-growth policy for enrollments because expansion is not consistent with its values. At the same time, administrators speak about forming strategic alliances and partnerships. Administrators overall at Fielding see for-profits as a challenge to them. While admitting that they could learn a great deal from the for-profits, one administrator at Fielding expresses the need for their actions to be consistent with values:

"I think you pick out the successes that fit with your culture, your cultural values."

Heritage College is quite far from a for-profit business model, yet it also is sometimes confused with them because of its nontraditional characteristics. Heritage uses a "low tuition, low unfunded aid model." Tuition is low: $6,800–8,000 for the full year, and much of that for its student population comes from financial aid. As with the for-profits, Heritage has learned the importance of facilitating financial aid for first-generation college students with little knowledge of the confusing catacomb of regulations; it has developed a very active financial aid office that pursues the regular federal aid awards, as well as special scholarships for which students might qualify. Additionally, it has some entrepreneurial programs, such as one for school counselors, that generate revenue beyond their expenses, or make a "profit." Finally, it is also very aggressive about grants to help fund the faculty and other campus-provided services to the community.

What does Heritage College think about the for-profits? The president states that she does not have anything philosophical against the market model, "provided that the value system that it is operating is reflective of educational values that serve students." However, she fears that some of the for-profits "are embodying values that would not be good for society in trying to reach students who have big economic barriers. It is counterproductive to recruit students but neglect the level of support, both financially and academically, that they need to persevere and succeed." Additionally, she claims that institutions such as the University of Phoenix "tend to skim off the students who can pay themselves or who can easily navigate the student loan system, and students who are already motivated towards a degree." This makes it harder for the other institutions such as Heritage College, because it takes away some of the students that would make it easier to balance the finances and leaves an unrealistic picture of what it takes to educate nontraditional students. This in turn discourages public legislatures from providing adequate support for students who will not participate successfully in a University of Phoenix–type program but have talent that society needs developed.

Since the University of Phoenix, DeVry University, and Argosy University are publicly traded companies, meeting shareholder expectations is a necessary aspect of their respective missions. However, as administrators repeatedly point out, this pressure is not unlike budget pressures experienced in traditional higher education institutions. Those interviewed spoke at length about balancing the revenue growth pressures with academic quality. Additionally, there were repeated indications that the event of going public put pressure on the institution to once again focus its mission and make it more productive. Therefore, on an organizational level, the pressure of shareholder expectations may have made the for-profits more efficient and alert to the core mission.

CUSTOMER SERVICE AND EFFICIENT LEARNING ENVIRONMENTS

> Every aspect of what we do has the student focus in mind. (For-profit administrator)

A focus on serving students, very much in line with a business philosophy of being customer-based, permeates the for-profit universities. This customer service emphasis is not only a focus for student services, but also leads to a learner-centered pedagogical approach. Throughout the interviews, administrators and faculty members speak both about the importance of customer service and the need to create the most productive and efficient learning environments. "I consider my students my customers" was a common remark heard at the for-profits.

The for-profits and nontraditional universities concentrate on accommodating the schedules and obligations of working adults. The following excerpt captures how this priority is seen as an organizational strength at the University of Phoenix and illustrates that its mission is limited and targeted on adult learners:

> A singular focus on that population, to some degree it's a luxury that we enjoy which our traditional colleagues don't. And that is that we can focus on one student in certain types of programs and really cater to their needs and create a learning environment that speaks just to them. The mandate of most four-year institutions is so broad that it's almost undoable in the larger sense.

The further appeal of this specific mission is that it allows the institution to focus on the shared problems of the students and can thereby better address the special needs of this population:

> Everyone in your class is going to have the same kind of problems. They're going to have kids, they're going to have church, and they're going to have social obligations. Everybody understands what the demands are on your time. We're just not going to waste it, we're going to make it as easy as possible to get there. It won't be easy, but at least we won't make it unnecessarily burdensome.

A faculty member talks about how the students attending the University of Phoenix have specific needs that require the institution to pay attention to student home life and other educational distractions:

> They have full-time jobs, some of them have second jobs. Many are single parents that are caring for children. They're caring for their own parents. They have long commutes and then they are full-time students. . . . If I were teaching at UC Davis or San Diego State [University] or Cal[ifornia] State [University] Dominguez [Hills], my approach would be different.

One of the strengths of the mission of the University of Phoenix is in the way it segments the market so effectively. The University of Phoenix consciously avoids the eighteen- to twenty-two-year-old student market, realizing that because its learning model incorporates work experience such an attempt would not be successful (although it has recently lowered its minimum age requirement).

An administrator at the University of Phoenix describes how teaching facilities are designed to center on student needs:

> We sat down and said, "When you come to school at night, we understand you arrive at about 5:45 and class starts at 6:00 and you have a list of things you have to do. How can we facilitate you accomplishing those things in the fifteen minutes that you have?" And then we designed a space around that. We staffed it with the people that answered the most often questions that they're going to ask. We put the materials in there that they need. We put access to the Internet and the computer stuff and all their curriculum materials in there, so that if they have forgotten something, they can go in and get it. If they have a disk and they didn't get it printed out, they can slide it in and bring their materials. If they choose to come early and meet as a group in order to do their work—we provide quiet rooms for them to be able to do that. We looked at what the things were the students needed to be successful and we designed around their needs. Physically around their needs, and then staffed it appropriately.

Here's another example of how a customer-service approach leads to online resources designed with students in mind. Observe how the organization starts with assessing student needs and focuses on student-defined needs. "So we asked them what it was that they wanted to access in an all-around-the-clock environment, and we took a list of what they wanted and we developed it." The FlexNet program, introduced in 2002, offering partially online and partially face-to-face education, is a further attempt by the University of Phoenix to meet student needs:

> We don't want our students to have to make choices between going to work, going to school, going to my church/community activities, et cetera. Our online program has become so recognized and students are wanting a piece of that that we created a model of FlexNet, which is a five-week undergraduate course. The student would meet with their learning team, their co–work group, in a classroom environment the first and last night of the course, and then the two- or three-course evenings sandwiched in between would be through the computer.

For this FlexNet program, the online courses, and face-to-face courses, online student services is another area where the University of Phoenix is working to meet student needs: "We get about 8,000 applications a month and each of those applications has to go through a filtering process." This enormous volume of applications is automated to improve customer service and speed admissions.

However, there is a distinction between a customer service orientation and always giving students what they want. The president at the University of Phoenix made this point when discussing the university's required attendance policy:

> The student as a customer is not always right. Customer service, to us, means that customers—both internal and external—are entitled to timely, accurate responses delivered in a courteous manner. It does not mean that the answer is always, "yes." It does not mean that they get whatever they want. It means that they are entitled to be treated with respect. One of the examples of that is when students say, "If you are so student-oriented, why do you have attendance requirements?" "Well, the faculty and I happen to believe that it's important for you to show up for class. Attendance isn't negotiable." While we have minimized the administrative burden as much as possible and believe adults have to take charge of their learning, they cannot do so if they are not present to contribute. Not being present in class also deprives the other students of the horizontal learning which occurs from every person's unique contribution. So in that sense, the student-customers would like us to do something different from what we're willing to do.

Nevertheless, the president points out the central role that customer service plays in a competitive higher education marketplace:

The number one differentiating factor we're going to have—and will continue to have—is an absolute, astonishing attention to student service. We have to be more service-oriented than others. We have to be at the level of a Ritz-Carlton in the sense of being attuned to what the students' needs are and then providing them with the best value proposition. Why do people buy Mercedes versus Volkswagen? Aside from prestige, there is some value attributed to having that car. They both run. They both have steering wheels. Why will people pay that extra money for a Mercedes? A good part of the reason is reputation for quality and service. We're not going to compete with Harvard or Claremont [Graduate University] or other top-tier institutions on academic reputation. We do not strive to be elite, we don't have the history and we are not enrolling the top one percent of graduating classes. We are serving a mass demographic, that middle bulk of people in need of education in order to hang onto or move up in their jobs. So there has to be a reason these students will choose us rather than another institution and I think one reason is amazing service.

Note how she speaks in business terms, much like a company would discuss product differentiation, when pointing to a high level of customer service as a distinguishing feature of the University of Phoenix. An administrator at the University of Phoenix emphasizes here how the student service and productivity questions are continually asked and examined:

The point is that we do ask those questions. We do need to look and say, "Is this being run and managed the most efficient way?" Generally, we do wait until someone cries or screams or the data shows that there isn't enough attention being paid, that with a very large span of control you start losing efficiencies. And we do a lot of management through reporting. Again, our job is to identify the key criteria that we value. What do we need to make sure is paramount in our efficiency effectiveness? And if we start seeing things slipping, then surely the first thing that comes up are discussions about what we need to change in that regard.

A theme echoed throughout the interviews that illustrates how the student focus leads to a structure and group of services that best supports the creation of an effective learning atmosphere is the direction of resources and energy to create effective and productive learning environments:

I think it [the goal] is to create the most efficient learning environment that we can possibly create for working adult students. And that has both an academic side to it as well as an administrative side to it. We need to create the most efficient learning environment that we can possibly create for them. That's one of the things that John [Sperling] has said that I really think is true. I quote it a lot of times. "If you can show people a very clear path to run down, they will do great work." And it's creating that clear path, creating that very clear, clean, efficient path to run down that will cause them to do great academic work as students and be real positive examples of graduates of our institution.

Another administrator describes more in detail what is meant by creating these learning environments and keys in on "affective" components of learning:

That whole affective side of learning, which has to do with both the environment as well as the kinds of skills we're imparting: the ability to speak. The ability to create self-confidence. How do you do that? You do it by giving them time to practice in groups for self-confidence and self-esteem. And all of those affective attributes of education that you don't hear about too much in higher education.

These affective characteristics are particularly important for the population it serves—first-generation college students. An interview subject responsible for the online campus points to responsive student services as a crucial part in creating effective learning environments. They assign students to what they call "customer service teams," which include an admissions adviser, a financial adviser, and an academic adviser who work together as a team. Administrators believe that if working adult students are given a clear path they will produce and succeed—but time is a premium for them: "If they're going to produce quality academic work, they've got to spend every waking hour doing that work, doing the work, not in any other administrative detail."

Customer service for the University of Phoenix and other for-profits is tied closely to the desire to provide access to diverse populations, the concentration on working adults, and the objective of serving the business community. This customer service focus helps to differentiate the university in the educational marketplace, increases quality (in a business sense), and suits the psychological traits of the adult learners they serve who often view themselves more as customers than traditional students. Those interviewed speak often about the central belief in creating efficient learning environments and clear paths to learning and meeting career goals for students.

TEACHING/LEARNING MODELS FOR EDUCATING
WORKING ADULTS

To facilitate cognitive and affective student learning—knowledge, skills, and values—and to promote use of that knowledge in the student's work place. To develop competence in communication, critical thinking, collaboration, and information utilization, together with a commitment to lifelong learning for enhancement of students' opportunities for career success. To provide instruction that bridges the gap between theory and practice through faculty members who bring to their classroom not only advanced academic preparation, but also the skills that come from the current practice of their professions. To use technology to create effective modes and means of instruction that expand access to learning resources and that enhance collaboration and communication for improved student learning. To assess student learning and use assessment data to improve the teaching/learning system, curriculum, instruction, learning resources, counseling and student services. To be organized as a for-profit institution in order to foster a spirit of innovation that focuses on providing academic quality, service, excellence, and convenience to the working adult. To generate the financial resources necessary to support the University's mission. (University of Phoenix, 2003, p. 2)

How do the teaching/learning models of the nontraditional universities align with the mission? What does the University of Phoenix mean when it talks about its mission as educating working adults? Why "working" as opposed to just "adults"? Why "adults" and not just the general public?

In the following quotation, a faculty member responds to a question regarding the role of the University of Phoenix in retraining workers and contrasts this function with the retraining that often goes on internally within companies outside of America:

> I think the majority of students who come to this school, their tuitions are paid by their employers. In other countries, companies take it on themselves to educate the employees in their house. . . . Recycling our displaced workers. I think that's what the University of Phoenix is doing.

The same faculty member distinguished the mission of the University of Phoenix from DeVry University, which aims for traditional eighteen- to twenty-two-year-old students with its undergraduate program. He describes the primary audience for the University of Phoenix as corporations looking to train their workers:

> The University of Phoenix really does not have a direct competitor. DeVry is a competitor. However, DeVry caters to younger students. They are maybe one or two years out of high school. And they're running on government subsidies. The federal government and the state government have lots of educational programs that the under-privileged population can take great advantage of. Eighty percent of tuition is coming from the government as far as DeVry is concerned. Here, it's coming from the corporate.

Tuition reimbursement polices are common in large American organizations. The lucrative market for these dollars compels traditional higher education institutions to compete with training organizations, as well as with the accredited for-profits. In its catalog, the University of Phoenix describes the reason it focuses on professional programs: "Because the great majority of adults who return for higher education do so to further their careers, these are the programs most needed and, therefore, in the highest demand by the populations served by the University" (University of Phoenix, 2003, p. 1). As we see, the university justifies its emphasis on professional programs by pointing out that these are most desired by adult students returning to college. At the same time, these are the programs that are most useful to the corporations that are often footing the bill.

Throughout the interviews, administrators and faculty members articulate how the university's stated mission of educating working adults distinguishes their audience from that of traditional two- and four-year institutions. An administrator discusses this mission of serving businesses and emphasizes the voluntary nature of student participation described in free market competition terms:

> Lots of large corporations use us. And so we know that they're looking for a certain set of outcomes and we have to make sure those students can do it. If the student has to improve their writing, it is our job to make sure they are better writers when they're done with their writing class. Otherwise, that organization is not going to feel as though we delivered the quality of education they came to us to get.

Here we see the emphasis on employer-driven outcomes. A faculty member describes the specific audience for the University of Phoenix courses:

> I would say to the student if they want to pursue higher degrees, going beyond master's and going to do research—pure science and whatnot—go to Stanford, go to UCLA. Go to one of those traditional schools. If you are a practically minded person who would like to

advance your career and have a real-life education—a practical education that you can use right now while you're going to school—come here. None is better than this one.

An applied, work- and career-enhancing education is what the University of Phoenix aims to provide for its students. An administrator describes University of Phoenix's student population and how the applied educational programs are geared to them:

> You have to keep in mind who it is that we're appealing to. We're never going to be an institution focused on eighteen-year-olds. The average age of our students is the mid-thirties. So what I'm telling them is: "You're a midcareer professional. What you probably want is number one a kind of no-nonsense approach to this. You want to pay for what it is that you are going to use. You're probably going to want to pay for some convenience element to that. And you have to have some perceived value. What makes this education more valuable to you is you're going to have an up-to-date curriculum. It's going to be taught by people that not only understand the content, but understand how it works in the real world."

Customer service is a crucial aspect of the mission at for-profit institutions because it links to the student-centered purpose and is the orientation by which they efficiently manage the educational experience for discerning corporate clients.

PEDAGOGY

The provost of the University of Phoenix points to the concrete objectives they are trying to achieve in the classroom: "Do our students know what they should know? Can they do what they ought to be able to do? Have we helped them to develop values that are appropriate to their professions or disciplines? Are they achieving their life and career goals? Answering these questions requires placing a tremendous emphasis on assessment." Notice the focus on measurable outcomes and assessment, part of proving themselves to the corporate market of their return on investment (ROI). This is important because the University of Phoenix is very much aware that corporate decision makers think in these terms when making choices about funding training for their employees. The particular pedagogical goals identified by the University of Phoenix are very much in line with the needs of its primary audience—the working adult population and their employers: "They have the ability to take principles and concepts and turn around and apply them to real world problems, because they have just done it over and over and over through the program." A faculty member elaborates on the applied and integrated nature of the University of Phoenix's teaching methods:

> The advantage of the University of Phoenix is that all of the classes revolve around real world issues that have to do with work. All the homework is designed to be applicable to what they would be doing at work. So the reports you write are all in a business format. There are some classes that do the academic stuff, but mostly geared so that you can go to work the next day and apply what you learned the night before. You can't do that at a traditional school.

Learning and work are integrated through the use of student work experiences and are designed to be immediately usable in current employment. This strategy has a strong pedagogical advantage by giving the students a learning handle to more easily assimilate the course content, while at the same time benefiting the employer through increased productivity. We find here and throughout the study that the mission of serving working adults is directly connected to the pedagogical methods that are used at the university.

In specific terms, John Sperling indicates that the formation of learning communities is a key way that the mission is delivered:

> The only time people learn effectively and joyously is if they're part of a learning community, so we say that we're group-driven. Every student must be a member of a class and then a study group, as well as the class. Half of all the assignments are study group assignments. And we run it like the marines. Attendance is mandatory. Completing one's assignments is mandatory. If you don't, you're out. You can have one excused absence, the second, you're out no matter what it is. In our online programs you have to be involved five days out of every seven to be in attendance.

The use of learning teams and group projects throughout all of the courses (online as well as face-to-face) is one way that the learning communities are implemented. The student focus is identified as a reason that distance learning formats are successful at the University of Phoenix because the faculty and administrators are more proactive in making sure student needs are met, and there is a focus on creating learning communities.

The following administrator at the University of Phoenix indicates how the focused mission leads to pedagogical practices such as using work experience as a group to explicate course content within the classroom: "I want to be able to take what I'm learning in the classroom today and apply it on my job tomorrow. They can do that here." A faculty member emphasizes the importance of students who are actively working, and describes what happens if they lack such frame of reference: "It is pretty critical. I have had students who were temporarily laid off, staying at home with small children, one thing or another; and it is a little more difficult for them to engage in the discussions and to even do the papers." The applied nature of the curriculum is a direct result of appealing to this working adult population. It provides a learning approach for adults, often uncomfortable with higher education, to use personal knowledge to grasp unfamiliar course content, while at the same time giving corporations additional reason to support tuition reimbursement for this education because it may apply to their employees' current work:

> That was what the university was based on—that whole notion of bridging. Most of the theorists say that adults learn best when we're able to make a bridge between the new information they are getting and their past experience and make it relevant in real time to them. And so I think that's one of the things that our model does. It marries theory and practice in ways that some traditional pedagogy doesn't.

It is an established practice in adult education programs to try and utilize life and work experience in the curriculum. The following respondent talks about this need for the student population at the University of Phoenix and how it connects with their general psychological disposition toward higher education: "We have people here who are upper level management people. They just never went back and finished their degrees. And now they want to do that. You can't treat such a person as though they had no life experience." Terms such as "respect" and "self-esteem" are used continually throughout these interviews at for-profits when administrators and faculty members talk about the adult students. In the following quote, we see how a teaching approach using student experience is contrasted to the transmission of knowledge, seen as more appropriate for younger students: "I would never recommend it to an eighteen- to twenty-two-year-old. Number one, this is an accelerated program. Number two, it's expected that you have life experience at work. I think the eighteen- to twenty-two-year-old crowd needs the traditional environment." Another aspect of the learning model mentioned here that ties in with the mission of serving working adults is their use of intensive format courses, individual courses over a six-week period. One administrator speaks about how the learning model of the University of Phoenix utilizes immersion and is particularly useful in working with the targeted population of working adults: "I really feel it's learning by immersion, if the student tends to take advantage of how the classroom and the learning experiences are constructed. The fast pace, the immersion in the learning team, the various responsibilities and roles." Furthermore, this administrator talks about how the immersion coupled with learning teams work to raise self-esteem in the learner—here again, a common issue for University of Phoenix students, and adult learners generally, seeking to complete their degrees:

> They even are, I think, not put off at the difficulty of it. They look at it as a challenge and kind of hold hands if you will with their learning team and get through it together. So there's a great camaraderie that's built in a way that I know people describe boot camp. It's kind of that as well. You're on a ten-mile run and if your buddies can do it, you can do it, too.

One instructor speaks about how the selection of faculty members is very much dependent on how well they will work with adult learners: "They're very—what's the word? Picky." This same faculty member comments further on the customer attitudes of adult learners: "Adult learners are much more vocal than twenty-two year olds think they can be. They feel like their hands are tied. Whereas here, they know they're paying money and so by gum it's going to be right." In response to this customer attitude prevalent in adult learners, a faculty member speaks about the need for less hierarchy in the classroom at the University of Phoenix:

> I think with more and more adults coming back to school, they're going to have to recognize that these people are not the eighteen- to twenty-two-year-old crowd and they do need to be respected as knowing something. I had a friend who worked at NASA JFC in Houston for twenty years and went back to get here Ph.D. at UCI. They didn't give a damn whether she had ever set foot in anywhere professional. It was: "You're an idiot. You only have a master's degree. We're the big honchos with the Ph.Ds and you know nothing." And that bothered her a whole lot. I don't think adults are going to stand for that anymore.

An administrator points to how a student/customer focus leads to pedagogical initiatives designed to accommodate learning styles, and create customized learning materials. This is the latest pedagogical innovation

the University of Phoenix is currently trying to implement. The desire
to meet student needs is leading the University of Phoenix to concentrate on discovering how to better accommodate differing learning styles
in online courses.

A faculty member responds to the common charge against the University of Phoenix—that is, that its curriculum goes too far in the applied
direction: "There is a balance. You can't just have all application. Otherwise, it's a trade school." One can see that the University of Phoenix is
not just focused on skill acquisition and, at least in relationship to information technology training, sees the greatest need in broader management
and communication training:

> A: The reason they [IT students] picked computers was they didn't
> like relating to people. And as they move in their career, they've got
> to relate to people at some point. And so I'm working with the
> Northwest Center—I don't know if you're familiar with them—up
> in Seattle. They're based out of Bellevue Community College. And
> they're trying to work out standards. And one of the things we're
> going to help them with is other kinds of standards for IT people,
> besides the technical standards that the certifications give you. These
> other ones, the communication, the analysis, the problem-solving
> standards. The person needs this other half of the picture to really
> be successful long-time.
>
> Q: It's very interesting because clearly you're saying that skills aren't
> enough. You're actually promoting a very traditional, academic point
> of view.
>
> A: I know. Except it's not a liberal arts one [laughter]. But it's the
> same philosophy. It is the same philosophy. But what we are trying
> to define are those things in the business world that are equivalent
> to liberal arts. You know? And there's very similar parallelism there.

This administrator talks about the notion of seeking to provide the equivalent of a liberal arts degree for the business world—a well-rounded, applied education. However, unlike a liberal arts education that seeks to
round the student with an understanding of religion, ethics, philosophy,
history, and other broader cultural knowledge, the University of Phoenix
attempts to concentrate on educating students in a way that leads to
workplace success. Of course, this is much more measurable than the less
concrete whole person development that the liberal arts degree pursues,
and measurement is important to corporations funding training. Nevertheless, it is interesting to note that in these previous quotations, the
concentration at the University of Phoenix on writing and communica-

tion skills, although with different objectives in mind, is similar to those often espoused by liberal arts institutions.

I learned from those interviewed that the mission of educating working adults is directly connected to the learning theory employed in the classroom, relying heavily on life and work experience. Furthermore, the particular psychological characteristics of adult learners with customer attitudes, self-esteem issues, and career needs are accommodated both in the student services and the pedagogical approach that utilizes learning teams, immersion, and bridging techniques. Additionally, the concentration on working adults serves the function of retraining displaced workers in new careers, and as a benefit to employees of corporations seeking to upgrade their skills and increase productivity. So I see evidenced in the mission of serving working adults both the identification of a specific and lucrative market, and a pedagogical approach tailored to meet the needs of this nontraditional student population.

COMPLIANCE

Given the difficult and often confrontational history of the for-profits and regional accrediting agencies, it is not surprising that compliance has become one of the main goals of these institutions. How does compliance as a goal mesh with the other organizational directions? What influence has compliance had in shaping mission?

An administrator at the University of Phoenix talks about how compliance is a stated goal for the institution:

> Quality, customer service, and compliance. Those are it. And everybody can articulate those. . . . The compliance really is viewing ourselves in the outside world, in the context of the rest of the world. Because of our culture, we can kind of get a little bit introspective. But the compliance is actually good for us, because it keeps dragging us back out into traditional academia.

Notice how compliance serves to test the organizational mission with external standards described as the "outside world."

When asked how much policy and procedures at the University of Phoenix have been driven by accreditation demands, the president spoke about the influence compliance demands have had over time:

> As an institution, we have passed the need to have quite an antagonistic a relationship, but clearly that has colored who we are. I think our accreditors grew along with us. Uncomfortable as it was, we

forced them to look at some of those things and say: "Okay. Is there really a demonstrated relationship between this requirement and what they are hoping to do?" And what we've said is: "Our focus is on learning. That's what we're about. We are a teaching/learning institution. So measure us in terms of whether we are teaching and the students are learning." We didn't veer from this—we really kind of forced this issue all along.

Observe in the quote how the president feels that the University of Phoenix with its unique mission is forcing the accrediting agency to change. However, the compliance concern has been also limited the organization. The president indicates that accrediting agencies are forced to change as a result of the University of Phoenix's mission pushing the limits of guidelines.

The recent entrance of other visible, nontraditional institutions has in some ways lessened the pressure on the University of Phoenix to conform: "I have to thank the Western Governors for a large part of this because they really forced the issue of the interregional guidelines." Another administrator speaks more generally how corporate and other for-profit institutions are now pushing the regulatory world making it easier for the University of Phoenix. Notice how the debate is framed in questions about training versus education and seat time: "I don't care if you call it training or education. The learning that takes place should have some outcomes attached to it. That's what I think all of these corporate training and technology training institutions are allowing us to do, is really focus on the learning outcomes and then determine where a learning outcome has applicability." The provost at the University of Phoenix also speaks about the demands of accreditation and regulation. Notice the particular debate the provost enters into regarding contact hours per day, and intensive format courses. One can observe that clearly not only is compliance part of the mission of the institution, but also that pushing the limits of regulation is a regular activity:

> These are adults who work in teams in the workplace and know how to get things done. We're still responsible for accomplishing the learning objectives. But what if I, as their instructor, concentrate on helping them master certain of those objectives and they, individually and in teams, concentrate on expanding their knowledge of those objectives and on mastering the others? If we measure the outcomes and the outcomes are equivalent to what they are in traditional academic settings, does it matter how they got it or does it matter more that they got it?

Compliance as an aspect of mission is a basic need for any educational institution. However, the especially hard battles the University of Phoenix and other for-profits have fought over the years with accrediting agencies have led to a particularly broad investment and focus on accreditation. We see here from those interviewed that this concentration has somewhat limited and altered the organizational mission. At the same time, many would argue that it has led to a baseline level of traditional notions of quality at the for-profits. Most important, both administrators and faculty indicate that the for-profits' nontraditional mission is serving to alter accrediting agencies and the domain as a whole.

ANALYSIS

For those unfamiliar with the University of Phoenix and the other for-profits, there are some surprising aspects to their missions, especially the sociopolitical grounding. In conclusion, there are two primary lines of analysis that emerge from this examination of the mission of the for-profits: one descriptive, the other proscriptive. Simply describing in detail the mission and goals for the for-profits is interesting in itself, because of their uniqueness and the general disinformation about them. However, the manner in which the institutions constantly test, reaffirm, and clarify their missions, as well as the way mission informs their curricula, are clear organizational advantages. Other higher education organizations might learn from these successful practices.

When describing its mission, the University of Phoenix stresses the primacy of serving working adults. What does that mean exactly? How is this mission different from, or similar to, traditional higher education mission statements? What are the organizational ramifications of such a mission? The following are the key descriptive elements of the mission of the University of Phoenix:

- Provide access to the underserved: its sociopolitical purpose.
- Serve corporate clients.
- Meet identified need.
- Set clear limits.
- Align with learning objectives.

Provides Access to the Underserved: Its Sociopolitical Purpose

The histories of the organization and the activities of founder John Sperling clearly reveal that a social purpose at least partially informs the

University of Phoenix's mission. Throughout the interviews, respondents spoke about the nobility of the University of Phoenix's mission and how it makes their work meaningful. Other for-profits, as well as the non-traditional institutions, articulate this value in the mission.

Serve Corporate Clients

Alongside the sociopolitical mission is what for some might seem counterintuitive: a commitment to serving the needs of corporate clients. Aiming to both upgrade current employees and retrain displaced workers, this focus on increasing productivity for businesses while at the same time providing access to first-generation college students is what makes the University of Phoenix unique. The other for-profits also focus to some degree on the corporate market.

Meet Identified Need

The mission seems to be effective partly because it has matched two needs—social and corporate. The social need to educate a population of first-generation college students not adequately served by traditional higher education institutions is matched with government and corporate funding sources. In this way social objectives to provide access to higher education are served while at the same time meeting corporate objectives to develop a skilled workforce.

Set Clear Limits

The mission is particularly effective in the way that it is designed to delineate the organization's core business. The respondents speak often about what their mission does *not* cover and regularly set and reset limits to the directions they pursue. Additionally, one advantage of the mission's limits is that it steers the for-profits and nontraditional universities clear of direct competition with better-positioned traditional institutions.

Align with Learning Objectives

Generally, the alignment of learning objectives with the mission is apparent. The concentration on working adults dictates in a very direct way the focus on communication skills, working in teams, and critical thinking—all needed in corporate environments. Pedagogical goals are plainly described as both oral and writing communication skills, critical thinking skills, and the ability to work in a team. Additionally, respondents discuss specific requirements of disciplines. Reliance on the student's work experience is repeatedly mentioned as a way of making learning concrete and utilizing personal experience in the curriculum. The pedagogical goals are also generally connected to specific teaching approaches such as required presentations and work in teams.

CONCLUSION

The key characteristic of mission at the University of Phoenix, and to some extent the other for-profits, is what one might call "organizational existentialism." Peter Drucker's admonition to organizations to ask their reason for existing seems to be employed in a dramatically successful way at the University of Phoenix. In the interviews with administrators and faculty it is not immediately apparent where the pervasive dynamism of the organization came from, or how this creative energy was sustained. However, in analyzing the qualitative data it is increasingly evident that the internal dialogue, debate, flat organizational structure, and decision-making process are all connected in some way to this continual testing of the organizational mission. At first, the tendency of the respondents to philosophize about their business seems to be simply a willingness to enter into discussions about nontraditional education. Upon further examination, it is clearly more than that. A plain strength of the organization that other higher educations might emulate is a conscious attempt to test, validate, and alter continually their mission. The result of this practice is organizational clarity, purpose, and uniqueness. While it has become commonplace the past decade or more for organizations to focus on mission, often expending significant resources toward this end, what I've learned from the University of Phoenix and other institutions studied is that this mission focus is a vital practice that needs constant, deep testing and communicating.

In the next chapter I turn to look at the culture of for-profit and non-traditional institutions in order to better understand the important ways in which they differ from traditional institutions.

CLIPPINGS

Blink and you could miss America's largest university. Its low-key roadside campuses are the antithesis of Oxbridge's dreaming spires. But then so too is the concept of the University of Phoenix. There are no Nobel laureates on its faculty, nor does it pioneer cutting-edge research. Its students are hardly the cream of the crop—drawn largely from the ranks of working adults who missed out on university the first time round. In fact, they are not even called students. Instead they are known as "customers," to whom Phoenix offers a stripped-back syllabus of vocational degrees and diplomas to enhance their employment prospects. It is also the only peer-review board-accredited university listed on the stock market, where its profits are the envy of corporate America. Many US academics turn their noses up at Phoenix, deriding it as a "McUniversity." But it could just be the single most significant mass-education phenomenon of recent times, and the success story is not lost on a growing number of traditional universities mulling how to cash in on their intellectual and cultural capital. Founded in 1976, some 150,000 students now throng to Phoenix's bricks-and-mortar and virtual classrooms. By comparison, the US's largest public campus, the University of Texas at Austin, has about 50,000 students. John Sperling, Phoenix's founder and, at 81, still its chairman, nurses a sense of vindication. "People now realize that the University of Phoenix model is that of the future of most of higher education and that they had better copy it or become toast." (Phillips, 2002, p. 18)

According to student registration surveys, the average student is in his or her mid-thirties (34 for undergraduate, 36 for graduates) and has been employed full-time for 13.4 years. The student population closely parallels the shifting U.S. workforce and population indicators for gender and ethnicity. Gender of entering students is 54 percent female to 46 percent male. Approximately 40 percent of entering students report being members of an ethnic minority. (University of Phoenix, 2003, p. 2)

CHAPTER 5

Junkyard Dogs: The Culture and Rhetoric of For-Profits

It was a culture war, very simply.

—John Sperling

To better understand how and why things are done at the University of Phoenix and other leading for-profit institutions it is useful to look at the specific cultural attributes of these institutions that often distinguish them from traditional higher education. Organizational culture might be described as the collective beliefs and practices of the members of a working community. While the University of Phoenix's culture is primarily profiled in this chapter and undoubtedly represents a somewhat special case, many of its characteristics reflect the for-profit environment generally. University of Phoenix interviewees often describe each other—with admiration—as "junkyard dogs," a phrase that aptly represents the relentless activity, determination, and lack of pretense in the for-profit university culture.

The University of Phoenix is culturally an interesting combination of the counterculture of the 1960s and corporate America. This is probably surprising to many, who might assume that for-profit institutions are uniformly corporate in character. While liberalism is not unusual in traditional faculties, their institutions generally do not combine this way of thinking with a corporate culture. The culture at the for-profits fuses corporate with a range of counterculture attitudes: combativeness, a belief in their mission, openness and encouragement of collegial debate and discussion, an appreciation of creativity and new ideas, a higher energy work ethic, informality, and the accommodation of family life outside of work.

COUNTERTRADITION IDENTITY

As a graduate of UC Berkeley in the 1970s and something of a counterculture product myself, I recognize the feel of that era in the culture of the University of Phoenix. In fact, John Sperling was a graduate of Berkeley (prior to the free speech movement), and the University of Phoenix's leadership is of the age to have been greatly influenced by the various sixties social movements. This backdrop of the people against the establishment, combined with the personal disposition of its founder, John Sperling, makes up one clear aspect of the University of Phoenix's cultural identity.

Sperling describes his love of controversy and struggling: "I have a, what would you call it—a perverse delight in controversy. I feel most alive when I'm in a fight." Nevertheless, he argues that the fear of the University of Phoenix many traditional academics express is unfounded: "We create new markets that they haven't touched. So if you looked at a graph of our enrollment versus the enrollment in traditional education, the overlap is about 15 percent at most." One can't help but feel that Sperling derives a little pleasure from the established universities' reaction to the threat he has created. This enjoyment of playing the rebel runs throughout the organization: "We kind of like being dubbed the Anti-Christ of Higher Ed. In a sense, we are the ones forcing everybody to reanalyze what they do. Because it makes us stronger. We kind of lock arms and walk down the street together." This image of marching together in protest clearly refers to the 1960s free speech and Vietnam War protest movements. In fact, one fear respondents repeatedly express is that as the organization grows and becomes increasingly mainstream, the University of Phoenix may lose this outsider identity: "We have gone from being way over in the fringe element to being pretty close to mainstream. And my fear is that we will be mainstream and we will lose our whole reason for being." As with many baby boomers, they seem to ask, "When you grow up and become part of the establishment, do you lose your political soul?" The fear of coming closer to traditional universities works to motivate the University of Phoenix toward more innovation in order to keep the non-traditional identity: "I think it's driving us to take that next step."

Although the university has been in existence now in some form for quite a few years, there is still a feeling of almost "playing" at being a university. In the following story, we see evidenced the way that longtime members of the University of Phoenix community think it is humorous to have the trappings of traditional universities:

> In 1996, when we had our last North-Central comprehensive visit, it was in the middle of the ballot initiative [for decriminalization of marijuana] here in Arizona. And he [Sperling] had given quite a bit of money in favor of that and there were protesters out in front of the university just when the team came. And we all laughed and said: "This is great! We're just like a real university [laughter]. We've made it!"

A faculty member speaks about how the nontraditional nature of the university is driven home by unusual sponsored gatherings and events: "The first faculty meeting people attend as new faculty is a harbor cruise, but it prepares them for the fact that this isn't gonna be what you thought when you thought I am gonna teach at the university level; this is different."

Part of the counterculture feel of the organization comes from a strong and consistent value system. The leadership of the University of Phoenix express great self-confidence and widespread belief in the mission. In the previous chapter, how the mission is formulated and constantly tested were displayed. In addition, the culture supports a strong belief in the mission's rightness. Of course, this conviction stems from the founder's point of view, which he identifies as religious and cultural: "I was raised in a Calvinist household, and Calvinists believe they can determine the difference between sin and virtue. They don't have any doubts. And although I'm no longer a Calvinist, that habit of mind has carried over. So once I decide to do something I never have any doubts." Another administrator speaks about the link between personal beliefs and organizational mission: "I don't think I would of have stayed with the institution if my personal beliefs and values didn't align with theirs." Longtime and devoted employees of the University of Phoenix perpetuate these counterculture roots of the organization. This counterculture disposition for the organization separates the University of Phoenix from DeVry University and Argosy University to some extent. While some of the leadership is of the age to have been influence by the sixties movements, the organizations themselves are older than the University of Phoenix. What is interesting to note here is that the University of Phoenix is both more counterculture and at the same time more directly tied to corporate America than are the other for-profits. One would think that this would be an uneasy alliance, but other aspects of the University of Phoenix's culture are similarly closely linked with corporate values. The nontraditional institutions, Fielding Graduate Institute and Heritage College, have a similar counterculture origin and feel to them—especial Fielding.

OPENNESS TO DEBATE

Perhaps the most important aspect of the University of Phoenix's institutional culture, because of its impact on innovation and organizational structure, is its openness to intellectual debate. One administrator describes how open discussion is consistently encouraged: "What is valued is that John [Sperling] is totally willing to take the most off-the-wall suggestion and entertain it." This quality exhibits itself in various ways, but especially in commitment to open communication regardless of position. This doesn't mean that the University of Phoenix manages by consensus, but there clearly exists the opportunity to be heard and listened to. Administrators continually speak about how they value the contribution of their colleagues: "We have highly qualified people in the organization who have wonderful ideas. And if we don't capitalize on that we're missing out on a great resource."

One way to gain additional understanding of an organization's culture is to look at the language that is commonly used, and repeated. Often these key phrases and terms reveal shared values and approaches to the work they do. While one wouldn't want to make too much of an informal analysis such as this, it does help to give us a feel for the organization. Often the importance of communication throughout the University of Phoenix is emphasized with positive phrases such as: "get message out," "talking more about this," "great comment," "establishing expectations," "socialize the concept," "affecting positive change," "good suggestion," and "you make it successful." These phrases reveal an understanding of the importance of communication in implementing changes, of socializing change. A group of phrases are often used to characterize and deal with real or potential problems including: "going to be pushback," "don't want to dictate from corporate perspective," "are we going to be able to do this?" "we don't want to go there," and "not written in stone." These phrases indicate both an expectation of dissension and a willingness to compromise and hear feedback throughout the organization.

Terms and phrases generally used in corporate settings were heard throughout the interviews, the observations, and my faculty training experience. The common use of such terminology would undoubtedly surprise or even shock many traditional academics. New academic programs are described like new product roll-outs with corporate phrases like "beta" and "alpha" used to label various versions of the educational merchandise. The customer service emphasis is evident with the repeated use of phrases like "manage to student perceptions," "manage to them," "ask what the student wants," and "value students." The admonition to "manage" is heard over and over again. Phrases such as "relationship management," "manage business in standardized way," "management skills," "managing grievance," and "managing within process" are heard continually. In addition to reflecting the organization's corporate model, they tended to communicate an approach that differs distinctly from traditional higher education where "building consensus" and "shared governance" are ideals. Again, to manage well is a University of Phoenix ideal and goal. However, notice that terms such as "order," "direct," or even "lead" are not detected as prevalently. Managing well at the University of Phoenix involves good communication and an openness to discussion.

The following quotation shows that the open discussion of ideas works to involve personnel in their work and helps build the enthusiasm and dynamism exhibited in their culture: "There is a collaborative environment here that enthuses people and locks them in to the institution. For example, we have a deans' meeting every Monday, and we actually talk about theories of learning and education—every week." The staff members at the university are accustomed to discussing and thinking about innovation in higher education, from administrative practices to learning theory. From an interview with one of the leaders, it is clear that the organization continually anticipates the next step, the next innovation. What is the next step? "Let's take on the publishing world next." The administrator points out that although academic institutions rely heavily on the publishing industry, they don't have a lot of say in how books are designed. Upon further reflection, the University of Phoenix realized that it was large enough and had the leverage tell the publishing industry what it wanted. Once understanding this, administrators said to themselves, "Okay, let's revisualize what it is that a textbook is about. Let's ask that question." So they started to disaggregate the book and really ask, "What's of value in here? The cases? I don't want them in the book. I want them on the Web. Because I can update them and I can get newer cases. The questions would be better to offer interactively by the Web." In their discussions they ask basic questions such as, "Is reading important? Is there a place for multimedia?" They examine the course and book content and ask, "Where does it add value and what is its purpose philosophically?" in deciding how to construct these new custom textbooks.

One visible attribute of the University of Phoenix's culture is its almost obsessive preoccupation with new ideas and innovation. Those I interviewed express a feeling of freedom and lack of limits: "Pick your goal. Because this institution will not limit you." On a personal level, a number of the interview subjects comment very simply on wanting to do interesting work. "I think my calling is really to do interesting work wherever I happen to find it." "Interesting work" is linked to new ideas and projects, and innovation. A faculty member describes the atmosphere of innovation where individuals with the will have the freedom to try something new, and to fail. "They innovate. They are not afraid to try new things." Willingness and ability to change direction and try something new is indicated often in the interviews as part of their culture: "They are so flexible and so willing to turn on a dime that I don't really know what is going to happen in higher education in the next few years, but I am positive University of Phoenix is going to be at the forefront of whatever it is." In Chapter 4, it was revealed that the willingness to discuss and test common goals was a central characteristic of the University of Phoenix culture:

> I think it's very clear in our minds who we are, what we are, and what are the philosophies driving us. I've never been at an educational institution so aware of educational philosophies, like learning theories and what the profile of the adult learner is and outcomes, objectives, the difference between an outcome and an objective in an assessment. Those discussions are continual.

Even basic beliefs of the organization, such as who they serve, are open to debate and discussion. This is clearly a culture that encourages challenging norms. In fact, one administrator points to the willingness to discuss educational philosophy as the "research" of the University of Phoenix: "Learning is what our research is all about here."

A clear aspect of the culture of the University of Phoenix—consistent with its counterculture attitude—is its combative nature. One administrator speaks about how frequently scrutinized the institution is and as a result how guarded they have become. This examination has hardened the institution to outside criticism:

> We've got to be the most highly analyzed institution out there. We've had more accreditation reviews from NCA and programmatic accreditation reviews. And every time we go into a new state they do a review. It never ceases to amaze me how many of these reviewers come in and think they're going to cut through that Potemkin village they perceive as here—that there is some smoking gun they're going to uncover. I can't imagine any rock that has been unturned

in this place. There just isn't anything that's a secret anymore. There have just been too many people here looking for it.

Administrators repeatedly talk about the way that outside attacks have had the effect of drawing the group closer:

> I think that we still have detractors out there—lots of them. But for the most part, the people that are the most vocal about being detractors are doing so out of what John Sperling calls "willful ignorance." It's because they are not willing to come and look at what we do. They just kind of look at the veneer of the fact that these are corporate office buildings, that we don't have a football team, that our library is all virtual as opposed to big dusty books on shelves. And they assume all those things mean there is no quality here—that we are a giant ATM machine sticking in Visa cards and out pop diplomas. That really isn't what we're all about.

Given the intensive and long scrutiny it is not surprising that the administrators at the University of Phoenix are thin-skinned. One administrator describes the culture as "hypersensitive" because of years of criticism from traditional institutions that leads to a focus on assessment to prove the successfulness of what they do: "I think we're hypersensitive, and I think it's blocking us a little bit of being able to cooperate as much as we could and share as much as we have at this point with people, because we were always on the defense." The University of Phoenix has a culture that values debate internally within the organization and externally with outside agencies and critics.

LOYALTY

It is not hard to see how a belief in the mission of the organization and constant attack from outside would lead to a great sense of dedication toward the organization. Through the interviews I conducted, administrators and faculty members of the University of Phoenix expressed a strong sense of commitment toward their organization. Starting from the top with John Sperling, this sense of loyalty is valued throughout the organization: "I think loyalty is very important, but you only get it by giving it. . . . We always, whenever possible, promote from within. Every company is devoted to growth, because only through growth can you create new opportunities for people in the company." The University of Phoenix has a relentless, seemingly endless fascination with growth. At times administrators explain this as the nature of a business, but Sperling connects it with loyalty to staff through opportunity to grow and make changes on an individual basis. This principle of involvement/investment in an organization because of structured opportunity is distinctly different from traditional higher education that is reluctant to change and minimizes individual effort to some degree. Loyalty, integrity, and ethics are linked directly to improved individual performance. Loyalty to John Sperling himself is part of the equation at the University of Phoenix. Many of the top administrators who have been longtime employees indicate loyalty to Sperling and their desire to get his approval: "You know your work is excellent if he buys into it. And for some of us—probably for a lot of us—that's really important."

At DeVry, administrators also speak about having many long-term employees. While they tend to have higher turnover in admissions, or sales staff, they have a very stable group of adjunct faculty. Administrators talk about recruiting employees who are motivated by the education mission, and then are rewarded and recognized for their productivity. Loyalty was also very evident at the nontraditional institutions, Fielding Graduate Institute and Heritage College, undoubtedly partly a result of clear and inspiring institutional missions and values.

A common thread in the interviews at the University of Phoenix was found in comments on teamwork, the lack of infighting by employees, and the general collegial atmosphere. One administrator made the distinction between a hierarchical organization and a decision-making structure:

> I think it's a very traditional hierarchical organizational structure. But the decision making isn't extremely hierarchical. So I think the traditional structure is important. Again, I'm going back to the issue of discipline and structure. Discipline and structure are important for organizations. And if you have the discipline and structure—which we have very much, because of our for-profit status and needing to pay attention to the academic side and not mingle the business side with our academic decisions and so forth—that's why I think the structure is incredibly important. But within that, because we're not a real hierarchical organization in terms of our culture.

A clear organizational hierarchy exists, but decisions are made using input and communication from all levels. I will look more at the organizational structure and decision-making process in the next two chapters, but here at the level of culture there is an openness that tends to involve and invest employees in the organization. Openness of communication and access to organizational leadership are central qualities of the collegial atmosphere found at the University of Phoenix.

Of course, this doesn't mean there aren't disagreements and internal power struggles. Infighting among organizational units also occurs at the University of Phoenix, as shown in the following quotation; the online and satellite campus groups appear involved in a struggle over the new FlexNet program: "We've got kind of a little bit of this the online campus versus the ground campus, a little bit of tension there. We need to work through that." In interviews and observations it was also clear that there is some tension over the implementation of the digital textbooks as well.

INFORMAL AND HARDWORKING

The interesting combination of counter and corporate cultures in the University of Phoenix can be seen on one hand in its apparent informality, and on the other in its relentless drive and work ethic. In scanning the new business environment, particularly in high-tech companies, it is not unusual now to see businesses where employees dress in jeans and polo shirts while making million-dollar deals and competing for dominance in their industry. For higher education, certainly informality in dress is far from unusual, but there is a strong hierarchy and formality in processes. The culture at the University of Phoenix expressed by those I interviewed is very critical of traditional academic pretensions and often contentious positions taken especially by faculty with vested interests. "There's a lot of humor and not very much pompousness. They don't allow you to be very pompous in this place." Another administrator speaks about the anti-intellectual or antiacademic atmosphere with little tolerance for traditional academic pretensions: "They're going to have to leave their degree at the door, and they're going to be judged on their thought and their concepts and their ideas. And everybody's ideas count at the table here. It could come from anybody. It can come from John or from a brand new person. So there's that openness." Informality links directly to innovation and creating a safe atmosphere for risk-taking. Of course, having a leadership team at the University of Phoenix with longevity helps breed a sense of teamwork and fun: "People are very professional, and yet there's a lot of fun. In this organization, because there are a great many people with longevity here, there's a sense of knowing each other and a great sense of camaraderie." One administrator describes a positive and negative aspect of informality: "We're a very large institution for its informality. I just walk to other people's offices, and I go around and get everybody else excited and everybody starts talking about it. That works great. . . . But on the flip side, we're an awful big organization to run it that way [laughs], just kind of informally." Here again is revealed the somewhat counterculture attitude of the kids running the shop.

However, some commented that organizational formality has increased as a result of becoming a publicly traded organization. Moving from an entrepreneurship to a professionally managed organization forced them to create models or structure, and more regulation. While they try to keep the bureaucracy as minimal as possible, there does have to be more formality as they get bigger and more distributed.

Underlying this informality is a belief in the goodness and importance of hard work. Once again, this organizational characteristic seems to start from the top as expressed by Sperling: "I like to go back to the biblical phrase: 'By their works shall ye know them.'" This reference reveals an essential aspect of the hard-driving culture of the University of Phoenix where working, creating, and getting things done is valued. One question asked in the interviews was who is admired and what characteristics they admire in their organization. One administrator comments on the admirable work ethic of a colleague and the hard work of the front office/student services staff:

> I'll tell you what. She sets a work ethic pace that the rest of us are well aware of. So that's a great thing. But truly the qualities I admire are the people that are on the front line talking to students every day. . . . I admire the people that are at the front lines that don't probably have thirteen years experience at the university and maybe haven't seen as broadly as I have the impact that the university has made in people's lives, and yet they come to work every day and they do fabulous work every day. They are the good work of the university, in my opinion.

One interview subject claims that the profile of people attracted to working at the University of Phoenix includes people who tend to be hardworking: "They're work-a-holics. They like to get things done. They're doers. That kind of classification. And they like it to have a beneficial aspect to society. And they don't mind making money." Notice here the observed characteristics of both wanting to serve a social purpose and make money: a key characteristic of the University of Phoenix.

While demanding jobs aren't always seen in a positive light, those I interviewed tended to speak appreciatively of challenging work: "I stayed here because you're really challenged and stretched—and it's very unusual." Problem-solving demands are seen as satisfying aspects of their work: "That we are encouraged to solve problems, to be innovative. Not always to make money, although sometimes that's implied. To be innovative. To be held accountable for our results. And really to do very interesting things." For many ambitious, go-getting overachievers, the University of Phoenix is a good fit:

> This is the first institution that has been ahead of me. Normally I've had ideas that I would have liked to have done, and I was frustrated. Here, John's going, "You're not done yet? You didn't start that yet? We're not going to roll with e-books in every course in September?" "No, John. It takes time." . . . I haven't been in the situation of having the resources to then make it happen. And as fast as I can go.

A crucial aspect of the atmosphere of innovation is the access to resources allowing innovation. Nevertheless, other organizations may have similar resources but may be unwilling or unable to direct them so quickly at innovators.

For any visitor to the central offices of the University of Phoenix in Arizona, the one first clear impression emerges: This is an aggressive, driven organization. A faculty member comments on the culture and atmosphere of the university: "You can feel this drive. This school wants to get somewhere. Everyone wants to get somewhere—they want push. Other schools where I teach, I don't feel the same thing." On the surface this description might seem to apply to any large corporation with performance expectations and staff scrambling to compete internally and externally. However, the felt impression of the atmosphere is distinctively positive, exciting, and upbeat. Not only is the personality of the organization exciting and upbeat, but so are the personnel who are attracted to work at the University of Phoenix. John Sperling characterized his own qualities that have led to success as "high energy, focus, and doggedness." A top-level administrator claims, "You will never find a greater amalgamation of Type A personalities anywhere in the United States than in the University of Phoenix." Another administrator focuses on the growth push of the institution as part of the reason for the impression of such dynamic organization: "It's in a growth, constant motion mode. Which I like."

In one instance, an administrator speaks about how the hard-driving culture of the organization leads to problems with bringing in new people to hold positions of responsibility:

> One of the things we found is that this is a tough place for someone to come into a high level position—a campus director position or higher—without having previous University of Phoenix experience. Because we're so different. People who come out of a traditional academic environment often have a difficult time here coming in.

Things move very fast. We make decisions quickly. There is a lot of collegiality, but we move and there is an expectation that we move. There is a level of passion here that I have never found anywhere else. And it makes for an interesting place to try and break into in a way. You have to be a University of Phoenix–type person I have found because there is a certain passion for it.

Obviously, the speed of decision making and action alone separates the University of Phoenix from traditional universities accustomed to a laborious process of building consensus and thoroughly vetting initiatives before moving forward. Additionally, there is a level of accountability for the administration that appears to be stronger at the University of Phoenix than at traditional institutions. A respondent talks about the demanding atmosphere of the university culture requiring aggressive behavior and attaining specific and measurable goals: "In this organization, you'll get stepped on. Things keep moving forward. If you can't keep your campus moving forward, you can't keep meeting the goals, you're going to get trounced on. So you've got to be ambitious. You've got to be creative. You've got to be entrepreneurial."

As businesses, the other for-profits tend to also emphasize hard work, a quicker pace, and visible accomplishments. At DeVry, the university's entrepreneurial beginnings were crucial to its current culture. It strongly focuses on the customer, serving the customer, and making sure the needs of the students are met. Additionally, DeVry tries to treat its adjunct faculty respectfully and shows them that they are valued for the contribution they make. Like the University of Phoenix, there is a strong work ethic at DeVry. Administrators at DeVry speak about looking to hire personnel who are dedicated, motivated, and work very hard.

TIME FOR FAMILY

Although the University of Phoenix and the other for-profit institutions are clearly demanding, hard-driving cultures, they also appear to understand and appreciate the responsibilities of their personnel's family lives. Administrators and faculty members I interviewed repeatedly commented on how the University of Phoenix is very supportive and flexible toward employees' family ties, and appreciates the need to allow time for family regardless of workload. The challenge of seat time in the classroom also seems to extend itself to a liberal understanding of the need for flexible work schedules, focusing on measurable work outcomes rather than time at a desk: "The university looks at my results and I am held accountable to how well I perform. . . . I move my schedule and flex it as I need to. The university is very good about providing that kind of balance." The focus on bottom-line performance issues allows the university to accommodate flexible schedules undoubtedly feeling that there is a built-in check against abuse. As an organization that pioneered Internet-based learning, it is not surprising to find that telecommuting through the extensive use of e-mail is commonplace:

> This organization very much allowed me to balance and still feel good about being a new mom, trying to establish that. And now I think because of technology that has allowed us to evolve even more. I can work days at home if I've got e-mail connections. We teleconference. Half of our day is talking to people at a distance. Meetings very seldom occur face-to-face anymore.

However, one interview subject commented on how sometimes conflicting attitudes about the work and family balance come into play. While the top leadership has family commitments and is therefore sympathetic toward trying to strike a balance between family and work, there is also a culture of obsessive attitudes toward work led by the founder, John Sperling. Administrators speak about expectations of overachievement and constant availability, while also recognizing the importance of family: "So I would say you get mixed messages sometimes. Achieve, achieve, achieve! But try to balance your life." As with many professional people in various industries today, the push at the University of Phoenix seems to be to do it all. Is this a blurring, or integration, of family life and work? Administrators talk about a basic value or "social ethic" or understanding about the importance of family. This leads to a lack of attention to specific hours worked, and a general expectation that all work will get done on time, and done well. Undoubtedly, in such a large organization there are various degrees of integration/disintegration of family life with work. However, the willingness of the University of Phoenix to accommodate family responsibilities when combined with the personal investment in the organization would seem to help support a positive integration of the two worlds.

CONCLUSION

In this chapter the culture of the University of Phoenix and the other for-profits is revealed as an interesting mix of corporate and informal or counterculture characteristics. The University of Phoenix, as well as the

nontraditional institutions, have roots in the 1960s free speech and anti–
Vietnam war cultures, which inform their tendencies toward a belief in
the rightness of their mission, their combativeness with traditional higher
education, openness to debate about higher education practices, and an
appreciation of creativity and innovation. As businesses, they are also
hard-driving and demanding organizations. Nevertheless, these organizations tend to create an atmosphere of loyalty and collegiality, promote
from within, and make accommodations for family life outside of work.
Especially at the University of Phoenix, I found an unusual mix of business and countercultures.

In the next chapter, I look at specific attributes of for-profit organizational structures. I examine many of the characteristics in their culture
that inform how they are structured, how they operate on a day-to-day
basis, and how decisions are made.

CLIPPINGS

Teaching the World a Lesson

SOCIALISM aspired to put what were once the privileges of the few
into the hands of the many. As a historic movement, it may have
foundered; but for one left-winger whose political instincts were
formed in the radical trade unions of the 1940s, its vision has inspired
a capitalist triumph. John Sperling, former sailor, academic and union
organizer, is ironically enough one of America's richest men. (Olsen,
2002, p. 29)

Sperling is constantly dreaming up new ideas. The notion of clon-
ing, for instance, came to him at his weekend home in San Francisco
one morning five years ago when he and Hawthorne were having
breakfast. They were in the middle of a discussion about Dolly the
sheep, which had just been cloned by scientists in Edinburgh, Scot-
land, when Sperling looked around the room, saw Missy lying hap-
pily on the floor, and joked, "Hey, we should clone Missy." . . . Since
1996, Sperling has poured $77 million into these four projects.

Anti-aging	$44 million
Drug law reform	$13 million
Pet cloning	$10 million
Saltwater agriculture	$10 million

(Warner, 2002, p. 98)

In 1976, the leading edge of the Baby Boom generation was just turn-ing 30. That same year saw the introduction of the first personal computer, the Apple I—an event that signaled the birth of a new economic system in which intellectual capital would eventually sup-plant industrial might as the dominant economic force. These mile-stones marked the beginning of a sea change in higher education, though many (perhaps even most) within that system did not rec-ognize it at the time. Considered together, these phenomena sug-gested that the jobs that would make up the workforce of the future were only just beginning to be created or imagined. In order to fill those jobs, the bulk of the new workforce would require higher-level knowledge and skills than those needed in a manufacturing economy. At the same time, the largest-ever age cohort of the population, working adults, would be going through the stages of life during which they would be most affected by the coming economic dislo-cation and would need advanced education to adapt to these changes. It was in this historical context in 1976, that Dr. John Sperling, a Cambridge-educated economist and professor-turned-entrepreneur, founded University of Phoenix. (University of Phoenix, 2003, p. 1)

CHAPTER 6

Organizational Structure: Managers, Not Administrators

> In business you'd never call anyone an administrator, you'd call them a manager, a leader. That's what I do. I don't concentrate on what we're doing today, but where we can go.
> —DeVry University administrator

The organizational structure of the for-profits, especially the University of Phoenix, differs vastly from that of a traditional university (see Table 6.1). Although the administration has unusual qualities, the central difference is the faculty in the overall structure. The University of Phoenix has neither tenure nor a faculty governance system. Although in recent years it has created a network of curriculum chairs, roughly equivalent to department chairs in traditional institutions, the power and authority of faculty members are nothing like that found at traditional institutions. The University of Phoenix is essentially a collection of adjunct faculty (labeled "practitioner faculty") who work on course-by-course contracts. Many of the University of Phoenix faculty members teach at traditional universities as adjunct, or even tenured, professors.

The other for-profit universities studied for this book have a similar business-leaning organizational structure, but perhaps to a lesser degree than the University of Phoenix. For instance, Argosy University has a campus executive committee at each satellite location that includes all the academic heads, as well as different management groups, admissions, and library services. The interests of the faculty are directly represented in the executive committee, but there is no controlling faculty senate.

Table 6.1
Management vs. Administration

Professional Management	Administration
Accountability	Appointment
Teams	Committees
Risk-taking	Risk-adverse
Venture capital	Allotments
Career mobility	Stable careers
Centralized policies/local autonomy	Autonomy
Standardized curricula	Faculty determined
Part-time faculty and multiyear contracts	Tenure system

This campus executive committee is responsible for the operational end. In addition, there is a separate academic council made up exclusively of faculty that make recommendations to the chief academic officer.

On the business side of the University of Phoenix's organizational structure, one finds modern methods and enlightened business philosophies that emphasize a flat organizational structure, strong employee motivation, risk-taking, change, and innovation. While some of these elements are present in traditional universities, few if any use this approach as broadly. These radically different organizational principles are a core difference for the University of Phoenix and receive detailed explication in this chapter.

SEPARATION OF ACADEMIC AND MANAGEMENT AREAS

A central difference between the for-profits and traditional institutions is in the separation of academic and management aspects of the organization. A manager at the University of Phoenix commented on this separation: "Our faculty do not get into some of the administrative areas of the organization. They focus on the real product. They focus on the curriculum and the students that are in the classroom." The president describes the difference in governance structure at the University of Phoenix:

> The AAUP [American Association of University Professors] statement on shared governance doesn't work here. This is not the same sort of organization. The University of Phoenix has always distinctly divided the academic issues from the management issues. The aca-

demic side has responsibility for everything academic. . . . The management of the organization and management of the campuses is
done by professional management, not by academics.

Notice in this quotation the description of "professional management" for
those controlling organizational decision making. Distinction in University of Phoenix's governance results from the use of part-time practitioner faculty members who have less leverage than tenured faculty in a
traditional institution. One administrator at the University of Phoenix
specifically argues that the lack of tenured faculty has allowed the organization to innovate: "I actually did a study as part of my doctoral work
on innovation in higher education. I interviewed presidents and chief
academic officers, basically trying to get their perceptions as to why they
couldn't be more innovative. Without a doubt, they perceived it to be the
faculty."

Recently, the University of Phoenix has added more full-time faculty
called "curriculum chairs," who also have some administrative responsibility. An administrator at the University of Phoenix comments on this
change, which adds a layer of academic administration: "They are full-
time faculty that have an area of expertise in which they are classically
and appropriately trained. Then they work solely with the faculty that
teach in their area." A faculty member at the University of Phoenix describes the academic organizational structure as "vertical": "All of nursing
reports into the nursing dean and they work on the nursing curriculum.
Now all those nursing people are located in twenty-four different locations throughout the United States, but they all have the same jobs.
They're all responsible for the nursing curriculum within their location."
In the next chapter I look in depth at this separation of academic and
business decision making, and the inherent tension between these two
entities. This separation is a common and distinctive characteristic of all
the for-profits studied for this book and is at the center of the organizational difference from traditional institutions.

ACCOUNTABILITY AND OWNERSHIP

A second distinguishing characteristic of the for-profits, as discussed in
Chapter 5, is the way it both empowers employees by encouraging them
to take ownership for their work, and then makes them accountable for
performing well: "That is what the University of Phoenix is about: outcomes and achieving them, from our curriculum to our managers." One
administrator at the University of Phoenix speaks about the importance

of communicating clear limitations and reasonable performance expectations:

> You know that to accomplish your goal within a set time and a set
> budget, you're going to need decent staff. It's going to take this long
> and cost this much. And if quality is an issue that just has to be the
> way it is. People always want faster. They always want it more ro-
> coco than it was intended to be. So on the one hand you want to
> try to be a team player. On the other hand you feel like you need to
> stand up for what you know it's going to take to get the job done.
> So the way I resolve that is I try to be honest about what I think it's
> going to take. And sometimes you're not very popular when you do
> that. And I've done it repeatedly, so I guess it must be relatively safe
> to do it. I'm still here [laughter].

The same interviewee speaks about how the University of Phoenix allows
and even encourages employees to take ownership for projects and see
them through to completion. On a personal level, this encouragement of
ownership leads to more fulfilling work:

> [At a previous job] I felt if I had stayed there for thirty years I would
> have never seen any project through. There would have been a lot
> of process, but no outcome. And it would be very difficult for me to
> point to what my contribution was. Here, I've been here long enough
> that I've seen some things that I initiated that have become stan-
> dard operating procedure. And that's very gratifying.

Another administrator talks about the freedom staff have to develop
projects: "If I dream up some project I want to work on and I can con-
vince a couple of people of its worth, probably I'll get to do it." The following quotation from an administrator reveals the extreme degree of
accountability in the organizational culture of the University of Phoenix.
Notice here that the accountability is framed as valuing communication
and teamwork:

> We have seventy managers. And they have to come to a meeting ev-
> ery single week and they have to present the performance of their
> group and its progress that last week, from enrollment to admissions,
> to finance to receivables, to academic recruiting to faculty recruit-
> ing, to faculty performance. We measure everything. We quantify ev-
> erything. Those seventy people have to come into a room every
> Thursday for an hour and a half and every single report, every single

person has to report on the progress of their group. It's only a 30 second deal. The flag goes up, they report, we move to the next line. But we're able to take a look and see trends. We've got seventy eyes trained on every single slide.

Accountability and reward structures are more important and central to the for-profit universities than in traditional higher education and partially account for their productivity.

TEAMS AND SHARED LEADERSHIP

The use of teams in performing tasks or working on projects is a common approach at the University of Phoenix. Known as shared leadership or a participatory management style, this approach deeply influences the organizational structure throughout:

> It's the team concept that we have. None of us has a single problem. I don't have one that is mine alone. I can assure you I can call the person in my role in Florida and talk about all the same problems. New names, different places. That sort of thing. But the problems are all the same. And so it's the sense that it's a common problem and that we're all going to struggle to resolve it.

In the following excerpt, the respondent distinguishes the decision-making process from convincing to more of communicating and answering questions:

> I've found that it isn't so much convincing. We're working on a project right now that's a pretty significant change. And the way that we're approaching it is a list of questions and answers. We'll do a presentation that talks to it, but we brainstormed all the possible questions. And we did that by sitting down literally with my team, and I gave them the presentation and just recorded all the questions that came up. They're normal people, those are normal questions that people would want answers to. We'll incorporate all that data in the final presentation to answer as many questions. Then we find that change is a whole lot less of an issue because we've walked through: "Here's what we were trying to do. Here's the strategy. Here's the design. Here are the pieces that are going to go into it. He's going to get ruffled and what we're going to do about it. Here's all the fabulous enhancements that are going to go with it." . . . Most people don't mind change. They just want to understand.

It is interesting to see that the respondent later advises that decisions be made more slowly so that interested parties have time to assimilate the changes, contradicting the usual image of the University of Phoenix as moving at break-neck speed.

One interview subject speaks about how teams are formed across organizational areas of responsibility in order to get the broadest perspective on change movements. "We set up environments where both functional and crossfunctional teams meet to talk about what the strategy should be at the organization." Again, one sees here the characteristic of two management styles working together: hierarchical and flat. The emphasis on hearing from frontline employees is linked to the assessment of student services and overall educational effectiveness:

> We have so much data internally that we collect. We do focus meetings. We'll pull groups of people together to say—Whatever we think is a problem—If we think our students are withdrawing at a higher rate in a particular program, we'll pull those students together. "Tell us why you dropped. What could we do differently?" Knowing how to get information and what to do with that information and when to act, that's all part of the challenge.

Furthermore, the University of Phoenix explicitly values the abilities of its employees to work in teams: When asked, "What qualities do you most respect and admire?" an interviewee answered, "Teamwork." An administrator talks about how his basketball coaching background led him to understand the importance of teamwork: "It's like starting out in the season with your twelve players and your goal is to get those twelve players to play absolutely as one and to win every single game that you play." Teamwork and accountability go hand-in-hand in the University of Phoenix management approach.

An interview subject gives an example of how group decisions are made about new educational programs, this one with an e-commerce emphasis:

> So what happens at that very highest level is people start talking about the philosophical question, how do we do e-business? Are we going to integrate it in our courses or are we going to actually do degrees? And those start becoming the conversations at the deans' meetings, at the high-level strategy meetings of our corporate leaders. The direction we were given is "do it." And be competitive. Get it out there. So the next step, after we decide we're actually going to do it, and we settled on e-business versus e-commerce, which

doesn't seem like that big a leap now, but at the time we were talking about it, everybody else was using the word "e-commerce," and even little things like that are really discussed. Is it going to be an e-commerce program? Is it going to be e-business? Once it was decided, we did research of every university in the country. What are they doing? We got this giant book and we looked at everybody's program in the country. Again, because we're a private company, to us that's business. You just hire people to go out and research everybody's program in the country. It's not like we worry about it being in our budget. We're a company. If you don't do that, you're not competitive. So we came back with what everybody was doing and what their strategies were and their courses. And then we start discussing that. What we noticed was a lot of them were pushing toward technology and not business. They were calling it e-business, but really they had added a bunch of technology, telecommunications courses, and stuff like that to their regular curriculum. And so we go, "Well, we're not sure that's what it is." So the next thing we do is we bring in this panel, one for e-business, three deans—undergrad, business grad, business and IT.

The process involves groups throughout from internal discussion, to market research, to program building, to expert team formation.

A respondent speaks about the flatness of the organizational structure and Sperling's rule about open communication from all levels: "That is John's number one rule. You can talk to anybody about anything at any time. There isn't such a thing as chain of command to talk to somebody. It just doesn't exist in this corporation as long as John is at the top of it." However, this interviewee is aware of the problems with this open organizational structure:

The downside is that sometimes we're very inefficient at doing things, because ten people are doing the same thing ten different ways at the same time and communication isn't real clear, because there isn't a clear chart. I can be dean and I can be part of Apollo, at the same time, which means I report to the provost, to the president on one side of the house, and I report to directly to Todd on the other side of what I'm doing. And that doesn't make for a very tight organization. So things like communication aren't as good as they could be if you had a very structured organization. Who's responsible isn't always real clear, because we've got five people doing corporate education right now in totally five different ways. . . . It allows innovation, but on the flip side, everything doesn't always get communicated well.

A faculty member who teaches business courses sees the organizational structure at the University of Phoenix as part of the trend toward participatory management style seen in many corporations:

> It is almost like participative management in a forward thinking corporation. In a corporation they do not—well if they are forward thinking and healthy—the executives don't sit in the ivory tower and make all the decisions. They have focus groups. They have employee task forces. Those kind of things. That is more of the analogy that holds up for me.

Here we find that rather than viewing the organizational style of the university as a new form of academic governance, the respondent sees the University of Phoenix approach as linked to current trends in corporate management.

CENTRALIZED OR DECENTRALIZED?

One of the crucial issues for large multicampus academic organizations such as the University of Phoenix, DeVry University, and Argosy University is to decide on the amount of centralized practice and control needed to meet objectives. Rather than being an either/or proposition, in many cases institutions decide to lean toward centralization in some ways, and decentralization in others. The decentralization emphasis at the University of Phoenix apparently stems from Sperling's notion of innovation originating from various efforts made independently and simultaneously throughout the organization. The central office gives campuses resources and in turn has to follow central policies. However, the campuses have quite a bit of latitude: "We don't meddle in the details of their campus business." Sperling's appreciation for innovation at the local level leads to allowing a certain amount of autonomy. The philosophy is that if you have ten people do the same things you only get one result. Whereas if you have them do ten different things, you are more likely to find something particularly good. An administrator summarizes the decentralized attitude as, "If you want to go start this, go ahead. We don't care. You don't have to get anybody's approval, just go do it. We want you to integrate it back in at some point, but for now you can go do it."

The following administrator describes a key decision point in the organization's history when it committed to give more autonomy to the individual campuses: "You can pinpoint one of those large leaps [in growth] as being the time when they decentralized. Because given a little more freedom and a little bit of running room, each of the campuses exploded in their own way, and that percentage of growth by each campus made for a huge growth for the organization." One important approach indicated by those interviewed was to standardize processes, then allow freedom for innovation or variation within that overall scheme. Notice in the following quotation how an example of a discussion of standardized accounting procedures concentrates on common outcomes, not processes: "Is it okay that your accounting department looks different than mine? Probably. We both close our month-ends to the penny at the end of the month. You do it differently because it reflects your thought process and your skill sets and who you hired to do it. I do it differently." This focus on the end point allows the organization to accommodate individual differences and innovation within a general framework. The University of Phoenix extends this centralize-decentralize balance to academic matters such as the faculty recruitment process: "They must do training that is comprised of certain elements. They must do some certification, etc. But the way they choose to deliver that is within their control to a large extent. If they want to do their certification over six weeks, one night a week. . . . Again, it's kind of that many roads lead to Rome, but you must get to Rome."

A main element of this decentralized-centralized balance is the splitting of academic from business operations. A result of this split is that one can be centralized, while the other remains more autonomous. Additionally, faculty members have diminished power over the educational enterprise and administrative issues. Administrators see this as a gain for students:

> The faculty are absolutely responsible and should be driven to be accountable for what we do on the academic side of it. The curriculum, the instruction, the learning, all of that is the faculty responsibility. The business side of it is responsible for the business side of it. The administration, the customer service, the technology, and all of those things. That is really helpful because it allows us to put the student in the middle of the process and say we can build around the student. The administrative systems and decisions we've put into place, what we charge for tuition, how we deliver materials, how we counsel students financially, how we counsel them academically, and all those things that provide service to students are handled on the business side of it. And so they're not handled or driven by the needs of a tenured faculty.

Notice in the quotation that the stated result of the split is that faculty members do not control student service operations. The use of standardized course materials is probably the most prominent aspect of the cen-tralized-decentralized approach to traditional academic areas of respon-sibility:

> We have a very interesting mix of centralized and decentralized. For example, we design curriculums centrally, but when it's delivered, we expect it to be delivered by the individual instructor using their own style, talents, and their own view of the world. So we don't expect it to be delivered the way it's designed. What the central design en-sures is, for example, we design the whole program to make sure that every course has touched all the topics that we want touched and that there's as little repetition in those courses as possible and that courses really do feed courses. So that when you go into one of our courses, the instructor knows the competencies that the person is walking in with from previous courses, but we also know that later-ally, across the country. So if somebody has transferred from a Cali-fornia campus to Phoenix, we know if they took this course, these were the objectives of the course, this was the material that was cov-ered in the course. How it was covered, what the exact assignments are, we don't know. That was determined by the instructor.

Consistency in what course material is delivered and in the learning ob-jectives is more important at the University of Phoenix because of its lack of full-time permanent faculty, who at traditional universities are the guardians of the curriculum. The large number of practitioner fac-ulty at the University of Phoenix expedites the centralized approach to academic content. The second way the academic decisions are decen-tralized is through relying on business and industry for curricular input: "I have access to corporate leaders on a peer or one-to-one basis that I wouldn't have had as an academician. . . . So there's certain connections to industry that are peer connections, because we're viewed as a publicly traded corporation that understands business and has the same quarterly filings that they have." Finally, an administrator justifies the centralized approach to creating course materials because of the input from faculty teams: "People get scared of the word 'centralized.' But we're using our faculty to do it. We're bringing in teams constantly from our campuses that are actually the ones that are doing that development. It's more under our leadership that it's happening." One characteristic of the University of Phoenix is an effective approach to centralized-decentralized structures. Economies of scale and quality control are achieved through centralization, while local efficiencies and innovation are encouraged through decentralization.

DeVry University also has a distributed system with fifty-eight sites at last count. Since the sites are small, they can handle anywhere from 100 to 400 students. The staff often crosstrains and customer or student service is emphasized. The small size allows the individual sites to infuse their operation with a small school feel. Administrators speak about a recent effort to change what had been Keller Graduate School and DeVry campuses into combined DeVry University locations serving both undergraduate and graduate students. They call combining of locations a move to "DeVry University Centers," which means part of that effort is reorganization. As a result they are currently reorganizing the center's reporting. Previously they were a very centralized organization with policy in almost all divisions occurring in a very uniform way. This reorganization has led to a process of reassigning responsibility of the sites to local managers who are closer to the market—a typical business approach. DeVry leadership has also decided to move to a uniform academic calendar; previously they were on a quarter system at the graduate level and a semester system at the undergraduate level. As part of this shift, DeVry changed the structure of their courses to more of a hybrid delivery in which both in-person and online meetings are used. Their program is called "iOptimize" and is very similar to University of Phoenix's FlexNet program.

The decisions made in the wake of the Keller-DeVry merger illustrate the organization's thinking about best management approaches. Academic institutions often emphasize uniqueness both in academic programs and management. For instance, many large public systems give great autonomy to individual campuses so that they have different majors and degrees, as well as different management schemes and policies. Conversely, the for-profits strive for a balance of centralized-decentralized structuring. The decision to combine DeVry and Keller operations is characterized as "creating greater value" for the organization because of the market decision, and consistent branding of the name of DeVry University. Administrators emphasize the marketing advantages of a more centralized and consistent DeVry University. This recent reorganization seems to have been part of a long-term process of converting what had been a fairly traditionally formatted three-year, daytime undergraduate program into more of an adult education model. They began by adding undergraduate courses at the Keller Graduate school sites and realized that the working adult population could benefit from this approach: "We felt we could serve the undergraduate market of working adults as we had been serving the graduate students." The leadership at DeVry feels that one advantage is their ability to replicate practices and programs quickly. For instance, once they saw the advantage of reformatting their undergraduate program, they moved quickly to expand this change through the reorganization process.

RISK-TAKING AND ALLOWING FAILURE

The organizational structure of the University of Phoenix is designed to allow, if not encourage, risk-taking. Yet again, this characteristic comes from the founder. In the following quotation one sees how Sperling reacted to failure early in his career: "When you look at it from an economic viewpoint, there's not a great opportunity cost of failure because it opens up all the things that you never considered while you were deeply involved in the activity that led to that failure." Sperling describes how he learned to understand the temporary nature of defeat: "No matter what happens, a few days later I've got another scheme and I'm off chasing that." He, and the organization, seems to understand that other new opportunities will come along: "Now I don't get depressed over it. I know, 'Oh a new idea will come, just don't worry about it.'" Sperling even sees his unhappy experience leading the faculty union at San Jose State University, in retrospect, as a positive change: "I built a professors' union and got kicked out of it. That was the most traumatic event in my life. And then out of that came a whole series of educational experiments and then finally the first company that formed the basis of the Apollo Group. And I think, boy that was the best thing that ever happened to me." However, one shouldn't confuse this willingness to make mistakes with confidence in his decisions: "I'm never sure of the right course of action. You try and you hope it works and if it doesn't work you pull back and do something else." Sperling's approach is to test ideas out in practice rather than to spend a great deal of energy analyzing new projects: "You never know whether the decision is right until you operationalize it." How does he evaluate the effectiveness of decision making? "Bottom line is a powerful feedback." This drive to innovate was continually remarked upon by interview subjects: "We are encouraged to solve problems, to be innovative. Not always to make money, although sometimes that's implied. To be innovative. To be held accountable for our results. And really to do very interesting things." Once again the comment on a desire to do "interesting things." Administrators comment on the way that innovative ideas are brought forth by finding support in the organization: "I feel like it's still a place where if you have a good idea and you can find people who will champion that idea, structure be-damned basically. They will find a way to incubate that idea. They will find a home for it. I've experienced this a number of times, so it is something that I believe." The following interviewee describes the innovative nature of the University of Phoenix:

> In some dynamic organizations there is too much work. Anybody who picks up work can run with it. And nobody gives a hoot. Hey, you took it on your own. Good for you—do it! That kind of thing happens here. They're doing so many things. And once in a while they are falling flat on their face. But that's what I see happening in this school. They innovate. They are not afraid to try new things.

Innovation is also clearly appreciated at the other for-profits, as well as the nontraditionals studied for this book. However, the tolerance for risk and culture that supports risk-taking was less clear at these other institutions. Nevertheless, because of the for-profit nature, which makes them focused on the market, it is likely that at the least they are more responsive to innovation and risk-taking than are traditional higher educational institutions.

PUBLIC POLICY AWARENESS

One attribute that is evident about the for-profits, particularly the University of Phoenix, is that they understand the importance of actively trying to influence public policy. This priority is reflected in the resources put toward monitoring policy efforts. John Sperling comments on the importance of public policy to for-profits: "You have a highly motivated workforce with a product that the consumer wants and a political structure to support it. It would be dismantled in a couple of years without the political structure." This has led to the university's active attempts to influence policy:

> Well remember, education, most professors don't know it, but it's one of the most intense political activities in the country. For instance we have four national lobbyists and thirty-five state lobbyists, all have to be in place in order to protect the Apollo Group and its interests—a constant attempt by the educational establishment even now to do everything possible to avoid having to deal with the University of Phoenix.

Sperling speaks about the University of Phoenix's particular struggles: "One Dupont Circle has a gaggle of national educational organizations with a powerful lobbying force in Washington, and they do everything possible to cause trouble to any for-profit educational entity." He understands the specific way in which traditional higher education tries to marginalize nontraditional and vocational education in public policy decision making:

> For instance we constantly have to watch over the educational re-authorizations act of 1972. So we have to be in there lobbying or they'll have sections of the law that would just cause for-profit education all sorts of trouble. We're constantly being reviewed by the Department of Education as they are being agitated by One Dupont Circle. Every state has a licensing entity for higher education that is almost always controlled by the educational establishment. So you have to fight your way into each state, and you have to have a lobbyist there because almost every year somebody's going to drop a bill that's going to cause you all sorts of pain and anguish.

An additional way that the University of Phoenix tries to affect policy is through the regional accreditation process:

> There are constant enemies in the accreditation community that have you in their cross hairs. It's a powerful entity. The educational establishment is very conservative, likes change like it wants a hole in the head. And it is powerful because it controls the state educational agency and it has an enormous installed base among the graduates of these institutions in the legislatures. In state legislatures, almost every bloody state legislator is a graduate of the state university and the state university is in there lobbying like hell against you at every opportunity.

The accrediting challenges presented by the online delivery system used for about a third of the university's courses represented another accreditation challenge. Sperling points out the difficulty of starting a new university, particularly a nontraditional one, because of the resources necessary to protect the institution's interest in the policy arena. Without that huge political structure that costs millions of dollars a year for institutions like the University of Phoenix, another institution starting out now would have a difficult time.

VENTURE CAPITAL ACCESS

The ability to fund innovative programs and projects because of access to capital through the public offering of the University of Phoenix is a strategic advantage. Sperling remarks on this access: "Once you finally get it built, then you go out to the capital markets and they shower money on you like it's going out of style." A dean comments on how substantial resources are budgeted for new program development: "As a dean, I have a budget for this. I have a substantial development budget. It's not just my staff. . . . I have my staff budget, but then I have a development budget that's much larger than my staff budget." Representatives from DeVry and Argosy speak of the revenue as "venture capital." They argue that the difference from traditional institution's revenue sources used for new program development is that those funds always come with political or private strings attached.

This cash advantage also has substantive influence on the organizational culture and structure. The following administrator from the University of Phoenix talks about the increased professionalism and efficiency that the market requires:

> We had to have more internal discipline. If you look around at what we do, we're a very different organization from most academic organizations. What makes it work is the discipline that we bring to what we do. And that added more discipline to it. Yes, we are highly regulated. We've always had accreditation reviews and lots of state boards and state regulatory bodies look at us. But this added another layer. Now we have Wall Street analysts looking at us. And we had all of these analysts parading through when we first went public who had never been associated with any kind of nontraditional education. In fact, most of them who had been educated at traditional upper-tier organizations were very skeptical. Then we had to have the discipline of explaining ourselves to them and to the outside world in a way that we never had before. And let me not forget to add that going public brought in an additional source of funding, which, obviously, brought in millions of dollars into our coffers. We've been able to pour much of that money back into the academic side—adding more degree programs, adding more staff, adding more discipline to how we do that and how we watch over it.

Clearly, access to ready capital to fund new programs is an advantage for the for-profits.

CHARISMATIC LEADER

One apparent characteristic of the University of Phoenix's organizational structure is the same charismatic leadership for its entire history. As one interview subject puts it: "John is almost like a legend in the company." The top leadership of any company or university, particularly its founder, helps form the personality of that organization. For-profit and nontraditional universities have often benefited from leaders who articulated the values and beliefs of the organization well and were good at motivating others to join their endeavor. Aspects of this leadership at the for-profits include the ability to come up with new approaches to higher education, to communicate the organizational vision to the employees, and then to see new programs and innovation through to implementation. In the following quotation, an administrator speaks of the importance of Sperling's leadership to the organization: "A clear vision from John and a clear charge from the very top that this is the direction in which we're going to make it work. And once he has said that, then people are willing to come together. We don't generally have a problem getting people to rally around something like that once that clear voice rings out." Notice Sperling's role here in motivating the organization into collective action. Furthermore, respondents point to Sperling's recognized leadership role in the domain of higher education as a whole: "One of the reasons this place is the way it is was that John was the voice in the wilderness calling for a new way of doing things. He saw potential for an institution that would serve a greatly underserved population in a different way, provide them access well in advance of others recognizing that this was going to be a need." The "voice in the wilderness" from the founder of an organization combined with other leadership qualities makes for a particularly compelling leader.

CHURNING PERSONNEL, MENTORING, AND GROWTH

Undoubtedly partly influenced by the extreme growth of the University of Phoenix, there is a tendency for staff to move from one role to another within the organization: "Generally it's not people leaving the university, but it's churning. They're moving into new positions. Otherwise, because of our growth, we have to bring in a lot of people from the outside and teach them our model very quickly." The organization pays attention to providing career paths for successful employees so that their skills can be utilized at increasingly higher levels:

> I would say that over the last three years, they have paid a lot more attention to career pathing within Academic Affairs proper. And then out in the campuses we have seen instances where someone who was a Campus Director of Academic Affairs became a Campus VP. The first time that happened we almost fell out of our chairs because it was so unusual. You would see someone who was a Campus Di-

rector of Operations become a VP. So I see evidence that good work, regardless of function, is recognized. And it's recognized by promoting people to more and more responsibility.

Informal mentoring seems to occur regularly at the University of Phoenix. Undoubtedly, partly because employees often come from either traditional institutions or outside of education altogether and need to learn the university's unique organizational structure. Sperling denies any intention to mentor his executives: "I'm on the phone to them suggesting, cajoling, whatever, but I don't have any sense of mentoring them. See, my view of management is that you just want people to do what you want them to do and you'll use any technique possible to get them [to do that]." However, in the following quotation he sees his role as trying to help his staff be successful: "I am absolutely dedicated to their success, and in so far as I mentor them, my job is to knock down barriers to let them achieve what they want to achieve and I try to make sure that they do that for the people that report to them and on down the line." Sperling himself is mentioned many times by respondents as a mentor:

> When our organization was very small, John made it a real point to get to know his employees. Spouses, kids' names. Really he was actively involved. Always gave us opportunities to talk, to brainstorm. He was a real pusher. And he still has a sense of identifying people who, I believe, can add value to the organization and steer them into maybe even driving themselves a little harder and generating back that greater self-esteem, that you can go that one step further than perhaps maybe your plans were for yourself. He was certainly one of my mentors.

Note here how the push to perform at a high level is combined with a personal interest in the respondent. The same respondent reflects on the influence of another mentor and how the sense of humor and balance has a positive effect: "We've had a lot of battles to fight with the University of Phoenix, and I think the kind of personality you bring to the table and how you send the message is just as important if not more important than what the message itself is." A female administrator speaks about how John Sperling was a mentor and how he has a particular history of helping women advance in their careers:

> I've had mentors like John who have taken an interest in seeing me promoted and work well in the organization. Early on, I did some projects for the organization that caught his attention. And it was

really my writing skill—the fact that I had a great liberal arts education and had good writing skills. I was doing a lot of document
preparation for accreditation and licensure. We were fighting a lot
of battles in those days. He noticed that and he decided that maybe
I was smarter than I looked or something [laughs]. He sort of sponsored me and he sponsored many women. He's very good at doing
that for women.

Another administrator talks of Sperling's broad influence: "He was not a
mentor in terms of showing me how to do the job, but he was a mentor
for a lot of us in terms of his approach to education, his approach to life,
his approach to business. A lot of him has rubbed off, in my opinion, on
a lot of us." As part of his information mentoring, Sperling himself reflects on the need to instill a strong sense of personal ethics in management: "You have to teach them to tell the truth. The truth is very, very
painful, most of the time. And you just say, you can't tell different things
to different people. You must be consistent, and that's hard for most of
them to learn. You have to say, 'Now look, I told you, you can't do that
or your reputation is not going to be very good around here.'" One interview subject speaks about the informal and dispersed nature of mentoring
at the University of Phoenix:

> It's an informal process, or certainly was at that time. The univer-
> sity has designed it to be a little more structured in the ensuing years,
> but I had lots of people that served as mentors. Frequently they were
> in other physical locations, located geographically dispersed from
> where we are. But they either had similar roles to what I had or they
> understood the type of role I played in the organization. And they
> came forward with ideas, communication, developmental opportu-
> nities, help on occasion, a helping hand, in order to teach me and
> show me the ropes in every position that I had.

Others denied any influence from mentors: "No. I am not much for
mentors. I like to learn it on my own." However, mentoring is a structured part of the training for new faculty members: "One of the things
that the university does is set every new faculty member up with a faculty mentor—somebody to kind of guide them through regardless of their
prior experience. And that really helped a great deal in the teaching art
of things."

Personal growth is encouraged at the University of Phoenix. Sperling
commented on his attitude toward individuals in the organization: "Success comes in all shapes, sizes, sexes, genders, you name it!" One respon-

dent verifies how personal growth is encouraged and nurtured in the organization: "I have watched really wonderful individuals come into our company, find the right alignment for themselves and a career path that worked
for them, and watch them excel at what they do because they discovered
the enthusiasm and the delight and the passion for what their role was."
Another interviewee links the growth of the company to the opportunity
for employees to move up and grow with increased responsibility:

> I think what makes it special is that it's a living, growing organiza-
> tion. I know enough about organizations that when they're very static
> and not growing it creates a pall or stagnation that goes through the
> whole organization. But when an organization is growing, there's a
> lot of vitality. The reason why is that there's lots of room for people
> to move up. You're growing, so you're opening new positions at the
> top. People at the bottom are constantly moving up. And that al-
> ways makes people happy. They increase their standard of living and
> they're doing better all the way around.

An administrator speaks about the competitive advantage he enjoys in
recruitment because of the reputation for the organization of promoting
from within: "I have an advantage, because they know that there's opportunity. And if they come with great ideas, they have a chance to do
something."

Linked to the focus on employee career development, growth, and
mentoring is the notion of reward for good performance at the University
of Phoenix: "I think that we acknowledge that recognition is important
in our organization." Financial reward is not the least of the recognition
gained: "And it's rewarded. That's the last part. It is financially rewarded.
Let's be honest." Formal reward systems, especially for upper management,
were described at both DeVry and Argosy Universities. Additionally,
DeVry and Argosy, as most businesses, tend to have a stronger accountability and reward system for their employees than most traditional universities.

For-profits tendencies with their personnel include promoting from
within, stressing of both accountability and financial rewards, and attention to the mentoring and grooming of promising staff.

CONCLUSION

I found in this chapter that for-profit organizations structure themselves
differently than traditional universities, concentrating on managing organizations rather than maintaining structures. More like a business, the

for-profits tend to separate their academic decision making from their management decisions. Many of the for-profit institutions have distributed locations and try to balance centralized and decentralized functions—generally, they are more centralized than traditional higher education. Often decisions regarding centralization are made for business values such as economies of scale, marketability, quality control, and branding. For-profit organizations tend to encourage risk-taking and have access to venture capital to quickly respond to opportunities with new initiatives. They emphasize ownership of tasks and accountability. Leadership is generally flat and often shared. It is common for for-profit organizations to promote from within and reward productive employees.

Given the organizational structure, how are decisions made at the for-profits? Specifically, how is the natural tension between academic and business aims managed? The next chapter addresses these important issues.

CLIPPINGS

Lobbyist Watch: The University of Phoenix has been working hard to build stronger ties to the Republicans who will be in charge of higher-education policymaking in the White House, Education Department, and Congress. The Apollo Group, the university's parent company, has appointed William F. Goodling, a former Republican congressman from Pennsylvania who headed the Committee on Education and the Workforce in the House of Representatives, to the university's corporate board. ("Ways and Means," 2001, p. A21)

Really, the only dim spot in the Apollo Group's bright future lies with the power of pesky government regulations and regional accreditors, both of which have the power to cut off the for-profits' access to Title IV federal loans and grants, the 1964 program founded with the express purpose of providing financial assistance to low-income students who would not otherwise be able to pursue a college education. Without Title IV funds, few for-profits could afford to exist—their students are about twice as likely to receive federal aid than students at nonprofits. And they get a lot of it: At the two-year level, for-profit schools get an average of $6,974 in aid per student. Public junior colleges get $2,609. For education corporations, students are simply a conduit for their piece of the $35 billion federal loan and grant jackpot. The Apollo Group is particularly motivated to loosen the Title IV restrictions. In 2000, an Education Department audit of the $339 million in loans and $9 million in Pell Grants distributed by the University of Phoenix found that the school failed to meet some basic standards, including giving the students at least 12 hours of instructional time per week. Apollo paid out $6 million fines and re-turned more than $50 million in ill-gotten loans and grants. (Cox, 2002, p. 10)

Apollo Group, Inc. (Nasdaq:APOL), (Nasdaq:UOPX) announced that the U.S. Department of Education has issued the 1999—the most current data available—student loan default rate for the University of Phoenix. The 1999 rate was 4.6 percent. The national student loan default rate for 1999 was 5.6 percent as compared to 6.9 percent in 1998. ("Apollo Group, Inc.'s," 2001, p. 1)

WASHINGTON. . . . Rep. Howard P. (Buck) McKeon, a California Republican and chairman of the Subcommittee on 21st Century Competitiveness, which held the hearing, set the tone early on by saying, "If [a college] and its programs are accredited, the assumption by most is that it provides a quality education. The purpose of this hearing is to determine if that assumption is accurate." Leaning on Republican themes of accountability, Mr. McKeon said, "I am extremely concerned that accreditation agencies are imposing standards on institutions that have little or nothing to do with academic quality." (Morgan, 2002, p. A28)

University of Phoenix is accredited by the Higher Learning Commission of the North Central Association (30 N. LaSalle St., Ste. 2400, Chicago, IL 60602–2504; [312] 263–0456, [800] 621–7440). The Bachelor of Science in Nursing and Master of Science in Nursing Programs are accredited by the National League for Nursing Accrediting Commission (61 Broadway, 33rd Floor, New York, NY 10006 [212–363–5555]). The Master of Counseling program in Community Counseling (Phoenix and Southern Arizona Campuses) and the Master of Counseling program in Mental Health Counseling (Utah Campus) are accredited by the Council for Accreditation of Counseling and Related Educational Programs (5999 Stevenson Avenue, Alexandria, VA 22304 [703–823–9800]). (University of Phoenix, 2003, p. 1)

CHAPTER 7

"Creative Tension": Decision-Making Process at For-Profit Universities

How are decisions made at for-profit and nontraditional institutions? The previous chapter indicated that a central difference from other academic institutions is how the business-academic tension is managed at the for-profits. Effectively balancing business and academic interests, a flat hierarchy that encourages communication and debate, use of assessment and feedback systems, a reliance on personal relationships, and a culture of investment in the organization are characteristic of decision making at the for-profits.

CREATIVE TENSION

For-profit companies that are also accredited academic organizations face the crucial problem of managing decision-making processes so that business and academic interests are appropriately balanced. The for-profit leaders interviewed for this book are obviously accustomed to discussing this issue and have developed an institutional rhetoric to employ in these conversations, labeling such conflict "creative tension" at the University of Phoenix, "dynamic tension" at DeVry, and "productive tension" at Argosy. What do they mean by these labels?

"Creative tension" was the phrase used throughout the interviews at the University of Phoenix to describe the balance between the two organizational interests of pursuing increased revenue and sustaining academic quality: "We call that the creative tension within our organization, and we try and surface it. Because the tension isn't bad, it's just how we manage it that can be good or less productive." The University of Phoenix's position is that there isn't a conflict between making money and a focus on meeting the needs of students or customers, as they are sometimes called.

Administrators describe the separation of the academic and corporate interests as the central organizational difference of the University of Phoenix from traditional institutions where faculties have broader decision-making responsibilities. The University clearly separates its academic and management sides: the academic personnel having responsibility for everything related to academic programs, while the business decisions are made by professional managers. Articulating a theme echoed at the other for-profits, representatives from the University of Phoenix speak often about how the administrative elements of the university are professionalized rather than inserting faculty into the process. Like traditional universities, the tension surfaces most when the two sides compete for resources: "There's always a ton of what I would call creative tension in that there are decisions to be made about allocation of resources." It is difficult even in for-profit organizations to make decisions about the allocation of resources because inevitably some people will get less than they want.

Interestingly, those in what would be described as "academic" positions at for-profit universities do not necessarily feel that they are at odds with management. One administrator at the University of Phoenix claims that there isn't much conflict because of the centralized academic structure. Consequently, academic divisiveness experienced at traditional institutions is minimized: "The academic structure is more centralized and corporately driven. So we're very tied together as a management team. My Executive VP and my Provost and I make almost all decisions together, so that we can talk through the ramifications of doing anything." Administrators repeatedly speak of a give-and-take versus conflict, particularly around difficult issues such as faculty compensation. Undoubtedly, these conversations are easier because of a lack of tenure or faculty unions. Additionally, administrators talk about the need to prioritize goals and strategies and put them in alignment with resource allocation. In the following quotation, a meeting of the academic council at the University of Phoenix is described revealing the way the two interests are vetted with a specific example:

> She proposed that we consider allowing a pass/fail. As a general rule, we don't allow pass/fail grades at the university. So she is bringing change into this committee. So from an academics perspective, she's

looking at it along her lines. My immediate reaction then is—Okay, now put the business hat on—"I understand where you're coming from, but I got to tell you that employers do not reimburse on a pass/fail. So here's what's going to happen. You're going to create a pass/fail grade and my job—and you'll see prior learning assessment center falls under my jurisdiction—is to be profitable. Which means I have to have students enrolling in it. And if they're not going to enroll in it because their employer is not reimbursing them—and 80 percent of our students, 75 percent are being reimbursed—then I think we're going to sort of do a disservice to that."

One sees here that finally the balancing refers back to the interests of students. How then is the tension resolved?

What we decided is, "You know, you're right. You're right. We're just going to pull a small committee together." And I said, "Let's bring some teaching faculty in, because maybe we can have the best of both worlds. Maybe we can figure out a way, rather than just going directly to a pass/fail basis, let's look at the outcomes for that course and see if we can provide better guidance to the faculty on what to grade. What's the criterion that we're trying to accomplish in that course?" I can't speak highly enough of the mechanism of that academic council, because you have something very rare. You have the business, the academic, and the marketing side coming to the same table and talking about any item that's going to impact the institution. And that we understand there's going to be an intersection. And we don't want one to necessarily win over the other, we want it to make sense for this organization.

"Make sense for this organization" is a significant phrase in the passage, describing the reference back to value-based decision making. The goal, then, at this academic council level is to make the right decision for the organization as a whole, as opposed to advantaging individual competing interests. The following quotation demonstrates understanding the need for balance:

There is a dynamic and a creative tension between the business side of the organization and the academic side. If it gets out of balance, then we have problems. If it gets out of balance on either side. If the business side becomes too strong and makes the decisions, we paint ourselves into a corner. We make short-term bottom line decisions that will give us what we need right now but hurt us long term. If the academic side gets out of balance and all we do is focus on that, we won't be able to be a going concern. So it's finding that proper balance.

Administrators at the University of Phoenix repeatedly argue that the tension is not adversarial:

> I teach a two-day session in our Executive Development program. And we start that off by asking the question: "Are we a business that happens to have education as its product or are we a university that happens to be organized as a business?" And we have the people in that Executive Development program choose sides and debate that topic. What are the implications of choosing one or the other of those? Of course, the answer is: Yes. We are sometimes a business that happens to have education as its product when we are marketing, and at other times we are a university that happens to be organized as a business when I'm setting academic standards and say the faculty have responsibility for granting credit and grading. And administration can't change that. So the answer is: No. I don't see myself as the voice in the wilderness here. Because the business side is smart enough to recognize that if we don't put a good product in the classroom nothing else matters.

However, at other times administrators claim that they do play a role to some degree in advocating for academic quality issues. In the following quotation, a top academic leader in the organization describes a retreat and his insistence on meaningful academic quality. Notice how he describes the importance of vision communication:

> I'm going to contradict what I said earlier to a degree, but I feel like my job is to be the university's conscience—the canary in the coal mine. But the way to do this is to have a well thought out vision and to articulate it in something that people can believe in. Just anecdotal: We had an Apollo executive management retreat at John's [Sperling] house a month or so ago. And they were talking about the goal for the company to become the largest education company in the world and all those kinds of things that you do at strategic planning retreats. This much in revenues and this many—and I said: "One thing I just would like—and I am taking a risk by saying this in this group. But when rank and file employees hear about keeping the stock price up, for example, they don't give a damn. That's not what makes them get up in the morning. In fact, if we talk about that it makes it sound like we're trying to make money for the fat cats at the top. What they want is to be involved in something that is interesting and worthwhile and useful."

The administrator argues here for communicating essential values of the organization that motivate the organizational members, and comments later that he feels "good" about his argument and the positive reception it received at the retreat. Here one sees the alignment of the articulation of institutional mission with personal enrichment and satisfaction.

At DeVry University, the tension is described as "dynamic" and is managed by representation from both academic and business interests:

> I think we've always had, what people refer to here as a "dynamic tension" between the need to uphold quality, maintain quality, ensure the processes that maintain that, and not let that decay and slip to meet the demands of the market. Those two trends get mediated by senior management, management committees, and structures of groups of committees that are comprised of academics as well as operations people.

There is admitted tension when the perceptions from the academic side are not in line with those of the operations people or the marketing people. Nevertheless, one administrator claims the tension is natural and less ominous than one might assume: "I don't think there's inherent conflict. The process creates tension, which needs to be resolved."

How is the tension resolved at DeVry? Much like at the University of Phoenix, leaders at DeVry emphasize good communication and a willingness to listen to multiple perspectives. One administrator focuses on helping others understand the overall value of multiple perspectives in the decision-making process: "Helping people understand that others look at things differently, and the value that brings to decision making." Long-time leaders in the organization who articulate strong collective values help mediate this tension. An administrator at DeVry speaks about how the value of maintaining quality education is "inculcated" through the culture of the organization. In for-profit organizations tension is managed through assigning a different role for faculty in decision making. While faculty members are consulted, they do not ultimately have control of larger nonacademic judgments. Nevertheless, administrators report that decisions are always made with academic quality in mind, and they claim that they never make choices where they feel this value is compromised.

At DeVry University, the way they maintain their values within the culture is through individuals, training, and demonstrating that principles are not just institutional rhetoric. Additionally, the accreditation process has forced the for-profits to share to some extent external values, those common to the higher education domain as a whole. Academic quality for many for-profits has been a chief concern because of the importance of regional accreditation and a good reputation necessary for financial success. The following description of the role of accreditation and academic quality captures the sentiment found at all for-profits:

> To receive accreditation at the graduate level in the early seventies was a big move [laughs], it took a lot. And so the founders, Dennis Keller and Ron Taylor, making all the decisions that they made, realized that it was extremely important that they consider academic quality as much as the business approach because we were being scrutinized by the nonprofits, the traditionalists, to see what we would do. Because at the time for-profits were matchbook schools, that what they were considered by most traditional higher education. So we had a lot to prove. So we almost went to the extreme to try and prove ourselves.

Administrators at DeVry, as at the University of Phoenix, often speak about how allowing decisions that adversely affect the quality of the institution's education would be bad on a purely business level: "What business can make a decision that isn't for the customer and in the interest of the business? In the long run that won't work."

At Argosy University, administrators admit some tension with the faculty over the push for growth. However, growth is seen as bringing in more resources that can be used to support academic quality. In this way the for-profit status, they argue, helps support the academic mission. The administrators claim that even with growth the same faculty to student ratio is maintained.

In the nontraditional universities studied for this book, administrators are not nearly as conscious of the academic/business tension. At Fielding Graduate Institute, an administrator talks openly about how he doesn't see a conflict in their organization because their planning and administrative approaches are not used for accountability—and this may be a problem: "We're still pretty loose, I think we're weak in measurement systems and accountability." The administrator speaks about how the board for the university had become populated with more corporate representatives and that this led to some misunderstandings about academic organization, especially how decisions are made. The leadership admits there is always scarcity of resources, but both the academic and management sides emphasize academic quality first. Another administrator at Fielding speaks about the cultural difference between the academic and corporate world: "I mean academics love to talk about things, and discuss it; they don't actually always get to steps. People in business like to meet and discuss things and then make a decision." One interviewee admits that there is tension around issues such as faculty thinking too much is spent on marketing and not enough on hiring more faculty. Overall an emphasis on marketing and admissions is equated with business. Fielding utilizes strategic planning instruments to give voice to both academic and financial needs in the organization.

For-profits are conscious of this tension between corporate and academic interests and recognize the importance of the issue to external observers. Does the fact that these institutions have a for-profit status alter how they make academic decisions? Administrators feel that both their extensive assessment practices as well as the need to satisfy a demanding market help assure academic quality: "The real measure of how well we're providing what our customers are looking for is our ability to keep that continued enrollment." Additionally, an openness to debating decisions, wide involvement throughout the organization, and reference to their institutional mission all constitute ways that the for-profits manage the tension. Finally, the leadership at for-profits describes collectively held values that are consciously structured to protect against a dominance of business interests over academic quality.

HIERARCHY AND DEBATE

A level organizational structure is one of the things that is constantly referred to by those I interviewed at the for-profits. At the University of Phoenix, John Sperling insists on a policy of open access called "Comments to the Chairman," and if any employee feels his or her voice is being restricted in any way, they just writes him a letter or e-mail, or leaves voice mail. This policy, described often in the interviews, promotes the value of open communication throughout the organization, and decisions based on open communication. The Comments to the Chairman policy is announced and reaffirmed every year, and all employees are expected to have a card with the free speech ethic in their cubicle or in their office. This access to top leadership extends to the president and cabinet:

> [The president] is the most responsive person in the organization. I'll send her an e-mail saying, "We have an idea. . . ." And she'll send me an e-mail within a very short period of time, six hours, three hours, and she'll have itemized: "Here's what you need to do. Here's what I'm going to look at. Here are the outcomes. Go do it and let me know how I can support you."

Sperling understands the importance of gaining wide support for decisions throughout the organization: "The whole organization has to believe, 'Hey, this is a good idea,' or it won't happen. Anytime I've tried to impose an idea it just doesn't work."

At DeVry, administrators characterized the administrative hierarchy as informal and "boundary-less." Managers throughout the organization express an ability to communicate openly about any matter regardless of area of responsibility. Overall, there's a sense that the best way to solve problems is to have the people contributing freely throughout the organization in this boundary-less format.

One general characteristic of the for-profit's process of decision making is encouragement of open discussion of ideas. Both formally and informally the organizations employ a circular feedback system where tentative decisions are vetted and commented on, adjusted, and then updated quickly. While one could argue that traditional universities use this process, its participants are often faculty members, not the organization as a whole. Conversely, the University of Phoenix advocates a question and response system specifically aimed at involving the organization at all levels.

One benefit of the open and broad discussion is that it makes the subsequent implementation easier. I see here an awareness of the need for organizational assimilation to change in University of Phoenix's leadership team.

Representatives at the other for-profits similarly described a need for dialogue and discussion. More generally, at DeVry administrators speak about the advantage of for-profits in decision making because of the lack of political control. Additionally, for-profit institutions can be more responsive to the marketplace by providing the type of programs that are in demand and not limited geographically, and doing things that traditional education couldn't do quickly enough given its governance schemes. Administrators at DeVry speak of a flatter and less formal decision-making process, claiming that almost all of the decisions are made jointly by those representing the organization's business and academic sides. Additionally, there isn't much emphasis placed on either hierarchy or obvious signs of power in the organizational culture.

At the nontraditional institutions like Fielding Graduate Institute, the strategic planning process plays a key role in decision making and thereby serves to make the final decisions more formal, but also more inclusive. Fielding apparently uses this process to reconsider its values, and in so doing evidently inadvertently prompted the resignation of its president:

> In a sense it precipitated the departure of the previous president be-
> cause it was a highly collaborative process across the institution.
> After he saw where the institutional process ended up, he decided
> he didn't want to lead the institution forward. There are many iro-
> nies associated with that. Since we wouldn't have had the vision to
> come to those conclusions without his leadership.

Administrators at Fielding comment that overall this strategic planning process has led to greater involvement by the faculty and created a more active board.

ASSESSMENT

One value that drives decision making at the for-profits is a focus on student needs. Throughout the organization, the University of Phoenix concentrates on a student-centered approach: "They should be devoted to the welfare of the customers and then through that devotion, the company continues to grow and prosper." The university regularly collects data from the students on how to improve both the academic and student services ends of their operation. Assessment is part of the question-and-answer structure at the University of Phoenix because it gives feedback to the decision makers to refine judgments. Not only does the University of Phoenix assess its success at meeting educational objectives by students, but it evaluates every aspect of its operation: "If it moves, we measure it." They measure students not only in the cognitive fields, but also in the affective realm with pre- and postinstruments in their degree program. At the University of Phoenix, they manage through attention to data on customer service and on meeting educational objectives. A primary part of this assessment process is to identify the key criteria that they value, and then measure how well they are meeting that goal. Again, administrators focus very directly on decisions based on specific collective values.

The extensive use of assessment of student learning and program evaluation is also central to the for-profits' decision making. According to the University of Phoenix catalog (University of Phoenix, 2003), the university has two key assessment systems: the Adult Learning Outcomes Assessment (ALOA) and the Academic Quality Management System (AQMS). The university's ALOA system is a comprehensive cognitive and affective assessment system for working adult students, and the AQMS provides adult students with useful information about their current education skills and abilities—both at entrance to their academic program and again at graduation. The University of Phoenix tests specifically for what it calls Professional and Educational Values Assessments (PEVA): the values students place on professional knowledge and skills. All of the skills assessed relate to the university's pedagogical and student service approach including teamwork, preferred learning style, sense of competence, educational goals, professional values, and career success factors. One unique assessment instrument for the University of Phoenix is an employer survey. Since 41 percent of entering students report that they expect to receive tuition reimbursements from their employers, companies are queried to determine the benefits provided to their employees and to their organization by attending University of Phoenix. Furthermore, the University of Phoenix even surveys academic governance and faculty participation.

Active and broad debate is one strategy clearly used in the for-profits' decision making process. For-profits manage such discussion in slightly different ways, particularly in the degree of lessened role faculty members play. While faculty involvement in nonacademic decision-making varies, as a group they do not control the process. Overall, the for-profits promote a flat or boundary-less organizational structure that serves to increase the communication leading to better decision making. The for-profits are particularly strong at using assessment to inform their decision making both in academic and student service areas. Given the flat organization structure, decision making at the University of Phoenix often relies heavily on personal relationships. Given the long history of the individuals in the organization and the generally informal atmosphere, a great deal of the communication takes place in-person. Surprisingly for a company that is a leader in online education, the University of Phoenix relies to a great extent on personal relationships to make decisions: "It's almost all just personal communication." Trust based on positive past behavior within the group seems to be a basis for the communication. There's a general sense that if someone is level-headed, has a good track record, and really cares about making the right decision, one can work with them. This personal approach begins with Sperling, who declares that he never writes memos.

However, given that the University of Phoenix is a distributed organization, extensive use of e-mail is necessary: "John likes to kid me by saying the sun never sets on the Apollo empire or some crud like that. But it really is hard to communicate with people in Rotterdam at the same time as you are communicating with people in Hawaii." Some speak about the struggle to change from a cohesive, informal community to a large distributed one, realizing that they are an awfully big organization to run through informal decision making and personal relationships. Many at the University of Phoenix talk about the increasing difficulty of communicating across a distributed organization that has grown to be so large: "It's certainly more difficult to communicate than it used to be. We knew everybody. And you could get things done just by personality, if nothing else. And that's not true anymore."

CHANGE MANAGEMENT

How does change occur at the for-profits? One of the standard questions I asked was: "If you had to make a major change how would you go about it?" Decision making is perhaps more self-conscious and important at the for-profits because of their preoccupation with change. Change is embraced, valued, and actively pursued by the University of Phoenix. In effect, the university tries to institutionalize change so that employees coming aboard very quickly learns they are in a rapidly changing organization. Administrators claim that the organization has literally been built for change management. They have consciously asked themselves how to best manage change. Their model allows many to be a part of the decision-making process, although they consider carefully who they want to contribute. First, they identify ownership. Who is the champion or owner of a particular change? That owner does a return-on-investment type of analysis. For academic decisions, the initiative next goes through the balancing process of looking at academic and business issues connected to the proposal. This is followed by a process of getting feedback from a broader group, particularly those at the campuses implementing the change: "We have be more conscious about reaching out." Obviously, different types of decisions would be handled differently, but Figure 7.1 roughly illustrates the process at the University of Phoenix moving from the lenses of business, to academic, and then frontline staff.

Once decisions are made, an implementation process begins wherein the specifics are discussed widely and refinements made: "Once we get approval at that high level, we then take it down to what's called an implementation council. . . . Their job is to determine how best to implement. What are the timelines? Do we have to change procedures? How do we build a training program? Do we have to build new external documents, internal forms?" Notice in this quotation how project management has become a concentration in order to see changes through to successful implementation. One sees that main ingredients in the change model are an accepting and supportive culture and effective communication. The large difference in this model from traditional institutions is that the lat-

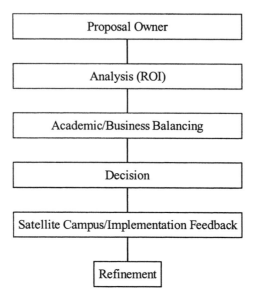

Figure 7.1 UOP Decision-Making Process

ter would either begin with (or consult) the change in academic or faculty bodies. At the University of Phoenix, the ROI and business concerns precede the academic.

The other for-profits also are very conscious of the need to manage change. Both DeVry University and Argosy University have been involved in numerous acquisitions over the past few years that have led to obvious change. Both organizations rely heavily on strategic planning. Interestingly, although the University of Phoenix is certainly very involved in strategic planning, the leadership doesn't refer to this process very often. At DeVry, administrators speak about diversifying in a time of downturn in the high-technology market and introducing a new biomedical program. They speak of "piloting" curricula and developing their distribution channels much as businesses would and talk about "rebranding" DeVry into DeVry University. Leaders at DeVry tell of various loci for change, including the board of directors. There is also a long-range planning process that involves creating a five-year strategic plan, a more focused three-year business plan, and a budget. The five-year plan and the three-year strategic plan get looked at annually again by the board and a group of internal managers they call the long-term planning committee.

DeVry's decision-making procedure is what the leadership describes as "fact based, data based, and research based." The leaders very consciously look at the marketplace and their students as customers. As the marketplace changes, DeVry tries to change in response. For example, the recent Ross University acquisition resulted when strategic planning ascertained that DeVry needed to diversify beyond technology and business. This "perspective" partially responded to the technology downturn as well the identification that biomedics, genetics, and pharmacology were educational growth areas, particularly in an environment with an aging population and increasingly expensive medical care.

Change at the nontraditional nonprofit institutions studied for this book is much slower and more traditionally accommodated. At Fielding Graduate Institute the process resembles a more traditional academic model wherein academic initiatives involve the provost and the Fielding Council, which parallels an academic senate. In addition, change occurs informally through individual discussions behind these formal processes. However, the university has standing meetings and committees where change issues proceed through an established process. Administrators at Fielding admit that their change process has some of the slowness of traditional academia, but is on the whole quicker. The leadership describes the institution overall as "open" and "entrepreneurial." They also say that they are not a hierarchical organization and that if one wants to do something generally one can "go out and make it happen."

Change at Heritage College was illustrated by a major transformation that the school made from being an open admissions institution to creating some minimum admissions requirements. Given Heritage College's mission to provide for underserved populations, this was a very significant adjustment. How did it occur? First, the change began in ways not unlike those found at the for-profits—they collected relevant data. The president drafted a proposal and brought it to her academic affairs counsel where it was very heavily debated, and strong feelings about the change expressed. Then the president gave a presentation to the faculty on how admissions providing for the underserved could still be met with the new policy. Later the policy was brought to other governing groups and nine months later it was approved. Overall, Heritage College has a traditional governance structure with an academic affairs committee comprised of all the full-time faculty. On the other hand, those entities may not be as politicized or polarized, perhaps because of both the small size of the institution and the strong belief in the institutional mission.

ETHICS

What role do ethics play in decision making at the for-profits? Ethical business behavior is something that is preached by John Sperling, who claims that one must have "absolute integrity" throughout the company, leaving no doubt as to how to act properly. This emphasis is undoubtedly coming partly from Sperling's own belief system, as well as a pragmatic understanding of the scrutiny that his company constantly faces. If you run a very controversial company, then you'd better have a solid ethical base: "It doesn't flow from my heart, it flows from my brain." Sperling's self-deprecating comments aside, the organization has become very aware of the legal ramifications of their actions. Sperling's world view suggests to him ethical behavior on the edge of legality in order to be as competitive as others with more power: "I have a concept of whatever is necessary, and I'll skirt as close to the law as I think I can get away with, you have to because the people with power are flagrantly violating the law and every ethical norm known to man. So if you're going to deal with them, you have to be absolutely as implacable as they are." In typically controversial form, Sperling claims that the dog-eat-dog ethics of the marketplace are more truthful than those found in higher education:

> A: Education is filled with half-truths or compromises, God knows what. They go around with halos over their heads and they can do the most awful things in the sense of self-righteousness.
>
> Q: Why do you think that is?
>
> A: Because there's no bottom line.

Tying back here to the notion of value-based decision making, one sees that higher education's lack of a clear bottom line leads to lack of accountability and unethical behavior in Sperling's mind. On a personal level, Sperling claims to respect honesty and plain motivations. Good work for him is clear objectives and straight-forward talk.

CONCLUSION

In summary, the decision-making process at the for-profits is unique in American higher education. In Table 7.1 one sees how traditional and for-profit decision-making processes contrast.

The difference centers on the way the inherent business-academic interests are managed and the reduced role for the faculty in operational decisions. Revealed is a flat organizational structure that encourages

Table 7.1
Traditional vs. For-Profit Decision-Making Process

Traditional	For-Profit
1. Faculty/Administrative Source	1. Proposal Owner
2. Faculty Approval	2. Analysis (ROI)
3. Administrative Approval	3. Academic/Business Balancing
4. Budget	4. Satellite Campus Feedback
5. Decision/Implementation	5. Decision/Implementation

open discussion, the use of data and assessment instruments from all aspects of the organization, and a culture of support for change and growth in the organization are characteristic of decision making at the for-profits. Change is very consciously managed and sought as much as traditional universities actively avoid anything new. On an individual stakeholder level, satisfaction at work is fostered by the perception of the organization's prioritization and how conclusions are arrived at to act in purposeful ways. Administrators express pleasure at the self-actualized ability to get things done. Clearly as the organizations move forward, controlling seemingly unlimited change is a challenge. As one administrator at the University of Phoenix puts it: "We used to just throw things to the wall. What stuck we'd go with. And that was a part of John Sperling's culture of being autonomous. 'Go out there and do it.' To now saying, 'How do we rein some of that in? How do we make our people understand that standardization or best practices—is it a bad thing?'" This chapter concentrated on the overall decision-making process and I found that for-profits tend to position their faculty so that they are less involved and in control. In the next chapter I look at the important issue of faculties in for-profit institutions.

CLIPPINGS

No more lugging around bulky 500-page textbooks. In what may be the next step in education's technological evolution, the University of Phoenix has begun phasing out the standard book. Phoenix, a commercial venture for adult learners and the largest higher education institution in the country, began a program in November in which some 2,000 students have become textbookless. Students get their study material—interactive multimedia programs, articles and electronic books—entirely online. (Rowe, 2002, sec. 4A, p. 7)

The FlexNet degree program combines classroom instruction with the interactive convenience of online study. This program is geared towards those professionals who desire to earn their degree but travel frequently, work rotating shifts, or live too far away to visit the UOP campus each week. "FlexNet courses combine the best of both worlds—on ground and online. Students and faculty come together twice during a six week course and then meet online the remaining four weeks," said Lori Santiago, vice president and director of Oklahoma campuses. ("University of Phoenix Uses Internet," 2001, p. 1)

CHAPTER 8

Faculties

Imagine a respected professor from a traditional school teaching at one of the University of Phoenix's satellite campuses. In the vast open parking lot, he looks up and sees a glass-and-steel building instead of the familiar brick, mortar, and tree-lined walkways. As he enters in the evening to teach his first class, he finds an ethnically diverse, adult group of students waiting for him. The classroom with its comfortable and anonymous Steelcase furniture looks more like a corporate office than the familiar wood-floored classroom with beaten, one-piece desks with the right-handed plank for writing. Before beginning the class, he refers once more to the standardized course materials he was given detailing learning objectives, activities, and assessment instruments from which he created his own syllabus.

However, the biggest difference this traditional faculty member will find is in his role in the overall organization. Instead of attending faculty and senate committee meetings where he participates in crafting institutional direction and addressing issues of concern to peers, managers are chiefly responsible for such operational decisions. While as a faculty member he would be encouraged to contribute in various ways to the design of standardized curriculum and advise on academic issues, the traditional professor would be appalled by the faculty's lack of power at this odd academic institution.

In preparation for writing this book I taught a class for the University of Phoenix. I applied for a teaching position, went through a four-week training program, and taught a six-week graduate online course on adult development and learning theory. This experience has given me a much more textured view of the organization and the altered role faculty play in a for-profit organization. Although I would not want to generalize too much from my own personal experience, I have a few impressions that might be useful in framing the chapter's discussion on for-profit university faculties. The three main differences I experienced in teaching for the University of Phoenix were the training and evaluation of faculty, their overall status or power within the institution, and the altered teaching role and methods.

First, the University of Phoenix is serious about evaluating and training faculty members before they are hired. After the initial application process, which is very similar to that found at other universities, applicants are required to go through an intensive four-week faculty training session. This training serves as a way for the University of Phoenix to evaluate faculty candidates in action while teaching, and provides training on key elements unique to the university including its specific teaching approach, the mission and history of the organization, adult learning theory, as well as specific policies and procedures. In addition, all faculty candidates must successfully complete a six-week paid mentorship in which they prepare and teach a trial course while a mentor works with them. During this mentorship, the candidates must reflect on their teaching, communicate regularly with the mentor, and be evaluated weekly by the mentor and students. All together this training is ten weeks long, and for me amounted to about thirty hours per week of work—easily the most comprehensive faculty training I've ever seen in higher education.

Second, basing its teaching model on adult learning theory (specifically the work of Malcolm Knowles), the University of Phoenix promotes a form of teaching that is more about facilitating learning rather than presenting knowledge. In this model, faculty members give short lectures, but are encouraged to lead discussions, relate course material as often as possible to the personal experience of students, and to use real world experiences and case studies. Additionally, the University of Phoenix's pedagogical model relies on collaborative learning and therefore students are required to complete some assignments in every course in an assigned learning team. While many faculty members in traditional universities may employ part or all of these approaches, generally one does not find this facilitation model employed so systematically and universally.

Third, it has become fashionable for traditional universities to claim that they are "student-centered," but at the University of Phoenix this is real in a way that would be impossible to duplicate in an institution with faculty governance schemes. While faculty members are a valued resource at the University of Phoenix, it is clear that they do not have the power they possess in traditional universities. How is this manifested? Overall, the University of Phoenix seems to position the management so that it becomes almost an advocate for the student in relationship to the faculty member. Combined with the altered pedagogical role, this student-centeredness leads to a palatable overall reduction in the comparative power of the faculty in the university.

The status of faculty members at the for-profit universities is probably the single most controversial aspect of the organization (particularly for faculties from traditional universities). In fact, typically traditional universities only reserve the term "faculty" for those who are on a tenure track—all others are simply "lecturers." Faculties at traditional universities often see the University of Phoenix as a symbol of the worst sort of exploitation of higher education professionals through its practices of almost exclusively using part-time faculty without tenure, insistence on practitioners with real world experience rather than research scholars, and giving them comparatively little power within the organizational governance scheme.

In reality, for-profit institutions have a variety of ways of structuring the role of teaching professionals from the use of primarily full-time faculty with long-term tenurelike contracts to course-by-course contracts with part-time instructors only. The part-timers who make up the large majority of the faculty at some of the for-profits are also often the same faculty teaching at traditional two- and four-year universities; the rise of the University of Phoenix in particular has coincided with the increased practice for the past three decades of using part-time faculty in traditional higher education. From a traditional faculty point-of-view, the motivation for using part-time professors is to reduce expenses, and the result is lowered academic quality.

There are some crucial differences in the use of faculty at for-profits that are central to the way these organizations run. First, the use of part-time practitioner faculty is in line with the overall mission and strategies of many of the for-profits, especially the University of Phoenix, with its emphasis on adult learners, professional programs, and the use of standardized curriculum. Second, the for-profits often have specific processes and resources in place to assist part-time faculty. Third, since there are no tenured faculty members there is not the hierarchy common to many traditional institutions. Fourth, a conscious attempt is made at the for-profits to involve faculty in administrative decisions, course and program development, and the overall values and culture of the organization. In this chapter we will learn how faculty members are positioned within the for-profit universities, explore their attitudes toward the organization, and see practices that might be useful to traditional institutions.

NONTENURE AND LACK OF HIERARCHY

While some have long-term teaching contracts, most for-profit institutions do not have a traditional tenure system—indeed, this is one of their defining characteristics. The University of Phoenix is a case in point. As a result, one of the university's distinguishing characteristics is that it has a flatter academic hierarchy. Nevertheless, there is a classification system based on number of courses taught and other contributions to the university through administrative leadership roles. The recent change referenced earlier at the University of Phoenix toward a greater number of full-time faculty may mean a slight shift toward more shared governance in decisions affecting academic practices. It is probably fair to say that most part-time faculty at traditional universities feel a pretty limited sense of loyalty toward the institution. This would tend to be the case because part-time faculty members are often professional teachers working at multiple institutions out of necessity. These "freeway fliers," as they are commonly known, are unlikely to feel much investment in any one of the particular institutions where they teach. However, one comment heard repeatedly in the interviews was that part-time faculty at the University of Phoenix are treated much better than at traditional institutions. This is largely a result of the absence of tenure system and the flattened hierarchy. An administrator talks about the difference: "At your institution, they're the bottom of the food chain. They only get to teach in times and places when the 'real' professors don't want to. They have no voice. What do you expect? You don't have any loyalty to them. Why should they have any loyalty to you? At our institution, they are the faculty." One administrator speaks about how part-time faculty members have an opportunity to make a very large impact through helping to design and revise standardized course materials, as discussed earlier: "They have the opportunity to affect hundreds and thousands." One might wonder about how cohesive this large group of full-time faculty are as a group. While this solidity seemed to vary from place to place, interview subjects did relate stories indicating a sense of community among the faculty formed during quarterly meetings for specific subject areas.

In place of tenure, some for-profits use long-term faculty contracts. At Argosy University, faculty members are on extended contracts and are described as having a great deal of input into the direction of the curriculum. The campus executive committee, with faculty representation, decides the direction for the campus, and there's also an annual faculty meeting where faculty have direct input into the process. Every faculty member has a yearly review, during the summer, and they are provided financial support for their continuing education and to present at conferences. As with the University of Phoenix, administrators point out that at Argosy there is more immediate feedback for faculty members: "I think that people know where they stand and what is expected of them." The other way that teaching at Argosy is different is in requiring faculty to bring professional and real world experience into the classroom, as practitioners.

The merger of Keller Graduate Institute and DeVry generated a mix of approaches to the use of faculty. At DeVry University, only about 5 percent of the faculty at the graduate level are full-time, but at the undergraduate level they have about 75 percent full-time faculty. There are a few full-time faculty at the graduate level who have administrative responsibilities, but primarily they only teach. At the undergraduate level all of the faculty have some administrative responsibility in addition to their teaching. There are many traditional advantages for the full-time faculty such as sabbatical, personal development, and personal renewal leave programs. As with the University of Phoenix, DeVry prefers that part-time faculty be employed somewhere else full-time in order to bring the value of their real-world experience into the classroom, particularly for the professional and technical programs. DeVry, like the University of Phoenix, prides itself on training faculty members to teach: "We really do believe in excellence in teaching." While they involve faculty in decision-making processes, DeVry administrators insist that such processes be quick and productive.

How invested and loyal are the faculty at for-profits given their somewhat diminished role within the organizations? At DeVry University, much of the work with faculty is done at the local centers through professional development and regular assessment activities. As with the University of Phoenix, faculty members at DeVry have the opportunity for involvement in curriculum development. They seek to hire faculty who want to teach, and do not have a research requirement for them: "It's not research for self-aggrandizement, it's not community service, it's not some abstract way that they meet their job requirement. They teach." Like the University of Phoenix, DeVry is aggressively student-centered: "The basic structure of what we do is focused on teaching our students. People who have a problem with that don't come here." Additionally, administrators say that they go against the usual notion of academic freedom by wanting to offer the same DeVry University degree at twenty-five large campuses and forty-one small teaching centers through standardization: "We want a student who gets a degree at our Fremont, California center to get essentially the same education as someone who attends the North Brunswick, New Jersey campus." Faculty members are free to make their own assignments, choose textbooks, do what they want within the framework of the course, but the structure of the course is established with terminal learning objectives that fit the preceding and successive courses: "For example a faculty member teaching the initial financial accounting course, if he happens to have a research interest in, let's say, cash management—no. You may be able to develop a course in cash management, but probably not. You need to teach this financial management and control class and do your research outside of the class." Course learning objectives are developed with central direction. Then the course outline gets sent out to the faculty at different locations, and the actual content is developed. The course is faculty developed, but centrally directed. An administrator at DeVry notes about the course development process: "Probably most traditional faculty would find that to be an unacceptable intrusion into their prerogatives."

At the nontraditional institutions studied for this book, the role of faculty members much more closely resembles that at traditional institutions. At Fielding Graduate Institute, an administrator comments on this fact: "For a dispersed institution that began as a kind of counterculture institution the role of the faculty has evolved now to be much more like a faculty member at a traditional institution—for better or worse." The faculty members at Fielding have a good deal of autonomy, partly because they live and work at a distance from campus. They have commitments to what are called "cluster meetings" of students, as well as regional meetings, national sessions twice a year, faculty retreats, and conference calls with their various governance teams. Fielding has a governance structure where every faculty member is part of some faculty committee: "In our structure I'd say our faculty are more responsible for the learning than at most traditional institutions." They do all the curriculum development, identify all the learning outcomes, and are responsible for the doctoral dissertations. Fielding is close to the for-profits in emphasizing student-centeredness and accountability for the faculty members. Overall, administrators at Fielding report that their faculty members are more concerned with service to students than at traditional universities: "We hold the faculty much more accountable for faculty service." As an institution founded to some extent on adult learning theory Fielding is particularly aware of the altered role of faculty in teaching: "We have endless arguments about do we teach or do we facilitate." The newer faculty aren't so quick to embrace this adult education philosophy, believing that there needs to be some teaching with the facilitation.

PRACTITIONER

A fundamental distinction from traditional institutions is the for-profit's reliance on what they call "practitioner faculty" who are not full-time teachers, but are instead working in the field in which they are teaching. Of course, this model is not new to traditional higher education that has for years relied on practitioner faculty in staffing professional schools and continuing education divisions. However, a few distinctions need to be made. First, practitioner faculty only make up part of the teaching staff at traditional institutions and are not nearly as pervasive as they are at the for-profits. Second, the use of practitioner faculty is built into the curriculum design at for-profits that heavily depend on both the instructor and students relating the course material to their own real work experiences. Third, practitioner faculty in the professional schools of traditional institutions have conventional governance schemes and employment status including tenure.

An administrator at the University of Phoenix describes the thinking behind the use of practitioner faculty: "An adult who goes back to school doesn't want to learn about business from somebody who has never been in business. They want to know that this person really understands how theories work in the real world." Given the heavy reliance on applied business-related courses of study, it is hardly surprising that many of the part-time faculty members come from the corporate world. The faculty members who do best in the organization are those who bring a mixture of an academic background and a practical business background. The use of practitioner faculty closely links to the institutional mission of serving working adults, who are more likely to appreciate faculty members with relevant personal experience in a field rather than those with abstract research knowledge. As opposed to more traditional schools of thought in universities that often are suspicious of personal, applied sources of knowledge, faculty qualified in this way are sought at the for-profits. This kind of hybrid faculty member is especially well suited to the University of Phoenix. One clearly problematic area for the for-profits is in how to apply a practitioner model to general education courses. As the following respondent explains, the University of Phoenix needs to offer humanities courses in order to allow students to complete their degrees. However, this use of more traditional academics stretches their practitioner model:

"What constitutes a practitioner in the humanities is a different creature from what constitutes a practitioner of business."

Nontraditional nonprofit institutions serving adult students also tend to emphasize practitioner faculty members. At the nontraditional institutions studied for this book, there is a scholar-practitioner emphasis for both the faculty and the students. At Fielding Graduate Institute, many students come into the program and are professionals already, but haven't had time to reflect on their practice. The university's educational program lets both the faculty and the students fill in the missing parts of their background, whether it is research in a particular area or additional practice in another.

CURRICULUM MODULES

For-profit universities often use standardized curricula in order to both maintain a level of consistent education and take advantage of economies of scale. Indeed, the pedagogical approach that the for-profits take in the extensive use of part-time faculty and the multiple campus organization is dependent on the use of standardized course materials. These "curriculum modules," as they are called at the University of Phoenix, are course materials developed by teams of faculty and content experts over a period of time.

Administrators at the University of Phoenix agree that the modules provide standardization and a baseline level of quality. However, individual faculty members are expected to enhance the materials and individualize them to the specific group of students they are teaching: "We expect that they're going to give real-life examples as a part of that, or talk to them about some real opportunities." During the annual summer meeting at the University of Phoenix referenced in the preface to this book, faculty members revise the curriculum modules. The academic teams divide up by their areas of expertise and conduct curriculum reviews. From this meeting they create their master schedule. The deans listen to all of the ideas at this annual meeting, make lists prioritizing and assigning people responsible for working for it, and at the end of that two- or three-day process leave knowing exactly what they're going to accomplish in the way of curricular enhancements. Those interviewed at the University of Phoenix claim that administrators are very good about listening to what's going on in their professional fields. They ask key questions about the curriculum on what to include and how to meet the needs of students.

Critics of the university point to these materials as a further diminution of the faculty. However, one University of Phoenix faculty member talks about how he is given standards and then within a loose framework can make alterations as he sees fit. An often-repeated phrase at the University of Phoenix is that the standardized course materials give faculty members more "freedom" by relieving them of the burden of preparing these materials and can instead focus on student needs:

> We'll give a series of activities that you can do to accomplish this, but you don't have to do those. You can do your own if you happen to have your own. Or if you're looking for ideas or you need a little imagination boost, you can go into the list of activities and ways to approach this. Then, depending on the size of the group you're teaching, you may do it one way versus another based on group size.

In response to a question about how faculty personalize and change the standardized materials, a faculty member at the University of Phoenix emphasizes the need to leave learning outcomes unchanged:

> You don't change from the outcomes. We still need to achieve the certain outcomes that are specified within the module. And the students hold the faculty accountable. "We are going to learn these ten things in this accounting course and, by golly, we're going to learn it." And they'll talk to you about it if they don't learn it, if the faculty member skips something or doesn't manage their time to cover all of those ten. But if, while you're at it, you have something else that you'd like to bring in or a particular area you would like to demonstrate, that is absolutely encouraged.

Standardized course materials provide a level of consistency and quality control necessary in a geographically dispersed organization so heavily dependent on part-time faculty.

In designing its standardized course materials, DeVry University, like the University of Phoenix, begins with assessing the broader environment, the economy, and overall educational market. This assessment is necessary because DeVry does not receive funding to develop new programs from the government or private donations. Typically, it looks where there is great growth in the foreseeable future—for example, in medical devices, drug development, and healthcare delivery areas. According to DeVry administrators, they ask themselves, first, "Which fields are extensions of our mission?"; and second, "Which are growth areas with the likelihood of good jobs for graduates?" Recently, biomedical engineering was identified as one such area for DeVry. Administrators conduct traditional market research, use focus groups, and call in professionals from the field, analyzing what they call a breakdown of "knowledge, skills, and abilities" that anyone in that profession would require. They try to concentrate on the skills and competencies that graduates will need and then divide the content into four- and five-hour courses, and an eight- or nine-semester program. Then for each course they write a curricular guide including the catalog description of the course, the terminal course objectives, a sample syllabus, an example lesson plan, exam items, a recommended textbook, and alternative textbooks. As with the University of Phoenix curriculum modules, DeVry creates what the faculty members will need to teach that course. Like the University of Phoenix, DeVry doesn't give the entire course to the faculty member, only a guide. Administrators at DeVry University describe the difference in the role of their faculty as focused more on teaching. Expectations for their faculty are fourfold: teaching, professional development (of which research could be a piece), program involvement (they want faculty to be involved in curriculum building), and service or miscellaneous duties.

Overall, the standardized course materials used at for-profits are often much less proscriptive than one would imagine. While faculty members are given a twenty-page syllabus containing learning objectives, sample assignments, an assigned text, and readings, all the lectures as well as a specific syllabus for the course need to be created by the faculty member (it is interesting to note here that the University of Phoenix is now moving to standardized lectures for the online courses). In reality, the course materials are not that much different from a detailed syllabus used at a traditional university. The difference is that the course materials are more consistently systematic and thorough than one is likely to find at a traditional university, where individual faculty members are often given a great deal of latitude in not only teaching the courses, but also documenting what they teach.

RECRUITMENT AND TRAINING

The type of faculty hired and the training they receive are key aspects of the for-profits. Because of a need to recruit faculty at a volume far higher than that for traditional universities, the University of Phoenix understands the importance of continually finding and placing faculty members. Unlike traditional institutions that have a base of full-time permanent faculty to draw upon, the University of Phoenix almost completely depends on the use of part-time faculty who are hired on a course-by-course basis. Many of the over 10,000 faculty members come from referrals, approximately 85 percent by one account. In fact, faculty are clearly one of the "audiences" for the University of Phoenix, as one can see when looking at its Web site, which profiles users as either potential "students," "faculty," or "corporate clients."

Once identified as potential faculty material, proper screening and training are emphasized. While many traditional universities have a process for faculty orientation, required presentations for evaluation, and other ways of judging and training new faculty, few are as systematic and thorough as the University of Phoenix's. The four-week training program consists of hands-on practice using the university's teaching methods and technology tools. Most important, the university spends a great deal of time on teaching candidates adult learning theory and the history, mission, and approach to learning espoused by the University of Phoenix. Of course, the training program also serves as a way for the university to screen candidates by seeing their teaching in action.

The mentorship is a formal process whereby a candidate is assisted closely in the first course taught. Two weeks before the course starts, the mentor works with the candidate in crafting lectures and discussion questions, and revising the course syllabus (built from a standardized model). During the course, the mentor closely watches the candidate teach the course, gives regular feedback, and answers any questions that might arise. The first course a faculty member teaches is part of the training and is much more labor intensive than teaching a course later on. The faculty candidate is responsible for completely documenting what he or she does in the classroom, as well as reflecting daily on the teaching experience. This all then becomes part of the permanent faculty member record.

The university does use some full-time faculty, and in fact during the interview period in 2001 was involved in restructuring this system by creating campus college or curriculum chairs that had both teaching and administrative responsibilities. There were at the time about 250 spread throughout the system. Every University of Phoenix academic program now has an Academic Program Council, composed of a dean or an associate dean and an equal number of full-time and practitioner faculty members. Reportedly, that group has total responsibility for a specific curriculum, although it might bring in people from the outside or from administration to advise them. Additionally, there are deans for each subject area.

So one sees that recruitment is particularly important for the for-profits because of the reliance on part-time practitioner faculty. Compensation at the for-profits is often lower than at traditional universities, and faculty have less prestige—both factors some candidates would consider.

ANDRAGOGY

The for-profit and nontraditional universities often apply adult learning theory in designing their teaching approaches. Using Malcolm Knowles notion of "andragogy" to distinguish adult from child learning (pedagogy), faculty are often schooled in adult learning theory that emphasizes self-directed learning and facilitation rather than lecturing. The University of Phoenix's stated approach to teaching is based on various adult learning theory models. According to the university's catalog, the student population of working adults dictates a teaching-learning model grounded in the research on adult learning and cognitive psychology. Their stated approach involves "active learning," "collaboration," and "emphasis on application and relevance." Furthermore, the university focuses on practical psychological and sociological issues in connection with learning with the understanding that adult learners have specific barriers to pursuing and completing a degree.

The active learning model assumes that the student's vigorous involvement in the learning process is necessary for learning. Both classroom and instruction are designed to encourage engagement and participation. Faculty members are repositioned as facilitators of learning, and students are expected to become engaged in learning. Collaboration structures that facilitate teamwork are central to the university's pedagogical model. The model uses the work experience of adult students to enhance learning with the stated emphasis on building "bridges" between new knowledge and learner experience. The students' experiences and current jobs are interwoven with subject matter in class discussions and learning team assignments.

The sociological and psychological aspects of its pedagogical approach involve the universitywide learning goals of professional competence and values accomplished through a standardized curriculum with clear learning objectives, convenient times and places for courses, student services geared toward adults, intensive five-week terms, learning teams, and practitioner faculty. The following are the university's stated general education goals:

- To refine students' abilities to apply problem-solving skills in many settings and contexts.
- To promote students' active awareness of their relationships to the natural, social, and cultural environments.
- To develop students' appreciation for and commitment to lifelong learning.

- To prepare students with competencies needed to fully benefit from and successfully complete their professional programs of study. (University of Phoenix, 2003, p. 1)

As part of the university's validation of adult work experience, it gives credit for prior learning. Based on the Council for Adult and Experiential Learning (CAEL) guidelines, the university's assessment process has been a model other colleges and universities have adopted for assessing prior learning. The other for-profits also refer to adult learning principles in their teaching approach, particularly in their graduate programs. The nontraditional Fielding Graduate Institute is perhaps one of the institutions with a curricular and teaching approach that is most directly based on adult learning theory.

As at most traditional higher education institutions, faculty members at the University of Phoenix also comment on the depressing lack of appropriate student preparation. A faculty member who teaches composition and communication courses notes: "There is hardly a student that doesn't benefit from the enhanced writing skills and the frequency of it. Students become very proficient at writing if they really pay attention to all the opportunities we give them to do that." More than for traditional institutions, this issue of poor student preparation is a significant problem because of the necessary sensitivity to appearances of exploitation of students lacking the skills and background to be successful in pursuing degrees. In my own brief experience with teaching for the university, I found students who were very good writers, mixed with a few students who were alarmingly underprepared. Having worked at other institutions with similar problems, I don't know that the University of Phoenix has an especially underprepared student population. Nevertheless, faculty members interviewed at the University of Phoenix do point to the writing skills issue as a chronic problem.

CONCLUSION

Traditional universities often see the for-profits, particularly the University of Phoenix, as symbols of faculty exploitation at the hands of administrators motivated by a desire to reduce instructional costs. However, the use of part-time practitioner faculty is in line with the working adult mission of the University of Phoenix and it has specific processes and resources in place to assist the development of qualified part-time faculty. Additionally, the flat hierarchy of the faculty as a group and the conscious attempt at the University of Phoenix to invest them in the organization seem to have a positive influence on the organization. Traditional institutions might learn from University of Phoenix's recruitment, training, and governance schemes, particularly in designing professional programs aimed at adults. There is no doubt in my mind that the for-profits are better at training, recruiting, and effectively utilizing part-time faculty than are most traditional institutions. At the same time, the faculty might be the weakest link at the for-profits. In terms of academic qualifications and teaching experience, the for-profits cannot compete with top traditional universities. The for-profits compensate for this gap to a large degree by disaggregating the traditional faculty functions, assigning primarily facilitating and grading duties to faculty.

In the next chapter I turn to the challenges that for-profits face and hear from the leaders of these organizations as they look to the future of higher education and their possible role.

CLIPPINGS

Some academic critics complain that Phoenix Online has stripped faculty members of their central role in higher education and replaced them with instructional-design consultants. Phoenix counters that professors at traditional universities who attempt online education are learning as they go, and often give students a bad experience as a result. (Olsen, 2002, p. 29)

Why 3 Liberal-Arts Scholars Moved from Traditional Academe to For-Profit Institutions

Who makes up this small band—just 300 of Phoenix's 10,000 instructors teach general studies—of full-time faculty members who teach the humanities to students in the business- and technology-driven world of for-profit higher education? Are they tenure rejects? Academics who didn't fit in with a traditional collegiate culture? Or are they people who want to teach, rather than bother with research, publishing, and administrative tasks that their brethren at traditional institutions face? These less visible yet necessary professors don't have the security of tenure. Instead, they work, as do many in the corporate world, without contracts or the protection of unions. A look into the lives of three who teach those fundamentals reveals that each has his or her own reasons for leaving conventional institutions. They make less money than their colleagues at top-flight research universities—the average full-time faculty member at DeVry Inc. makes $55,000—and don't get tenure, but the pressures to publish are gone, as are the bureaucratic entanglements. And while they can no longer lay claim to the leafy-green lawns or intellectual fervor of academe, the practical, businesslike culture of these nontraditional institutions works for them. (Borrego, 2002, p. 10)

So What Are You Good At?

Higher education has good brand names and does well at research but is no good at anything else, Alan Nelson, managing director of online learning resource provider Nelson Croom, told delegates at "The future of higher education: profits, partnerships and the public good." He said: "What are universities good at? Teaching? From my experience, that involved mumbling in cold buildings. Syllabus design? Three weeks on a topic that happened to be the PhD subject of the lecturer. Are you good at resource management? Are you good at coaching and mentoring? I remember a note on the door saying the lecturer was available on Wednesday mornings between 10 and 11 o'clock." (Goddard, 2002, p. 11)

Letters to the Editor: People Who Teach at For-Profit Institutions

My research on the faculty role and academic culture at for-profit institutions of higher education echoes the statements of the three faculty members interviewed for your article ("Trading Ivy for an Office Park," February 22). They are devoted to teaching, enthusiastic about their students, critical of the traditional university, and supportive of the goals of their employers. Academic freedom is not an issue, and the fact that they work in a for-profit environment seems to have no discernible impact on their teaching. They are not strikingly different from those who teach at traditional colleges and universities. . . . It is no secret that dedicated, hard-working faculty members who care about teaching can be frustrated by the mixed messages and conflicting roles inherent in the modern university. ("Letters to the Editor," 2002, p. 17)

Tech Talk: Tested Practices Buoy University of Phoenix Online

A big part of the model is to teach students in very small groups. On our campuses, we average about 15 students in a class. Online, we average between 10 and 11, but we don't ever let it go over 13. So the small group environment is number one. Number two, it's a completely instructor-led process. The instructor is as much an integral part in the process in an online environment as the instructor is in a classroom environment. A lot of institutions try to take the instructor's role and try to reduce it, and let media drive more of the learning. We never took that approach. (Roach, 2002, p. 54)

CHAPTER 9

Challenges for the For-Profits

While on many levels the for-profits are enormously successful institutions (particularly financially), they also face many challenges. In fact, over their history there are few types of higher education institutions that have been besieged so often by accrediting agencies and attacked by colleagues in traditional institutions. Since going public on the New York Stock Exchange, many of the for-profits are now additionally under the scrutiny of business watchdogs and stockholders. Perhaps the most relentless critics of these organizations are those on the inside, where a culture of continual improvement and restlessness rewards and encourages self-criticism. Additionally, many traditional universities have begun to use some of the for-profit methods through their extension divisions and are focusing their whole operation more on the growing population of adult learners. The for-profits in some ways are being hurt by their own success, which has made others mimic them while at the same time criticizing them mercilessly. Finally, the for-profits are both susceptible to some of the chronic problems that face higher education, and have unique challenges as a result of their nontraditional approaches to higher education. One of their most difficult problems is combating a poor academic reputation. In this chapter I examine both the self-reported challenges for the for-profit universities, as well my reflections on their weaknesses (see Table 9.1).

Table 9.1
Challenges at For-Profits

Challenge	Directions
Controlling growth	Assessment and standardization
Continue innovating	Rewards system and risk-taking
Acquiring new talent	Groom from inside and recruit
Student recruitment	More traditional academic model
Improve academic reputation	A struggle
Recruitment of faculty	A struggle
General education	A struggle

ORGANIZED GROWTH

Growth and constant change are hallmarks of the for-profit organization. One can only be amazed by the exceptional growth of the University of Phoenix, particularly in recent years. With the stated goal of reaching half a million students worldwide in the next few years, the challenge of maintaining the organization during extreme expansion is clear. Faculty members and administrators commented repeatedly on working hard as an organization to understand their own growth patterns and how to operate efficiently with an increasingly distributed organization, a new staff, and an evolving culture. One needs to appreciate this culture of growth at the University of Phoenix, which is more similar to the attitude of a business than that of a traditional university. Growth at the University of Phoenix is a given and thoughts of limiting or slowing growth are dismissed: "That's a taboo." With a ban on limiting growth and an annual rate of 30 percent, maintaining control is a major concern at the University of Phoenix and at some of the other for-profits.

A clear problem inherent in rapid growth is scalability. One administrator speaks about the constant need to understand how changes and new programs can be disseminated throughout such a large organization: "The thing we are constantly struggling with is scalability. Any process that I put in place now or any structure I put in place now may not serve us four years from now. Because we will be twice as big if the current growth work continues. So we have structurally tried to foster some individual campus local autonomy, but within some parameters." Consider here the University of Phoenix problem in comparison to some of the large public university systems in America where typically curricular and other key academic and administrative aspects of the organization are largely decentralized under the control of the local academics. Traditional institutions usually emphasize local academic control and individuation, whereas the University of Phoenix appreciates in business terms the value of economies of scale in reducing expenses. It has an aggressive growth plan to extend itself in three ways: through continued geographic expansion, through expansion of areas that are emerging or where there is an underserved population, and through increased online activity.

Scalability and controlled growth are particularly interesting to look at in the distance learning division at the University of Phoenix because of the natural advantages present in this format. A top administrator for the online unit describes the problem of facing extreme growth and maintaining quality. In addition, he focuses on the challenge of effectively integrating the face-to-face with the online programs. The administrator poses the questions: "Is the online division just another campus or are they really different? Can you maintain quality with extreme growth in distance learning?" The online unit faces two problems in growth: internal competition and questions of quality.

Many faculty members and administrators with long experience at the University of Phoenix comment on the growing pains associated with moving from a small to a large scale. An interview subject describes the challenge as retaining some of the characteristics of a smaller organization when making the transition to a very large one, particularly in their focus on customer or student service:

> Part of what has made the University of Phoenix so great for working adults is that we've tried not to become a huge bureaucracy. Yes, we keep the classroom intimate. But there are a lot of other things that happen. The students have to buy books, and they have issues that they need to deal with the administration on. If we become bureaucratic, then we're no different than State U down the street with their huge bureaucracy.

"Grow or die" is a phrase heard repeatedly at the University of Phoenix. However, how does an institution expand with high quality products and services? How does it manage yet another important tension in the organization? The for-profits use assessment and the collection of data about quality, very much reminiscent of the popular Total Quality Management (TQM) business systems approach from the 1980s and 1990s. "The way we manage that tension is to be as performance oriented and as quantitative and hold people responsible for those quantitative performance measurements as we can." Every course has a faculty profile that the dean who is responsible for that program must observe. Repeatedly,

administrators claim that their growth will not occur by easing enrollment
limits or putting unapproved faculty members into the classroom. Administrators talk about how the demand to grow needs to be countered by
strict performance assessments. A clear strategy for the university is to
create objectives and standards for performance and then hold staff and
managers to these expectations. This is a business-style approach to expansion. Performance assessment during a time of expansion is even
extended to academic issues, including holding the line to desired faculty
qualifications.

A challenge confronting the University of Phoenix is managing extreme and continual growth. Administrators express awareness of the
problem and look for ways to control and organize growth through performance standards, both administrative and academic. Nevertheless,
academic quality and organizational effectiveness is likely to be difficult
to maintain and improve with resources directed toward growth. Traditional higher education institutions would find this challenge to grow
quickly and maintain quality particularly challenging. However, with a
separation of administrative and academic management of the organization, the University of Phoenix has an advantage in growing quickly while
maintaining its same level of quality across the organization.

BRINGING IN NEW TALENT

One comment heard repeatedly in the interviews is that the for-profits have a history of promoting staff from within the administrative ranks.
An administrator speaks about a mentoring program to help develop the
skills of current staff:

> I think what we believe might someday be our Achilles heel is not
> having enough personnel strength, and if we can groom it within,
> we absolutely are going to do that. Absolutely. A couple years ago
> we started an executive development program where we select 25–
> 30 individuals throughout the company, corporate and campus alike,
> and we ask the question, "Who are our aspiring and capable lead-
> ers?"

While the policy of promoting from within has served the university well
for years and has increased organizational loyalty, it has also been a limitation. With a much larger and complex company, new competencies
need to be acquired: "I think we need to bring people into positions who
don't have that kind of history, who will shake things up and challenge

us." A challenge to the for-profits generally that many respondents commented upon is the fear that they are becoming too mainstream and increasingly unwilling to take chances and innovate: "We could come to a screeching halt, too, because we've reached the limits of this culture moving out, because it really is a view, a culture, a philosophy."

One respondent speaks about how the institution needs to form partnerships with outside organizations, particularly corporations, in order to continue to bring in new talent and innovate: "I don't think the university believes that within our walls we have all the answers." For-profits have a history of seeking out and forming strategic partnerships, and believe very strongly that it's critical to bring the right partners to a table to address challenges and solutions. The partnerships range from traditional academic institutions to nontraditional academics, corporate leaders, and community leaders. The University of Phoenix is particularly dedicated to forming partnerships of various kinds with corporations: "We were one of the first institutions that said, 'How can you build a bachelor of science in business degree without talking to employers?'" We see here that while administrators at the University of Phoenix are concerned about stagnation, they feel they have a competitive advantage over traditional institutions sometimes hesitant to turn outside for advice and a new perspective.

ADDITIONAL CHALLENGES

The self-reported challenges for the University of Phoenix revolve around controlling extraordinary growth in a complex organization dispersed across great geographical distances (now international), meeting the challenge of continual innovation, grooming and hiring new talent to lead and manage the organization, and fending off competitors adopting similar strategies. These issues arose repeatedly in the interviews with the faculty members and staff in new proposals and measures evidenced as demonstrated effort to effectively confront these challenges. To an external observer, these same challenges of growth and renewal are clear.

There exist additional challenges that for-profit administrators did not mention directly, but that surface in conversation, observation, and a reading of the institution's background information. These challenges include: improving academic reputation, recruiting high-quality faculty, positioning of student recruiters, and offering general education courses. Probably the largest issue for the for-profits is the need to increase their academic reputation. Administrators at for-profits realize that their "brand" is their weakest attribute and a potential long-term problem. Additionally, they know that academic reputations change slowly and that their battles with traditional institutions do not help. As a result, they are actively struggling with this issue. Generally, academic reputation is judged by faculty qualifications, research, and student qualifications—all measures where the for-profits fair poorly.

The other two areas of most serious struggle are in how to provide general education courses when they have a focus on business-related disciplines, and how to attract an increasingly large number of qualified faculty. Both of these challenges are tied to the academic reputation issue because they depend on faculty with strong traditional value (research, degree pedigree) that is not valued in for-profit models. For the most part, practitioner faculty models do not work well in general education.

As an institution heavily involved in technology skills training and education, DeVry was especially hard hit by the dot.com fallout and recession. As a result, it has emphasized diversification and the broadening of its curricula, and distribution through new campus locations, as well as through the Internet. It is very aware of increasing competition from both for-profit and traditional higher education institutions. It focuses on effective marketing and defining its own uniqueness within the marketplace as ways of meeting these challenges.

Argosy representatives focused on continuing challenges of the changing demographics, as well as making sure the curriculum and faculty are appropriate to meet student needs. Technology and the use of distance learning are leading to changes in the institutional and academic culture at Argosy, just as it is at traditional institutions. Cost is a primary concern and problem. Administrators within for-profits wonder how higher education is going to be funded just as traditional institutions are pressed by the pattern of eroding support.

For the nontraditional institutions such as the Fielding Graduate Institute, the main challenges are to somehow become less tuition dependent. Although Fielding began as a deliberately tuition-dependent institution, it now sees the need for additional support. One administrator characterizes this change:

> The founders' philosophy was that they didn't want to be beholden to soft money because you end up being very uncertain from one year to the next as to what is available. They were even more student-centered than we are today, in the sense that they wanted the students to vote every day, so to speak, with their pocketbook. If students weren't getting what they wanted, then we weren't doing

our job. But everyone is interested in keep improving services, and it is clear that we need more than fees.

CHALLENGES FROM TRADITIONAL INSTITUTIONS

The biggest challenge posed for for-profits seems to be the fear expressed that traditional universities are adopting in various forms for-profit methods: "I think the major emerging challenge is that we have had about twenty-five years with relatively no meaningful competition in the sense that nobody was able to put it altogether. People are starting to put it together now." The very visible success of institutions such as the University of Phoenix has led traditional institutions to look more closely at for-profit methods. In reality, very little of what the for-profits do hasn't been done in some way by traditional institutions. The use of distributed campus structures, intensive formats, distance learning, and programs aimed specifically at adult learners and corporate clients are not new to traditional higher education. Additionally, corporate management approaches to higher education administration and altered roles for faculty in governance, teaching method, and employment status have all been practiced before in traditional higher education. Extension and continuing education divisions within universities, as well as specific programs often connected to professional programs such as business departments within the university, have regularly used many of the same methods found at the for-profits. For-profits risk the ramping up of these methods, not their introduction in traditional universities.

As indicated in Chapter 2, enlarged competition is a general complaint in higher education today. In this increasingly pressurized environment, the for-profits can expect traditional universities to push back at them by using similar methods. Particularly for the small "at-risk" institutions described earlier (small in enrollment and endowment), they must attempt to be more entrepreneurial. Even at the nontraditional institutions such as Heritage College and the Fielding Graduate Institute that have very unique positions in the higher education market, and very clear identities, they feel competitive pressure. Administrators at Fielding note increased competition and the need for the institution to react more quickly than ever. Although in the past they have done very little marketing at all, they point to the importance of effective marketing and public relations. In part this is a response to the rise of for-profit institutions competing for the same students. As one administrator states: "More and more corporations, conglomerates are getting in on the act. And they have more money."

CONCLUSION

In this chapter indications are that for-profit institutions themselves face serious challenges including fighting a poor academic reputation, maintaining quality and control during times of rapid growth, and nurturing and recruiting talented employees.

I began the book examining the facts about for-profits, or the questions about who, where, and when. The middle of this book focused on the specific methods used in for-profits with a particular concentration on what might be gleamed for use by traditional institutions. This might be described as the "how" section. In the next chapter, I will try to make sense of what has been presented in this book in order to understand the question: Why for-profits in higher education? It is hoped that the concluding chapter will help us glimpse what the future holds for for-profit higher education and what those in leadership positions in higher education in America should do.

CLIPPINGS

A Gathering Storm in Higher Education?

Others feared the convergence of growing competition and shrinking public funding. A chief concern was that competitors would pick off the parts of higher education most likely to make money (or cheapest to provide) and leave traditional institutions with no way to fund socially valuable but financially unsustainable programs. (Think FedEx and the post office.) (Seebach, 2002, p. 27)

COMPANY THAT OWNS THE U. OF PHOENIX PLANS FOR A MAJOR FOREIGN EXPANSION EVEN AS IT CONTINUES to expand into new territory across the United States, the company that operates the University of Phoenix is laying plans for a string of campuses around the world. Company officials say their goal is to develop, acquire, or create partnerships with institutions in Brazil, China, India, Mexico, and several unnamed countries in Latin America and Europe. (Blumenstyk, 2000b, p. A44)

A Scholastic Gold Mine

While Reid, the police patrolman, is pleased with the quality of his education, a few of his classmates are disappointed. "The material in the courses is extremely redundant, and the quality of the instructors is uneven," says Stacy Modlin, 44, who is working on a master's degree in organizational management. Others deride Phoenix as a "McUniversity." In New Jersey, state regulators have blocked

Phoenix's attempts to set up shop, saying the school lacks a library—
though course materials and academic journals are available online
24 hours a day. Eugene Golub, president of a professors' union, likens Phoenix to "a school that teaches art by copying the Mona Lisa
using the color-by-number system." Alarmed by the competition,
other states are even trying to keep out nonprofit colleges. Old Dominion University in Norfolk, Va., has set up satellite campuses in
several states. But neighboring Maryland ordered the school to close
down its operations. "The states are treating us as if we were a foreign steel producer," says Old Dominion's president, James V. Koch.
(Marcus, 2000, p. 44)

Cybercritique
University of Phoenix Online Cleverly Uses "CTRL"

MARKETER: University of Phoenix Online
WHERE TO FIND IT: Yahoo! and more.
CRITIQUE: We here at Cybercritique HQ have always arched an eye-
brow at the fact that, according to Nielsen/NetRatings, some of the
highest click-through rates on (non-porn) banners come from ads
that look like computer error messages.

Not to mix metaphors, but this strategy sets up a sort of double-
edged sword of Damocles. The banners play off a computer user's
twitch reflex to click on all Windows-looking error boxes to make
them go away. The reflex exists because of the irritating nature of
error messages. Then there's the irritation of having not only the
faux-error go away, but the page of content the user was viewing go
away with it. Who pulled this dirty trick? Well, the click-through
gives the answer, and it won't necessarily be a positive branding experience. The University of Phoenix Online varies this theme to
make a much clearer and more positive statement. Running with a
computer like banner, it shows some of users' favorite keys: enter,
control, escape and shift. Each leads to a message about how a graduate degree from its online program will help the user get "ctrl" and
"esc" their dreary Dilbert lives by becoming the Dilbert's boss, the
Wallys at the top of the executive food chain. (Carmichael, 1999,
p. 38)

Despite pressure from colleges and legislatures, many state universities still make such transfers difficult by not accepting some community-college credits or not making their transfer policies clear. The
for-profit companies—particularly those that are becoming more
national with new campus locations and online operations—obviously see this as an opportunity, says Mr. Grubb. "They certainly are
reaching out more," he says. "Every place they go they look for as

many markets as possible." Articulation agreements help to establish the for-profit colleges as legitimate transfer alternatives. Mr. Grubb says he's still a bit skeptical about the for-profit institutions as a whole: He fears that their job-oriented curricula might not be serving students well in the long run, and is nervous about the way they talk about getting course work "out of the way" with compressed class schedules. Still, he acknowledges that the strategy helps the companies and students. Community-college graduates are more likely to succeed and require fewer remedial classes than those with less college-level experience, he notes, and "all that is to the good of the bottom line." And, he adds, "anything that facilitates the upward mobility of students" should be encouraged. (Blumenstyk, 2000a, p. A46)

Never Too Old: Two Universities That Target Adult Learners Expand Their Campuses

Two private universities have recently completed large structures in north Fresno, a testament to the soaring demand for degree programs that cater to working adults. National University and University of Phoenix each tripled their classroom space with moves from Shaw Avenue to buildings off Friant Road near Woodward Park. University of Phoenix, offering seven types of undergraduate degrees, settled into 21,000 square feet of space in a new building at Fresno Street and Friant in October. National, offering more than a dozen types of undergraduate and graduate degrees, moved into a 37,000-square-foot campus in November on the west side of Friant Road. (Ellis, 2001, p. C1)

Online U; Online Education

ANCHORS: LESLEY STAHL

STAHL: (voiceover) Arthur Levin, president of Teachers College at Columbia University, says the new online schools are catering to the new American college student.

MR. ARTHUR LEVIN (Teachers College at Columbia University): The image of the college student is somebody that's somewhere between 18 and 22, who attends college full-time and lives on a campus.

STAHL: Right.

MR. LEVIN: That person now makes up 16 percent of the college population. The rest . . .

STAHL: Wow.

MR. LEVIN: . . . are older, part-time, working.

(Footage of young college students walking on campus; Vicki Esposito walking up stairs; Esposito on a ferry; Esposito walking on sidewalk.) . . .

MR. LEVIN: They definitely do. Higher education is now being looked at as the next health care. There's a sense that here's an industry worth maybe $300 billion which people believe is low in productivity, high in cost, bad in management, doesn't use technologies. One entrepreneur recently told me, you know, "We're going to eat your lunch."

(Footage of Esposito working at computer; close-up of computer screen)

STAHL: (voiceover) The business plan: Give the customers what they want, stripped-down college without the frat parties and football games.

MR. LEVIN: So what older students are saying is, "Look, I'm looking for the same relationship with my college that I have with my bank, that I have with my supermarket, that I have with the ga . . ."

STAHL: With their ATM?

MR. LEVIN: Absolutely.

STAHL: Oh, wow.

MR. LEVIN: That's exactly what they're saying. "I want great service. Give me convenience, classes 24 hours a day. In-class parking wouldn't be bad, high-quality instruction and low cost. And I don't want to pay for anything I'm not using." They're prime candidates for instruction in the office or at home. . . .

MR. LEVIN: When I went to visit Phoenix, I really wanted to find a diploma mill.

STAHL: And you didn't?

MR. LEVIN: I didn't. Phoenix is offering a quality education. And it's one of the reasons I think they're attracting people. (Stahl, 2001, pp. 2–3)

E-Learning Today: As an Industry Shakes Out, the Survivors Offer No-Frills Education for Grown-Ups

No frills. "People aren't looking for an ivory-tower experience," says Sean Gallagher, an analyst with Eduventures, a company that tracks the education industry. Fathom, a Web site funded by Columbia University and featuring courses from the University of Michigan, the University of Chicago, and the Woods Hole (Mass.) Oceano-graphic Institution, among others, has been reduced to offering many classes free of charge. New York University and Philadelphia's Temple University have shut down their for-profit online divisions. A faculty committee at Williams College rejected a partnership with the Global Education Network, a Web-based learning company, after determining that each course would need to enroll as many as 3,000 students to break even. "We didn't think there was that large of an audience for the kinds of [liberal arts] courses that we specialize in," says Kim Bruce, a professor of computer science at Williams. Indeed, the largest audience for online education has turned out to be working adults who need to hold on to their full-time jobs while they get their degrees. (Shea, 2002, p. 54)

CHAPTER 10

Conclusion

I began this book by asking if there is anything that can possibly be learned by our respected traditional universities in America from for-profit and nontraditional higher education. In Chapter 2, I demonstrated that there are many challenges for higher education today including the lack of revenue, the necessity of maintaining and evolving institutional missions during a time of great instability, and the call to serve the increasingly large group of adult learners and first-generation college students. Concerns about financial support are not new in higher education, but institutions now appear often pressured to change their missions because of reduced funding, and are sometimes forced to behave in more entrepreneurial manners outside of their traditional missions. Stakeholders seem to be stratified more than ever and are pulling institutions in different directions. At the same time, higher education is more in demand now than ever, particularly with the adult student returning to college later in life. At a time of reduced funding and increased demand and expense, do for-profit universities furnish some answers?

SUMMARY OF WHAT I HAVE LEARNED

I started this voyage by looking at current challenges in higher education as represented by faculty and administrators from exemplary higher education institutions, and then analyzed how traditional institutions are meeting these challenges. In order to dispel common misunderstandings, I examined the current information on for-profit institutions in Chapter

3 and the historical development of vocational and for-profit higher education in America. I learned that the "threat" from for-profits is much less than advertised, with only 2.5 percent of all higher education students enrolled in for-profits, and just 10 percent of the for-profits having the important regional accreditation. Additionally, for-profits disproportionately serve ethnic minority students, enrolling 16 percent of all black students, 14 percent of Hispanic students, and 4 percent of Native American students. Those who lead for-profit universities often have similar values as those from traditional higher education and support institutional missions that have social change intentions. Although one can see the rise of the for-profit university as part of the general movement toward a privatization of higher education, at the same time the history of proprietary education in America reveals the increased legitimacy of these institutions because of changes in financial aid legislation pushing for-profits toward regional accreditation.

In Chapter 4, I looked at the unique missions at for-profits to serve working adults and the special characteristics of how mission functions within these organizations. I learned from the for-profits and nontraditional institutions how mission is made clear and relevant, is tested regularly, informs the educational objectives, incorporates diversity, and transforms the domain of higher education as a whole. In Chapter 5, I considered the cultures of the for-profits as represented in various symbols and forms of communication, as well as common attitudes and approaches to work. The culture of the University of Phoenix and the other for-profits is an interesting mix of corporate and informal or counterculture characteristics. They have roots in the free speech and anti–Vietnam War cultures of the 1960s, which inform their tendencies toward combativeness with traditional higher education, as well as openness to debate mainstream assumptions about higher education, and an appreciation of creativity and innovation.

In Chapter 6, I moved on to organizational structures and the balance of academic and business interests, decentralized functions, and the tendency toward risk-taking and innovation. In addition, topics such as awareness of public policy, participatory management style, and staff development were addressed. I found that for-profit organizations are organized differently than traditional universities and think of themselves as managing organizations rather than maintaining structures ("managing" rather than "administering"). Often structured more like businesses, the for-profits tend to separate their academic decision making from their management decisions. Many of the for-profit institutions have distributed locations and try to balance centralized and decentralized functions—generally, they are more centralized than traditional higher education. Often decisions regarding centralization are made for business reasons such as economies of scale and quality control. For-profit organizations encourage risk-taking and have access to venture capital to respond quickly to initiatives. Leadership is generally flat and shared. They emphasize ownership of tasks and accountability.

In Chapter 7, I looked more closely at the decision-making process at the for-profits, and explored how the tension between academic and business interests, variously described by the for-profits as "creative" or "productive," is maintained. I saw that a flat hierarchy encourages communication and debate, use of assessment and feedback systems, a reliance on personal relationships, and a culture of investment in the organization typically characterize for-profit decision making. How stakeholders are involved, the speed of implementation, and the resulting effectiveness all contribute to the decision making at for-profit universities. The way change is managed and how decisions are made are also key elements of their uniqueness.

In Chapter 8, the role of faculty members at the for-profits including the practitioner model and lack of tenure was examined. I learned that the three main differences in teaching for the University of Phoenix are the overall status or power of faculty within the institution, the training and evaluation of faculty, and the altered teaching role. I also looked at related pedagogical issues such as the problem of poor student preparation for college-level work and the use of standardized teaching materials.

In Chapter 9, I discussed the challenges that the for-profit universities face, including poor academic reputation, competition from traditional universities, and managing growth. Many of the for-profits are now additionally under the scrutiny of business watchdogs and stockholders, and traditional universities have begun to use some of the for-profit methods, focusing their whole operations more on the growing population of adult learners.

In this final chapter I conclude with an analysis of the distinguishing characteristics of the for-profit university in the context of higher education as a whole, and what practices might be useful to traditional institutions during a time of new external pressures and a quickly changing student body. I then spend some time considering the larger debate about for-profit higher education and positive directions for American higher education in the twenty-first century.

DIFFERENCES BETWEEN FOR-PROFIT
AND TRADITIONAL UNIVERSITIES

How are for-profit universities different from traditional institutions? With such a large and complex "system" of higher education in America, it is very difficult and treacherous to generalize—there are almost as many exceptions as there are rules. Nevertheless, I've tried here to summarize some of the general patterns that emerge from our look at these institutions. Table 10.1 shows the emerging challenges as discussed in Chapter 2, how the traditional institutions are responding, and the for-profit and nontraditional approaches.

The first row of the table (revenue) is a key difference between traditional institutions and the for-profits. Instead of reluctant involvement in recruitment, marketing, fundraising, and offering applied degrees, the for-profits are designed to efficiently produce revenue. One sees that the revenue pressure experienced at traditional institutions isn't an issue at the for-profits because of the corporate nature of the organization—they are at least partially organized and constituted to generate increasing amounts of revenue. In the face of the danger of commercialization, both traditional institutions and the for-profits talk about "balancing" the academic and economic interests. Traditional institutions address the problem of focusing less on social issues with service learning opportunities for students, increased access through distance learning technology delivery systems, and including multicultural perspectives in the curriculum. The for-profits have a consistent focus on access for a specific group: the working adult. Diversity as customarily defined is addressed through a deepened and broader role in the community for the respondents from mainstream colleges, while the for-profits respond with an increased customer service focus that strives to meet specific needs of their diverse student body. The related challenge of student preparation is confronted at traditional institutions with the use of existing resources, testing, and lengthening the time to graduate. Conversely, the for-profits are set up to teach students as they are when they are admitted. On the vocational education issue, four-year institutions arguing for whole person education are on the opposite end of the debate with the for-profits, which primarily offer applied degrees. In traditional institutions, change is notoriously slow and conservative, while change is valued and rapid at the for-profits. The problem of institutional identity is dealt with typically by emphasizing the uniqueness of the culture and mission in most institutions, while the for-profits actively address mission by questioning its relevancy. The rightmost column of the table shows how nontraditional institutions in this study, such as the Fielding Graduate Institution and Heritage College, might be positioned in relationship to their traditional and for-profit colleagues. Overall, these institutions occupy a middle ground between traditional institutions and for-profits. However, notice how a clear advantage of these institutions seems to be how their very specific and clear missions guide them in finding answers to these difficult contemporary issues.

HIGHER EDUCATION CHANGE MODEL

Traditional universities might learn from the for-profits how better to manage change. For-profit universities are built for change and help highlight how traditional institutions might evolve themselves. Given the increased pressures on higher education, why is it difficult for traditional universities to respond? The Study of Good Work in Higher Education has developed a model (Berg, Csikszentmihalyi, & Nakamura, 2003) for how universities develop and change over time, centering to great extent on evolving collective belief. Although we might all agree that it is important that educational institutions be guided by clear ideals, how does this occur? This process appears fairly easy to see in a small religious-based institution where the values are based on established religious doctrine, but these types of institutions are no longer the norm in American higher education.

One model of institutional change is to see it as coming about through the intersection of stakeholder values in institutional mission and actions (see Figure 10.1). Stakeholders include the government, local community, parents, students, faculty, staff, alumni, donors, and businesses. The values expressed in an institutional mission are really the mix of stakeholder values. While institutional values act as a lightning rod, the process of drawing those of like-mindedness to the institution as supporters is not always consistent and continuous. As the stakeholders change over time, the original institutional values may become irrelevant. In the current environment of rapid change and the necessary outreach of the university to new constituents, the pressure on institutional values is immense. How do universities cope with these forces of change?

The best higher education institutions, for-profit and nonprofit alike, have similar approaches to understanding value and mission. First, they are aware of the need to effectively balance economic and academic interests. The way that for-profit universities accomplish this balance is particularly enlightening, but the same need for balance exists at traditional universities. In addition, successful institutions make decisions in

Table 10.1
Traditional vs. For-Profit Solutions to Challenges

Challenges	Four-Year Private Institutions	Four-Year Public Institutions	Two-Year Institutions	For-Profit	Nontraditional
Need for additional sources of revenue	Fundraising, industry ties, marketing, professional schools	Fundraising, industry ties, marketing, professional schools	More cost-effective, but dependent on public funding	For-profit status, management	Tuition and financial aid dependent
Threat of commercialization	Balance economic and academic interests	Balance economic and academic interests	Less of an issue	Balance economic and academic interests	Less of an issue
Pressure for revenue-changing mission	Less of an issue	Forced to prioritize goals/audience served	Not an issue	Revenue pursuit is part of mission	Focused mission provides clear direction
Lessened focus on social issues	Less of an issue	Service learning, distance learning access, multicultural curriculum	Open access is continuing mission	Access for working adults consistent focus	Solid connection to mission
Diversity of students and faculty	Recruitment of ethnically diverse students	Infused in curriculum, broader institutional role in community	Not an issue	Age- and class-based, customer service focus	Mission-driven

Chronically poor student preparation for college	Increase selectivity (selective schools), focus resources (HBCUs, etc.)	Use existing resources, testing, educational career management	Open enrollment, heavy emphasis on student preparation	Open enrollment—teaching students as they are	Mission-focus
Increasingly vocational curriculum/de-emphasis of liberal arts	Promote whole person/liberal arts education	Promote whole person/liberal arts education	Vocational education mission	Applied/professional curriculum	Balance
Speed of change	Slow (few remedies)	Slow (few remedies)	Slow (few remedies)	Fast, risk-taking (not seen as a problem)	Medium
Trouble in differentiating institution and clarifying/maintaining identity	Emphasize uniqueness of mission and culture	Distinguish from two-year institutions, emphasize academic reputation	Not an issue	Constant questioning and testing of organizational identity	Clear, limited focus
Governance	Shared	Shared	Shared	Professionally managed	Shared
Decision-making process	Faculty controlled	Faculty controlled	Faculty controlled	Management controlled, faculty input	Faculty controlled, mission driven

181

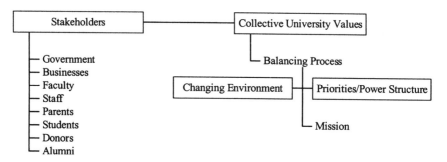

Figure 10.1 Value Formation in Universities

line with their values. Especially when considering new activities, the organization refers to its core values when making key decisions. This value-based decision-making practice is central to the success of these institutions. Particularly in large institutions, the tendency is often to become engaged in activities that drift far afield of the core mission. At times these activities evolve into practices that even run counter to their core values. Often the justification for these misaligned decisions is the need for revenue. In this way, public institutions with access missions can develop for-profit programs that serve elite clients, and religious-based independent institutions can develop educational programs with large returns to support their other activities.

One of the biggest challenges is for institutions to adjust their mission as the stakeholder values change over time (see Figure 10.2). If institutions are unable to do this, their missions become irrelevant and they no longer

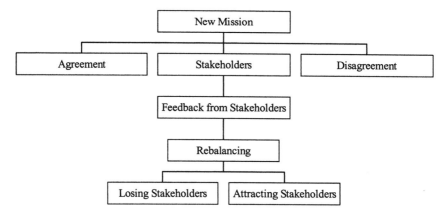

Figure 10.2 Institutional Value/Mission Change Process

have a mechanism for making value-based decisions—there is no reference point. For instance, a public institution in a community with a new demographic composition must adjust values and strategies to accommodate its shifting population. What different degree programs are needed?

There are two apparent ways that institutions sustain organizational values: through their culture and their organizational structure. When asked for symbols of culture and important institutional events at the for-profits, interviewees speak about the learning centers, student teams, and gatherings of administrators and faculty. These cultural artifacts reveal the strongly held value or concern for the particular challenges of the adult learner, as well as the flat administrative hierarchy and participatory management style.

Organizations often perpetuate themselves beyond their usefulness. Particularly in large, bureaucratic organizations such as universities, employees are more likely to want to protect their positions than to question their usefulness. Peter Drucker, the eminent business philosopher, suggests that the first question nonprofit organizations should ask of themselves is whether or not they still have a reason for existing. An example of this questioning would be a nonprofit designed to cure a disease such as polio. Once a cure for the polio is discovered, the organization is no longer relevant. Generally, this questioning of relevancy of mission isn't so stark. Nevertheless, Drucker's point is that an organization must continually question and test its mission to see if it is still meaningful and in alignment with the values of the stakeholders. The best institutions do this, and many for-profits, the University of Phoenix especially, are particularly expert. The reason for this is partially a result of their businesslike approach to understanding the mission and making their organization increasingly more productive. This testing and revitalization of the institutional mission is one thing that can be learned from the for-profit universities.

WHAT CAN BE DONE

While certainly it would be difficult and even inappropriate for traditional institutions with various missions to try and adopt all practices and approaches seen at for-profit institutions, there are some fundamental methods that they should consider.

Pay Attention to Mission

In Chapter 4 the centrality of how the institutional mission functions within the for-profit organization was discussed. The important aspects of the for-profit's mission that other higher education institutions should consider in examining their own organizational goals are to mix sociopolitical agendas with attention to the marketplace, understand how customer focus leads to increased diversity, align clear pedagogical objectives with the institutional mission, continually test the relevance of the mission, and use distinctive missions to test the limits of the domain.

Forward Social Agenda Through Attention to the Marketplace and Customer Service

Socially informed missions at the for-profits are probably the most surprising discovery for those familiar with neither the roots of the organizations nor the preoccupations of their leadership. This social meaning gives many of the organizations and individual employees motivation beyond simply returning greater profits to shareholders. Rather than seeing profit motives and social agendas at odds, traditional universities might learn from University of Phoenix's example how the two can work together. The for-profits do a particularly good job of balancing their social agenda with the demands of the marketplace. They seem to benefit from trying to provide education to underserved populations while at the same time paying attention to the market. At least partially, this has to do with the constant process of testing their mission, which leads to redirecting attention to their core business and competencies.

The for-profit's customer service approach leads to an ability to accommodate diverse populations in ways that state-supported institutions with similar missions haven't succeeded. In particular, paying attention to peripheral issues such as competing work, home and family interests, and psychological and attitudinal issues for first-generation, minority college students is a key advantage for them. Rather than simply making education available to these populations, the focus on customer service has increased the meaningfulness of this access to education. A specific example of how this student focus has led to increased diversity is the use of technology. Rather than focusing on the technology, as many traditional institutions have done with distance learning, the for-profits have concentrated on using technology to better serve students who need more convenient education that better matches the way they can successfully learn in college.

An administrator at DeVry argued that given the difficult time with the budget constraints, the issues higher education faces are very significant. The role for the for-profits is to continue to provide access when the traditional institutions cannot: "I think we as a member of the higher education community need to make sure that there is as much access as possible that people around the country no matter where they are have access." In for-profit terms, paying attention to the market means providing greater access.

Test Relevance of Mission

Perhaps the most important organizational discovery of how a mission functions at the for-profits is the fact that stated purpose is constantly tested. Throughout the interviews, respondents talk about debating the relevance and meaning of the mission. The sustaining of mission is tied to the for-profit's preoccupation with constant questioning and testing out what it is and what it should concentrate on operationally.

An interesting aspect of the for-profit's long battles with various accrediting bodies is that the fight has centered on asserting mission to these agencies. For example, rather than finding ways to comply with demands for full-time tenured faculty, the university has argued for a part-time practitioner faculty structure that better serves its students. This constant compliance battle has functioned to test and strengthen its organizational mission.

Align Pedagogy with Mission

The pedagogical objectives at the for-profits are clearly aligned with the desire to serve working adults who need applied knowledge that helps them to advance in their careers. In the process, they become more valuable employees. Since the for-profits, especially the University of Phoenix, have missions that direct them to focus on business needs, they are forced to prove to their corporate clients the value of the education. As a result, the learning objectives for the University of Phoenix are very lucid, specific, and link directly to its organizational mission.

Challenge Domain: "Challenge Authority"

For-profits have influenced regional accreditation because they have forced the redefinition of traditional standards and values. Obviously, this fits the counterculture posturing of the organizations. Administrators from for-profits ask, "What is the role of higher education in society?" There's a body of thought that says that the role of higher education is to preserve the culture, so that society invests money in, for instance, the art department, even though it doesn't have a utilitarian value. Then the other side holds the baldly utilitarian notion that education is just to train people for jobs. In fact, the for-profits and nontraditional institutions vary in their balance of the mix of applied and liberal arts curricula. DeVry thinks of itself as being somewhere in the middle: "We're not a career school, but we don't have a classical music playing quartet." An administrator at DeVry argued that the traditional higher education model was designed to serve an industrial age economy. The original intention of all public education was to teach students to be factory workers—"and we don't have any more factory jobs." He argues that the biggest problem is going to be providing access at an affordable cost. A traditional brick-and-mortar model is very capital intensive. Leaders at the for-profits argue that they serve a population that is not necessarily accommodated well in traditional institutions. Administrators at for-profits do not hesitate to challenge traditional practices: "DeVry will continue to innovate and take a leadership position in its educational approach, notwithstanding whether it is in-step or out of step with other institutions." Traditional institutions might learn from the willingness to go against the grain of higher education.

Concentrate on Learning Outcomes

For-profit institutions have been leaders in the use of assessment to control education quality. Partly, this concentration has come from attention to the corporate market, which thinks of training rather than education and a return-on-investment equation when analyzing their investment in staff education. Additionally, the scrutiny of accrediting agencies, as well as the demands of adult students, has led to the desire to prove themselves through assessment. At all of the for-profits studied, administrators consistently pointed to the need to be concerned with outcomes of the education they provide. With the success of the assessment movement, traditional institutions are following the for-profit lead.

Use Teaching Faculty and Practitioners

Traditional universities have already learned the value of using faculty with real world expertise, particularly in their professional schools. Additionally, traditional universities can study the importance of having faculty who are focused on teaching and advising rather than engaging in scholarship as a primary focus, particularly when serving adult learners.

Expand the Time, Place, and Way of Learning

The nontraditional student is becoming the traditional student. Many traditional universities haven't accepted that fact because they are much more comfortable accommodating eighteen- to twenty-two-year-old full-time students. As one administrator at DeVry said: "We need to make it convenient and practical for them." In paying close attention to student needs, the for-profits have expanded notions of time and place in higher education. This orientation has led to flexibility in format, location (online and distributed), as well as more convenient student services for adult learners. Overall, the for-profits have concentrated on the affective part of learning, as well as barriers to learning for adults, and looked at ways of minimizing student time to receiving a degree.

Times to achieve degree efficiencies are important: For example, students can complete a degree at DeVry in three years, compared to four or more years at a traditional university. In order to serve the students better, for-profits offer their programs year-round, three semesters per year at DeVry, five- to eight-week courses year-round at the University of Phoenix. This lessens the time required to obtain a degree and reduces student dropout rates. A student can complete a bachelor's degree in three years at DeVry: "Traditional educators usually react with, 'three years, that's not enough time.' Well, it is enough time. Three years you get nine semesters. In traditional schools you get eight semesters in four years." The reasoning behind the model is that for a student who has lots of distractions and other things going on, a continuous period of enrollment keeps them focused on what they're doing—they don't have opportunities to find other attractive uses of their time.

Administrators at the for-profits say that they turn their curriculum ninety degrees in order to help students who are not necessarily traditional learners to become engaged in an area of interest. Typically, in a four-year curriculum students have two years of general education and then enter their major for the next two years, developing more in-depth knowledge of their field. At DeVry, students complete the general education requirement throughout their time in the degree program. Courses in a student's areas of interest are started from the beginning, helping to keep them engaged.

Without question, location-independent education leadership lies with for-profit education. While for-profits only have 2 to 3 percent of regular enrollments, they account for about 30 percent of online enrollments nationally. A DeVry leader in the online area argues that they have learned that online education isn't just more convenient, it's a better way to learn. DeVry is known for an applications focus, for learning that can be applies very directly to the student's job and that tends to use less of a theoretical approach: "Learn by doing has been a DeVry hallmark." With the Internet, the university is now having students complete the lab work online from a distance. Using technology that it's both developed itself and acquired through partnerships, it simulates computer laboratory work for its technical courses.

According to a DeVry administrator, "Virtually all of the schools that were critical of us now have part-time night programs using practitioner faculty." When DeVry established a second location in Chicago it was one of the few to have multiple locations. "Now I'd say probably three quarters of the MBA programs have multiple locations," a DeVry administrator told me. In this way, many of the things that were not in the traditional model have been adopted as part and parcel of the current operating environment in higher education.

Collaborating with Businesses: Understand the Workforce They Need

For-profits understand that they need to pay close attention to businesses in forming their curricula. They typically involve business leaders as advisers in curriculum development and pay special attention to the placement of student in positions upon graduation.

Professionally Manage: Make Universities More Efficient and Productive

According to those interviewed at for-profits, traditional institutions could learn business efficiency techniques. The for-profits have been forced to be efficient as possible because all of their revenue comes from tuition—they have no endowment or government support (other than financial aid). As an administrator at one for-profit says, "[E]very department needs to run efficiently, and it is in your mind every day." An example of traditional higher education inefficiency is its focus on always expanding their physical campus. An administrator at DeVry argued that traditional universities are too much invested in brick and mortar: "That's a huge amount of capital that isn't really being invested for the student's benefit." For-profits do not spend a great deal of capital on buying property. The campuses are efficient, even Spartan. They lease spaces, which gives them a great deal of flexibility to either expand or contract space without a substantial penalty, and are careful not to spend too much on laboratory equipment for teaching courses.

On the academic end, the for-profit administrators claim that traditional universities operate on a guild or craft model comprising hundreds of small departments, each of which is run in an almost completely democratic way, making for a very complex decision-making process. At for-profits, they look at things from the point of view of the student, not from the point-of-view of the academic department: "I think the for-profits have that focus because they have to have it or they wouldn't exist."

LEARNING FROM NONTRADITIONAL UNIVERSITIES

Although the two nonprofit, nontraditional institutions studied for this book, Fielding Graduate Institute and Heritage College, are not the main focus, they may be the closest to offering a new direction for traditional higher education. The reason is that while they are utilizing a number of innovative and unusual methods, they still have maintained many of the core values and practices of traditional higher education. While the sample of institutions from this category is too small to effectively generalize about (and this category defies generalization), there are a few things one might point to as areas where traditional institutions might learn.

A leader at Fielding emphasizes the need for traditional higher education to rethink traditional practices: "I would encourage traditional institutions to question the basic givens of what constitutes higher education, and in particular graduate education, and ask themselves, Why do we still do it that way when it doesn't work for so many people?" Fielding was founded on the idea of serving adult students, which is why it doesn't have a campus and takes a broad view of educating its students including linking their learning to work in the community: "Our whole model is based on becoming involved with the whole stream of the student's life, from work to the community."

Especially at the Fielding Graduate Institute, I saw that from its inception the institution was founded on the notion of serving adult learners. Consequently, from the beginning they adopted an approach concentrating on adult learning theory that directly informed its "andragogical" approach. Additionally, much like the for-profits, it pays attention to the life situation and environmental context of adult learning and has developed a distributed system of learning that matches the need of its students. While institutions like Fielding Graduate Institute have similarities to the for-profits in the use of flexible scheduling and distributed locations, perhaps they could learn something from the for-profits about how to integrate individual flexibility with a more centralized program and curriculum.

According to the leadership at Fielding, one of their founders described the institute's students as "beautifully lopsided," meaning that they have deep knowledge and experience in some things, and limited knowledge of others: "They'll have someone come in who has been working with a degree in pharmacology that can teach biological basis to some of our faculty, who knows nothing about psychological assessment. Then they'll have someone else who is a psychology assessment person for twenty years, and knows nothing about biological basis." Traditional universities have trouble managing such educational diversity and could learn from the examples of Fielding Graduate Institute and Heritage College in this regard.

Perhaps the greatest lesson one can learn from the nontraditionals lies in their belief in the need to provide access to higher education for all. The president of Heritage emphasizes the point that higher education tends to emphasize selectivity and limited, restricted groups of those identified as higher achievers. The point she forcefully makes is that traditional higher education often fails to serve the broader population whose access is limited by income, culture, and location.

There is much that traditional higher education can learn from nontraditional institutions regarding how to work with low-income students. As the president at Heritage told me: "There's a whole constellation of things we've learned about low-income students." First, they do a lot of little things that add up to increased retention. The leader from Heritage describes how people with middle- or upper-class backgrounds have trouble understanding how small fees and other costs can lead to students not attending or dropping out: "If you live in a culture of poverty there aren't safety nets." For example, Heritage created an emergency loan program of $150 at a time for students, which they have to pay back before they can borrow more. "Say you need a pair of glasses, you can use your student loan money for the glasses. That's the money you were going to use for the math class textbook. You have to drop the class if you can't get the book." Heritage's emphasis overall is to make attending a university seamless and workable for them: "We are going to have to be prepared for more first-generation college, low-income, people whose families haven't had the experience or motivation to assist their kids to go to school." The leadership at Heritage sees an increasingly large population of first-generation, low-income people who do not have the benefit of a social network to help them through college: "How are we going to educate those people?" the president of Heritage College asks. One of the things Heritage models is placing an institution directly in a geographic area where they are needed. With approximately only 12 percent of the local high school students going to college, the community clearly has a need for Heritage. There are undoubtedly a great number of capable students who are not going to college because of finances, lack of understanding about education's importance, as well as, for various cultural groups, the family dictating that one needs to remain geographically close to their family.

How students are recruited is important. I learned from Heritage College that the whole process of recruiting and student services needs to be undertaken in a context of heavy involvement of the college personnel in the community they are trying to reach: "We have recruiters that will go to a home if necessary, sometimes a grandparent's home. Because the grandpa or grandma doesn't think it's a good idea for the student to go to school—because the grandparents don't know anyone with a college degree—he's not going." Recruiters also work through local church activities and local cultural groups so that college personnel are actually seen there frequently and are comfortable with the families.

Finally, the nontraditionals are similar to the for-profits, but retain many of the central values of traditional higher education. One key difference is in the role of faculty members. At some of the nontraditionals such as Fielding Graduate Institute, they have a contract, not a tenure system for faculty. At Fielding, a leader said, "We very deliberately don't have a tenure system because we don't want the tenure/nontenure schism." This is obviously a very sensitive issue, but it is worth noting here that there may be more reasons for considering contracts over tenure besides economic ones.

FOR-PROFITS AND THE FUTURE OF HIGHER EDUCATION: MONEY IN THE ACADEMY

Money will determine the future of higher education in America: how much, from whom, how used, and regarded in what ways. Money has many connotations in our society, but in traditional higher education it is often regarded with suspicion. Nevertheless, one can see what an institution values by looking at its budget. Whatever is valued is funded. All types of institutions are pressured to balance their budgets while trying to serve their unique missions. There are confused definitions of what attention to money means and the ethics of how educational institutions should behave in connection with revenue sources. In this quagmire, for-profit universities provide clarity and press the academy to elucidate themselves. Upton Sinclair, in his early-twentieth-century radical damnation of higher education, *The Goose-Step: Study of American Education*, argued that the control of higher education fell to a minority of the wealthy population who had an important stake in the type of education that is given, and who were educated: "Race prejudice is merely one side of the many-sided snobbery of college life. The college is the collective prestige of a mob of socially superior persons, and each and every one of them is interested to protect that prestige" (1923, p. 363). Eight decades later, the doors to the university have been pushed open with changes in public policy and larger society. Nevertheless, the goal of universal access is drifting farther and farther away. As shown in the second chapter, the public has underfunded higher education since the mid-1970s and has displayed a general unwillingness to financially support higher education at the same level as it has in the past.

Higher education in America is having trouble making financial sense, and it isn't just public institutions that are having problems. Although private universities have the advantage of sometimes large endowments, they spend 4 to 4.5 percent of their endowment each year on current operations. Selective institutions spend about $2,000 per each enrolled student for recruitment and have almost always increased their tuition levels more than the consumer price increase. The productivity of faculty is constantly lowered because while their salaries increase, the student to faculty ratio stays the same. In terms of governance, faculty members sometimes have trouble distinguishing what is best for themselves versus the institution and are often more like independent entrepreneurs, more loyal to their discipline than the institution. Beginning in 1994 as a result of the amendments to the Age Discrimination in Employment Act, mandatory retirement was ended, and tenured faculty members now have essentially lifetime employment. Government regulations have led to increased institutional competition by not allowing institutions to jointly communicate about admissions decisions. Additionally, huge deferred maintenance needs exist at most campuses—every time a building is endowed the cost for overall campus maintenance increases. Even beyond the direct public support of higher education, what many people do not realize is that the public supports institutions to a large degree by tax exemptions amounting to billions of dollars per year for their income, property taxes, and low-cost loans (Ehrenberg, 2000).

At the same time, according to a National Center for Public Policy and Higher Education study, Americans believe that higher education is more important than ever and is a key to middle-class lifestyle. Because of its importance, Americans feel that no qualified and motivated student should be denied opportunity to go to college because of price (Immerwahr, 1998). As a result of the combination of increased demand

and expenses coupled with reduced funding, higher education clearly needs to consider new models. Scholars in the field are suggesting that traditional higher education should consider examining the University of Phoenix and other for-profit universities to see how they are gaining competitive advantage and operating more efficiently (Embree, 2001). I want to end this book with a look at some of the crucial issues to consider in examining the role that for-profit and nontraditional institutions might play in the future of higher education in America.

One important and telling illustration of how money is regarded in academia is in organized sports. In the extremely well-document recent book *The Game of Life: College Sports and Educational Values* (Shulman & Bowen, 2001), the authors came to the remarkable conclusion that universities actually do not benefit monetarily from college athletics. Tracing the growth of college athletics to the entertainment industry and need for increased television programming, the authors argue that universities became caught up in a spiral of pressures from various sources combined with expectations of increased revenue through building big-time sports programs. However, the reality is that there is no statistically significant association between football records and annual giving at universities, and only a relatively small number of universities generate net income from sports. In fact, when all capital costs are accounted for, none do: "As a money-making venture, athletics is a bad business" (Shulman & Bowen, 2001, p. 257). The authors claim that as competition for admission of students increased, selective institutions moved away from finding a well-rounded student and instead focused on a well-rounded incoming class that allowed them to admit underachieving student athletes. Thus one sees that college athletics are a telling example of a lack of both efficient professional management, as well as an ironic crass commercialism, given the criticism of for-profits.

While perhaps the most significant threat is from unstable finances, the appreciation of increasing productivity has never been accepted as a value in higher education. In traditional universities, to question academic programs in terms of costs and benefits is to attack the core of the institution. As businesses, a simple production model applied to education includes deciding the desired profit margin, then pricing the product to produce the margin. If it can't make the target margin, the university doesn't produce the educational product. Most costs in education are wage-driven. As long as the faculty-to-student ratio stays the same, productivity will continue to erode as wages increase. Furthermore, the substitution of personal for institutional goals, as sometimes happens in the faculty-administration relationship, results in less productivity, using resources for personal use, or an obsession with rights and privileges. One wonders if any corporation could survive the administrative structure of a university, with lifetime employment for its workers. Some commentators such as Anderson and Meyerson (1992) argue that a bias toward risk and change in higher education is needed, much as found ever-present in the for-profits in this study.

An unpublished study of the University of Phoenix (Rutherford, 2002) found that there are three major themes that make the institution productive: a desire to accrue value to the consumer (students and employers), a willingness to improve business value, and awareness of the tension between the extremes found in academics and economic values. While perhaps nonprofit organizations assume a noncommercial attitude to keep themselves safe from being too controlled by the pursuit of revenue, the for-profits openly grapple with the tension between academic and business interests. The traditional institutions might do well to be as conscious of the tension and the need to balance the pursuit of revenue with sustaining academic quality. Often, traditional institutions criticize for-profits for turning students into "customers." Craig Swenson, the provost of the University of Phoenix, argues that the fear of for-profits creating an atmosphere of the customer always being right and in control is false:

> If that statement were applied uncritically, most businesses would soon be out of business. Bankers don't let customers set interest rates on their loans, nor do hospitals ask patients how to set broken bones. In the same vein, recognizing students as customers does not mean allowing them to dictate what topics the curriculum should include or what grades they should receive. (1998, p. 3)

In traditional higher education, the position of the student has changed as well, making these student or customer debates less relevant.

Throughout the process of writing this book I often wondered if "for-profit" was really the defining characteristic of this group of controversial institutions. David Harpool, in his recent book *Survivor College: Best Practices of Traditional and For-profit Colleges* (2003), argues that there needs to be a new terminology for for-profit universities and recommends labeling them "publicly funded/professionally or privately managed." He likens the stockholders to the taxpayers in public institutions, and centers on the primary difference being in the professional rather than academic management of the institutions. We've certainly seen in the previous chapters that the distinctions among these various types of institutions needs to be better understood. Particularly now with the birth of regionally accredited for-profit institutions, the simple for-profit versus nonprofit dichotomy actually is confusing. Throughout the interviews I found that a strength of the for-profits was a strong concentration on their mission. Part of this mission-centeredness helps them avoid business decisions that would harm their academic quality. As Harpool pointed out: "EDMC has passed on several key opportunities to increase revenue in the short term because the direction was inconsistent with its mission and/or values" (2003, p. 21).

In the future, traditional universities need to consider professionalizing the management of nonacademic aspects of their organizations. The AAUP Statement on Government of Colleges and Universities takes the impractical position that if something even remotely affects academic issues, then faculty should have some degree of control. "That model is neither realistic nor wise," according to Harpool. Why? The answer from the for-profits is that academics are not qualified to make management decisions for the organization, and that the institution is better off if managers control nonacademic areas. Furthermore, in some instances faculty members simply have their own professional agendas that tend to keep them from making decisions in the best interests of the university. Too often the dominant motivation is to advance and protect the status of the individual faculty member or department, and not to support the institution as a whole. In place of the employment guarantees that tenure offers, the for-profits often institute strong reward systems. For-profits encourage staff and faculty to invest in their organization, and many have profited greatly now that the universities are publicly traded. Harpool argues that if an institution treats its best employees the same as its worst employees then they will lose talent. As a result, the for-profits often have long-term employees, both staff and faculty. For example, 25 percent of University of Phoenix faculty members have been with the university for ten or more years (Embree, 2001).

In *Good to Great: Why Some Companies Make the Leap . . . and Others Don't* (2001), Collins found that in leading businesses, good leaders are ambitious for their organizations, not themselves. Often they are contradictions: modest yet willful, humble yet fearless. As I found generally (but not exclusively) in the interviews at for-profits, leaders tend to talk about their company, not themselves. Additionally, effective leaders rely on professional discipline instead of hierarchy. Many of the characteristics that Collins lists in his highly influential book fit the for-profit model, such as his admonition to use compensation and rewards to get the right people and keep them; not to encourage the wrong employees to be more effective; creating rigorous rather than ruthless organizational cultures;

concentrating on realistic data rather than rhetoric; fostering open debate; focusing on what they do best; using technology to amplify best qualities, not as a strategy in and of itself; and finally, preserving core mission while constantly focused on change. These are all characteristics prominently noted at the for-profits, and especially at the University of Phoenix.

American universities have always had a dual purpose of providing both religious and scientific education. The role of religion is a key to understanding American higher education. The primary influences on American higher education were the Scottish universities formed as a result of the Scottish Enlightenment—a moderate Presbyterian movement with an emphasis on finding compatibility between Christianity and cultural and scientific education. Science and Protestant religion went together because both believed in free inquiry versus arbitrary authority. Since there was such diversity of religious belief in American colonies, a discomfort existed in making one play a dominant role in higher education. Consequently, most schools had to tone down Christian teachings in public. The decentralized nature of higher education in America led to free enterprise and sectarian rivalry, resulting in most religions developing universities in America. Science, common sense, and religion were combined values in America that informed the development of American higher education. As shown in Chapter 3, vocational and applied education have a very long history in America.

America's first university, Harvard, was a product of the Puritan movement, and had a dual purpose from the start of providing servants of God and training for professions that underscored a belief in the sacredness of work. By the mid-nineteenth century, the training of clergy was no longer the primary goal of a university education. The German university model, which greatly influenced the nineteenth-century American university, was concerned with the goal of building character in a humanistic sense. As an outgrowth of philosophical idealism, the German emphasis was on developing the personal powers toward a kind of transcendent fulfillment. The German model also emphasized the state control and influence on higher education. In the 1890s most state universities in America held compulsory chapel services, and up until the 1960s almost all the leading institutions in higher education came from a Protestant tradition. Protestant independent institutions often regard themselves as essentially public institutions. The college served the church and the civil government. "Public" referred to the ruling class who had landownership and status in society—the same people who were often leaders in the church ran the civil government. What happened in the academy is that a Christian environment surrounded a scientific western curriculum: Christianity was retained in extracurricular activities, rituals, and symbolism. In the mid-twentieth century, a document called *General Education in a Free Society*, written at Harvard University, influenced for years the makeup of general education requirements across the country. In this report, the authors recommended that liberal Protestantism should be infused in the curriculum, but with no explicit Christian values expressed (Marsden, 1994).

A common criticism is that for-profits do not provide a broad, general, liberal arts education. In fact, out of necessity many for-profits do provide general education courses. However, the teaching of humanistic, religious, and ethic subjects is clearly not their emphasis. Administrators from the for-profits, especially the University of Phoenix, deny that adults need to have ethical education—that their moral and ethical selves are already formed. Some scholars in the field disagree, claiming that moral and civic development continues throughout adolescence and adulthood (Colby et al., 2003). In his influential nineteenth-century book *The Idea of a University*, Newman argued that the university is a place for teaching universal knowledge, not for research or religious training: "This implies that its object is, on the one hand, intellectual, not moral; and on the other, that it is the diffusion and extension of knowledge rather than the advancement" (1959, p. 142). Nevertheless, higher education in America, with its hierarchy of institutional types, has led us to a bifurcated system where professional training occurs some places, ethical and religious training at other places, and the "diffusion and extension of knowledge" isn't always the main thrust. We need to reconsider the role of higher education in society and the place of specific types of institutions in that equation, including for-profit institutions.

Some may ask why I have not focused on the limitation or the negative aspects of the for-profits. I certainly share the concerns that many have about the possible excesses of universities with a for-profit status. In many ways I believe the limitations and even failings of the for-profits are somewhat obvious. In fact, the administrators at these institutions are more aware of their own limitations than anyone from the outside can possibly be. This awareness has led them to not only be extremely conscious of limiting and testing their mission, but also of insisting on proving that they are doing what they claim they do through rigorous and constant assessment and quality control measures.

Like an administrator from the Fielding Graduate Institute to whom I spoke, I am concerned that the success of the for-profit institution in selling a version of higher education that is highly pragmatic and practical will cause students to lose the experience of education as a libratory experience. However, at the same time, if traditional higher education is not able to make itself more affordable or accessible to underserved groups, then it is failing. Better to examine our own failures in traditional higher education before criticizing those who succeed where others fall short.

FINAL THOUGHTS

The American university is one of the greatest achievements of the twentieth century and has been a key to the ascendance of the United States as a world leader. One of the reasons is that Americans have understood the importance of higher education. As a result, Derek Bok, past president of Harvard University, argues that the university is "the central institution in postindustrial society" (1990, p. 3). According to Clark Kerr, former chancellor of UC Berkeley, we are only now completely grasping the importance of higher education in our culture and how it has shaped the history of the world: "We are just now perceiving that the university's invisible product, knowledge, may be the most powerful single element in our culture, affecting the rise and fall of professions and even of social classes, of regions and even of nations" (1982, p. xiv). The strength of American higher education comes from its variety and complexity, which have made this country a great economic power and world political leader. After beginning in colonial times by trying to imitate the British college system appealing only to the upper-class, and then adopting the German research university model in the nineteenth century, the university grew to become uniquely American in the twentieth century. Higher education has become great as it has provided greater access to the public regardless of race, class, or gender. Access remains the root concern for those in the higher education community today. Access is the main issue in discussions of increased revenue demands, shifting missions for public institutions, evolution of thinking about diversity, and debates about the applied curriculum. Meeting access needs is where the for-profits and the other nontraditional institutions discussed in this book enter the picture, as they are often founded upon and grounded in open access for underserved populations.

Both in the interviews and in comments from scholars in the field, one sees that lack of access and an increasing inability to serve the social purpose that is a central part of the university mission are in the forefront of educators' minds today. The long debate in higher education about how applied the curriculum should be continues and is vital to an analysis of the for-profit institutions. Specifically, the perspectives offered here by respondents from a historically black college, as well as those views of the well-known scholar W.E.B. DuBois, contrast with the expressed approach and viewpoint of respondents from the for-profits when discussing their mission and role in providing access to underserved groups. Linked to this discussion of applied curriculum is the recognition across institutions of the changing nature of their student population with the entrance of the adult learner. Revealed in this book is an indication that changing demographics have led to a broader notion of diversity, one that includes access regardless of age and restrictions on learning brought about by geography, employment, and family responsibilities.

In my work linked to the Good Work in Higher Education Project, I have sought to understand the nature of excellence in American universities, work that is personally meaningful, respected within an organization, and appreciated by the larger higher education community. Clearly those interviewed for this book are good workers on the first two counts. Respect from the higher education community as a whole has been hard coming. Those of us working in the higher education community should be careful not to dismiss the work that is done by these professionals simply because they are employed by a business and not a nonprofit organization or government agency. Many of those leading the for-profits share the values of the traditional institutions and are working hard to encourage positive change and growth in their students and society as a whole.

I began this book with two images: one of a civilization sprung from a broken down car in the desert, and the other of a classroom with an open door to the wilderness. Now, at the end of this five-year journey around the perimeter of higher education, the lasting impression I cannot shake is that of Kathleen Ross, president at Heritage College, scolding traditional higher education for neglecting and writing off a large segment of the population with its elitist focus on selectivity: "Talent is distributed randomly," she told me, speaking of her students. It is found throughout higher education at for-profit and nontraditional institutions on the edge. Students and traditional higher education increasingly appreciate the values and practices of these institutions. What was once the edge is becoming the center.

APPENDIX A:
GoodWork Project

Since 1995 the GoodWork Project (GWP) has been investigating how individuals are able to carry out "good work" in their chosen professions when conditions are changing at unprecedented rates and when market forces are enormously powerful. "Good work" means work that is at once of high quality, socially responsible, and fulfilling to the worker. The GWP is a collaboration between Howard Gardner (Harvard University), William Damon (Stanford University), and Mihaly Csikszentmihalyi (Claremont Graduate University), and is supported by their teams at these universities. It is documented in the books *Good Work: When Excellence and Ethics Meet* (Gardner, Csikszentmihalyi, & Damon, 2001), *Good Business: Leadership, Flow, and the Making of Meaning* (Csikszentmihalyi, 2003), and the upcoming *The Moral Advantage* (Damon, 2004).

Since the project's inception, GWP researchers have interviewed over 700 leading practitioners in a range of professions, including journalism, genetics, theater, jazz, law, business, dance, philanthropy, martial arts, and higher education. They focus on individuals who exemplify the understanding of good work that the GWP has developed: (1) they are recognized as experts in their professional area; (2) they attempt to act in ways that are socially and morally responsible; and (3) they find personal meaning in their work. The ultimate goal of the GWP is to bring attention to the nature of good work and to attempt to increase its incidence throughout our society. In developing an understanding of what these individuals do, the GWP intends to create models of good work to encourage its practice in the future. For further information, visit the GWP Web site, www.goodworkproject.org.

APPENDIX B:
Research Methods

The data used in this book come from two distinct sources: the Study of Good Work in Higher Education and my own primary research. For the Study of Good Work in Higher Education, research focused on only one for-profit institution: the University of Phoenix. The research method used was to focus our attention on a small number of exemplary institutions, and individuals deemed most responsible for their current excellence. We asked what aims inspire each of these institutions and individuals and how they go about pursuing good work under the conditions that prevail in the profession today. We first surveyed the terrain of higher education and interviewed twenty scholars of higher education in order to identify current challenges in the domain and specific institutions that are currently perceived as outstanding. We then selected one or more schools representing each of five institution-types: community colleges, tribal and historically black colleges, other liberal arts colleges, teaching-centered research universities, and new-model providers (e.g., for-profit institutions).

We then focused on ten of the nominated schools (the "core" schools), where we asked a variety of each school's stakeholders to nominate the individuals most responsible for its excellence in undergraduate education. The resulting set of more than 1,000 internal nominations allowed us to identify "good workers" at each of the ten core schools. We conducted interviews with six to thirteen of these individuals per school, resulting in a sample of eighty-eight, including forty-three administrators, thirty-seven faculty, six trustees, and two others. We also interviewed the formal leadership (i.e., the president and/or provost) of six more nominated schools (n = 10), for a total sample of ninety-eight key individuals at national schools in a sample perceived as outstanding.

As stated in the Introduction, I set out to write a book on the University of Phoenix alone. After consultation with various colleagues and editors at different presses, I decided that this was too narrow and enlarged the scope of the book to include other for-profit and proprietary institutions. I chose the for-profit institutions based on a desire to cover the leading players (although DeVry Inc. was nominated by some of the experts we originally queried). For the nonprofit institutions chosen, I relied on the experts of the Good Work in Higher Education Project, who had originally mentioned both Heritage College and Fielding Graduate Institute as examples of institutions we should consider studying. For the interviews at these institutions I used the same semistructured interview instrument, and collected and transcribed the data in a similar fashion. The primary difference in this data collection was that most of the interviews were conducted over the telephone, rather than in-person. Additionally, I did not use an internal nomination process, but rather interviewed only the top leadership at these institutions. I personally conducted all of the interviews at the University of Phoenix (usually with a coresearcher), as well as all of the interviews at the other for-profit and nontraditional institutions. The one exception is the interview with John Sperling, which was carried out by William Damon.

REFERENCES

Anderson, R. E., & Meyerson, J. W. (eds.). (1992). *Productivity and higher education: Improving the effectiveness of faculty, facilities, and financial resources.* Princeton: Peterson's Guides.

Apollo Group Inc. reports fiscal 2002 fourth quarter and year end results. (2002, October 8). *Business Wire*.

Apollo Group, Inc.'s University of Phoenix student loan default rate 4.6%. (2001, October 3). *Business Wire*, pp. 1–2.

Berg, G. A. (2002). *Why distance learning?* Westport, CT: Praeger/American Council on Education, Series on Higher Education.

Berg, G. A., Csikszentmihalyi, M., & Nakamura, J. (2003, September–October). Mission possible? Enabling good work in higher education. *Change*. American Association for Higher Education, pp. 40–47.

Blumenstyk, G. (2000a, January 7). Turning a profit by turning out professionals. *Chronicle of Higher Education*.

———. (2000b, August 11). Company that owns the University of Phoenix plans for a major foreign expansion. *Chronicle of Higher Education*.

Bok, D. (1990). *Universities and the future of America.* Durham, NC: Duke University Press.

———. (2003). *Universities in the marketplace: The commercialization of higher education.* Princeton: Princeton University Press.

Bolan, S. (2001, March 23). News. *Computing Canada*.

Borrego, A. M. (2001, August 10). Study tracks growth of for-profit colleges. *Chronicle of Higher Education*.

———. (2002, February 22). Why 3 liberal-arts scholars moved from traditional academe to for-profit institutions. *Chronicle of Higher Education*.

Bowie, N. E. (1994). *University-business partnerships: An assessment.* Lanham, MD: Rowman & Littlefield.

Carmichael, M. (1999, July 12). Cybercritique. *Advertising Age.*

Clark, B. R. (1998). *Creating entrepreneurial universities: Organizational pathways of transformation.* Oxford, Great Britain: IAU Press.

Clowes, D. (1995). Community colleges and proprietary schools: Conflict or convergence? In Clowes, D. A., & Hawthorne, E. M. (eds.), *Community colleges and proprietary schools: Conflict or convergence?* San Francisco: Jossey Bass, pp. 5–16.

Colby, A., Ehrlich, T., Beaumont, E., & Stephens, J. (2003). *Educating citizens: Preparing America's undergraduates for lives of moral and civic responsibility.* San Francisco: Jossey-Bass.

Collins, J. (2001). *Good to great: Why some companies make the leap . . . and others don't.* New York: HarperCollins.

Collison, M. N. (1998, July 9). Proprietary preference: For-profit colleges gain momentum in producing graduates of color. *Black Issues in Higher Education.*

Cox, A. M. (2002, May 13). Phoenix ascending. *In These Times.* Institute for Public Affairs.

Csikszentmihalyi, M. (2003). *Good business: Leadership, flow, and the making of meaning.* New York, NY: Penguin Books.

Davis, S., & Botkin, J. (1995). *The monster under the bed.* New York: Touchstone.

DuBois, W.E.B. (1973). *The education of black people.* Aptheker, H. (ed.). Boston: University of Massachusetts Press.

ECS (Education Commission of the States). (2000, January). Report from the regions: Accreditors' perceptions of the role and impact of for-profit institutions in higher education. Denver, CO: ECS.

Ehrenberg, R. G. (2000). *Tuition rising: Why college costs so much.* Cambridge: Harvard University Press.

Ellis, A. D. (2001, April 11). Never too old: Two universities that target adult learners expand their campuses. *Fresno Bee.*

Embree, C. M. (2001). The University of Phoenix: A case study of a for-profit university. Unpublished diss. Teachers College, Columbia University.

Evelyn, J. (2000, January 24). A coming of age. *Community College Week* 12, no. 12.

Finkelstein, M. J., Seal, R. K., & Schuster, J. H. (1998). *The new academic generation: A profession in transformation.* Baltimore: Johns Hopkins University Press.

Forbes, S. L. (1991, May 27). Good school story. *Forbes Magazine.*

Forter, A. L (2002, December 13). National U. creates a for-profit company to run growing online programs. *Chronicle of Higher Education.*

Gardner, H., Csikszentmihalyi, M., & Damon, W. (2001). *Good work: When excellence and ethics meet.* New York: Basic Books.

Goddard, A. (2002, June 21). So what are you good at? *Times Higher Education Supplement.*

Harpool, D. (2003). *Survivor college: Best practices of traditional and for-profit colleges.* Chula Vista, CA: Aventine Press.

Henry, N. B. (ed.). (1943). *The forty-second yearbook of the National Society for the Study of Education—Part 1: Vocational education.* Chicago: University of Chicago Press.

Honick, C.A. (1995). The story behind proprietary schools in the United States. In Clowes, D. A., & Hawthorne, E. M. (eds.), *Community colleges and proprietary schools: Conflict or convergence?* San Francisco: Jossey Bass.

Hutchins, R. M. (1952). *The higher learning in America.* New Haven, CT: Yale University Press.

Immerwahr, J. (1998, spring). The price of admission: The growing importance of higher education. A national survey of Americans' views conducted and reported by Public Agenda. National Center for Public Policy and Higher Education.

Kelly, K. F. (2001, July). *Meeting needs and making profits: The rise of for-profit degree-granting institutions.* Denver, CO: Education Commission of the States.

Kerr, C. (1982). *The uses of the university.* Boston: Harvard University Press.

Lee, J. B., & Merisotis, J. P. (1990). *Proprietary schools: Programs, policies, and prospects.* Washington, DC: George Washington University.

Lenington, R. L. (1996). *Managing higher education as a business.* Phoenix, AZ: American Council on Education and Oryx Press.

Letters to the editor: People who teach at for-profit institutions. (2002, April 5). *Chronicle of Higher Education.*

Marcial, G. G. (2002, September 16). A gold star for Strayer. *Business Week.*

Marcus, D. L. (2000, January 24). A scholastic gold mine. *U.S. News & World Report.*

Marsden, G. M. (1994). *The soul of the American university: From protestant establishment to established non-belief.* Oxford: Oxford University Press.

Meister, J. C. (1998). *Corporate universities: Lessons in building a world-class work force.* New York: McGraw-Hill.

Merisotis, J. P. (1991). The changing dimensions of student aid: New directions for higher education. no. 74. San Francisco: Jossey-Bass.

Miller, S., & Haederle, M. (2000, March 6). Dollar scholar. *People.*

Moody's Investor Service. (2003, February). Higher education sector: 2003 industry outlook. Retrieved May 27, 2004, from www.citadel.edu/sacs/referencedocuments/financial%20documents/moodyindustryoutlook.pdf.

Morgan, R. (2002, October 11). Lawmakers call for more accountability from accreditation system. *Chronicle of Higher Education.*

Newman, C.H.C. (1959). *The idea of a university.* Garden City, NY: Image Books.

Nisbet, R. A. (1971). *The degradation of the academic dogma.* New York: Basic Books.

Olsen, F. (2002, November 1). Phoenix rises: The university's online program attracts students, profits, and praise. *The Economist.*

Phillips, S. (2002, May 24). Making it in a mass market. *The Times Higher Education Supplement.*

Rand. (1997). *Breaking the social contract: The fiscal crisis in higher education.* Retrieved May 12, 2004, from www.rand.org/publications/cae/cae100.

Roach, R. (2002, February 28). Tested practices buoy University of Phoenix online. *Black Issues in Higher Education.*

Rowe, C. (2002, January 13). Paperless chase. *New York Times.*

Rudolph, F. (1990). *The American college and university: A history.* New York: Alfred A. Knopf.

Rutherford, G. F. (2002). Academics and economics: The yin and yang of for-profit higher education—A case study of the University of Phoenix. Unpublished diss. University of Texas at Austin.

Schiller, D. (1999). *Digital capitalism: Networking the global market system.* Cambridge: MIT Press.

Schuch, B. (2001, September 1). Transcript—Encore presentation: Apollo Group CEO John Sperling looks to broaden boundaries of higher education. *CNN PINNACLE.*

Seebach, L. (2002, October 25). A gathering storm in higher education? *Rocky Mountain News.*

Seybolt, R. F. (1969). *Apprenticeship and apprenticeship education in colonial New England and New York.* New York: Arno Press and New York Times.

Shea, R. H. (2002, October 28). E-learning today. *U.S. News & World Report.*

Shulman, J. L., & Bowen, W. G. (2001). *The game of life: College sports and educational values.* Princeton: Princeton University Press.

Sinclair, U. (1923). *The goose-step: Study of American education.* Pasadena, CA: Economy Book Shop.

Slaughter, S. (1990). *The higher learning and high technology: Dynamics of higher education policy formation.* New York: State University of New York Press.

Stahl, L. (2001, July 29). Online U: Online education. *60 Minutes.* Burrelle's Information Services, CBS News Transcripts.

Swenson, C. (1998, September–October). Customers and markets: The cuss words of academe. *Change.*

Teaching the world a lesson. (2002, June 8). *The Economist.*

Thompson, J. F. (1973). *Foundations of vocational education: Social and philosophical concepts.* Englewood Cliffs, NJ: Prentice-Hall.

UCEA (University Continuing Education Association). (1998). *Lifelong learning trends.* Washington, DC: UCEA.

University of Phoenix. (2003). Catalog (electronic version). Retrieved December 10, 2003, from www.phoenix.edu/catalog/toc.html.

University of Phoenix uses Internet, technology to assist students; new programs help make pursuing a degree more accessible for adult students. (2001, November 20). *PR Newswire.*

Veblen, T. (1954). *The higher learning in America*. Palo Alto, CA: Academic Reprints.

Warner, M. (2002, April 29). Inside the very strange world of billionaire John Sperling. *Fortune*.

Ways and Means. (2001, February 2). *Chronicle of Higher Education*.

Wilms, W. W. (1974). *Public and proprietary vocational training*. Berkeley, CA: Center for Research and Development in Higher Education.

INDEX

About the Author

GARY A. BERG is Dean of Extended Education at California State University Channel Islands and author of numerous articles on current issues in higher education, educational technology, and media studies, as well as four books including *Why Distance Learning?* published by Praeger/ACE.